*To those who realize
that mastery of a handcraft means little
unless others are given an opportunity
to enjoy the finished work.*

Contents

Acknowledgments ix

Introduction x

1 CAPITALIZE ON YOUR TALENT 1
A Matter of Attitude 1
What a Home-Based Business Can Do for You 2
The Positive Approach to Selling 3
Proceeding on Your Own 4

2 MAKE IT EASY ON YOURSELF 7
Do Your Thing and Enjoy It 7
Minimize the Risks 10
IRS Requirements 15
Keeping a Positive Attitude 17
Goals and Objectives 18
A Practical Business Plan 20
Order and Organization 21
Brainstorming 23
Where to Get Help 26
Make the Most of It 30

3 DEVELOP A SOUND WORKING PLAN 33
Essential Benefits 33
The Working Document 34
Action-Oriented Goals 37
The Financial Plan 39

Budget Entries   43
The Business Structure   46

4   KNOW THE LEGAL REQUIREMENTS   51
A Word of Warning!   52
Naming Your Business   52
Licenses and Permits   54
Zoning Ordinances   56
Other Requirements   60
Self-Employment and Taxes   62
Employment Practices and Laws   63
Putting Your Family to Work   67
Do You Need Insurance?   69
Legal Business Deductions   71

5   PROFIT FROM THE HOME ADVANTAGE   75
Advantages   75
Potential Problems   76
Minimize the Problems   76
The Tax Breaks   79
An Effective Workplace   81
A Functional Office   83
Nook-and-Cranny Storage   84
What About Customers?   85
Stepping Out   87

6   PRODUCE FOR SELLING   91
What Consumers Want   91
Learn What Sells Best   93
The Appeal of Handmade   95
Variety and Quantity   96
Organize for Production   98
Quality, Price, and Profit   100
Establishing a Fair Price   104
A Basic Equation   104
Pricing Strategies   105
Inventory Control   107
The Key to Future Sales   108

7   MARKET YOUR PRODUCT
EFFECTIVELY   111
Defining the Market   111
Product Distribution Decisions   114
Building a Positive Image   116
Advertising   118

Publicity 121
Public Relations 124
Building a Clientele 125
Make It Count 128

8 SELL IT WITHOUT HASSLE — 129
According to Type 130
Confidence and Character 131
The Process 133
Prospecting the Easy Way 136
The Sales Presentation 139
Using Objections to Advantage 141
The Close 142
Follow-Up and Friendship 143
Evaluate! 144

9 HAVE A PARTY — 147
Practical Choices 147
The Advantage Is Yours 148
A Look at Alternatives 149
The Hostess Holds the Key 152
A Word About Gender 152
Getting Ready 154
Going to the Party 157
After Arriving 158
Addressing the Group 160
A Change of Pace 164
Wrap It Up 166
Review the Results 168

10 EXPAND YOUR HORIZONS — 173
Build on Your Success 173
Supplementary Practices 175
Open-House Sales 179
Craft Show Sales 183
Display Techniques 188
Open a Small Store 193
Borrowing Capital 195

11 KEEP TRACK & MEASURE YOUR SUCCESS — 199
Records and Books 199
Scheduling, Posting, and Retention 202
Simplified Bookkeeping 205

Sample Bookkeeping System   207
Some Helpful Hints   215
Net Worth Statement   218
The Pluses and Minuses   220

Appendix   Income Tax Form:
            Schedule C   223

Index   226

Acknowledgments

CREDIT FOR HELPING to make some of my topics meaningful goes to several individuals. Grateful acknowledgement is hereby extended to Alice Jacobe (leather work), Marilyn Blevins (beaded crafts), Jesse Wooten (ornamental concrete), and Fred Arnold (wooden crafts) for permitting me to photograph them and their work at Trader's World. The final expression of my appreciation goes to members of my family—to Linda, for sharing her expertise on selling crafts at home parties and for demonstrating how to address a group; to Ellen, for reviewing the experiences she's had operating a crafts store; and, of course, to Arlene, for her assistance in countless ways.

Introduction

EVERY CRAFTER who wants to do something with his or her products besides displaying them about the house can profit from this book. Whether you are producing quantities large or small makes no difference: Opportunities to make money from the work are there for the taking. If you have something of reasonably good quality to sell, basically the only other thing you need to step out successfully is the desire and personal drive to apply procedures of proven worth.

If you've worked at a craft for any length of time, chances are you've received compliments about it from friends, family, and other acquaintances. The motivational effect of a little praise like that can be substantial, but what could be more exhilarating than to have people not closely associated with you demonstrate their pleasure by buying your creations? Experience the difference, if you haven't already. Put your work on the market. It might be easier to sell than you think.

This book gives you all the information you need to earn an income from a handcraft. It is replete with procedures of practical value. Even if you've never before sold anything, you'll learn how to set up and operate a profitable handcrafts business—from start to taking orders—and you'll learn in the process how to release the talent hidden within you. By following the advice given, the joy of being your own boss and achieving worthwhile goals can be yours.

If, on the other hand, you are an experienced salesperson, this book can teach you methods and techniques of marketing and selling that are unique to this kind of business and must be known to be successful in it. Only those practices that have been proven useful are recommended within these pages. Among the many topics covered, you will find sections on bookkeeping procedures, legal requirements, and how to use one's home to advantage—all areas of significance to beginner and experienced businessperson alike.

Virtually any handcraft of appropriate quality will sell, whether made of ceramics, wood, metal, leather, textiles, or some other material. One reason is a strong buying market exists today for handcrafted articles. This book will teach you how to reach that market and how to capitalize on that knowledge, regardless of whether you make the products yourself or purchase pieces for resale.

This book also contains information on how to proceed while keeping the risks to a minimum, how to start part-time or full-time with little capital, where to borrow funds if needed, and what pitfalls to avoid in the process. It explains how and where to become licensed, which business structure is least costly, how to take advantage of the tax breaks, how to ensure a positive cash flow, where to go for free help, what to do to comply with the law and keep the IRS happy, and ways to avoid paying huge fees to legal or accounting professionals. Other topics include how to set up the workplace most efficiently, handle matters of quantity versus quality in production, price your craftwork for greatest profit, gain leads with little effort, advertise and get free publicity, avoid paying certain taxes—and many more tips of value to those of you now selling or about to sell handcrafts.

Rest assured, the methods of selling described and recommended in the text are entirely workable. Some are used extensively, such as selling at craft shows and through retail stores. Others, though often the most profitable and most easily applied, are not well known or commonly practiced in handcraft businesses, such as selling by the house-party plan. Procedures are explained for getting the most from the different practices, including setting up a small business at a mall and selling from carts or a kiosk.

Unlike some books that have been written by people who never practiced what they preach, this one is based largely on first-hand experiences—my own and those of my daughters, Linda and Ellen. In writing this book, I have drawn upon our work extensively. Each of us has sold articles of different kinds—Ellen as a partner in a crafts store, Linda as a sole proprietor selling crafts from her home and at house parties, and myself after being trained years ago to sell by the house-party method. In addition, all three of us have been and continue to be engaged in making crafts of one kind or another. It is these experiences that give meaning and substance to much of the book's content.

A strong feature is the manner in which the methods of selling are explained. The house-party method, for example, is detailed step by step, from the point of preparation clear through to closing individual sales and evaluating the experience. Because this method can be the least expensive and most profitable way to sell your handcrafts, I have covered everything of importance—from recruiting the hostess and instructing her how to invite guests (a captive audience, prepared to buy), to using motivational gifts, presenting the crafts, and applying special sales techniques. Anyone seriously considering selling handcrafts will want to study this topic. The method is easy to manage from the home, and it can be very profitable.

How profitable could you expect a business of your own to be? That depends mainly on you and the strength of your motivation to succeed. There are no guarantees in this business, nor is there any suggestion you will become rich by following this book. The evidence shows, nonetheless, that people of average education and no previous experience can learn to operate a handcrafts business profitably. Valuable suggestions for making the experience a positive one are given in each chapter. Responsibility for their implementation is entirely yours.

A few suggestions are included here as to how you might proceed. If you are a beginner aspiring to entrepreneurship, read the chapters through in the order presented. However, if you are already selling hand-crafts, you might want to pick and choose specific topics. Whatever the case may be, you will probably profit by keeping a copy for reference when the need for review develops.

After an initial reading, you will want to avail yourself of the supple-mentary literature identified from place to place. In particular, obtain publications of the IRS. You will need the latest regulations for filing taxes. For certain business procedures, IRS requirements for small businesses are highly complex and outside the scope of this book. (Commissioner Fred T. Goldberg, Jr., grossly understated the fundamental problem when he said, "Your government must simplify the tax law.") In an effort to ease the burden of understanding in this area, I have singled out some topics that should be given further study. Suggestions for gaining the maximum in deductions and for paying no more tax than necessary are among the subjects so noted.

1
CHAPTER

Capitalize on Your Talent

CONGRATULATIONS! You have taken an important step toward being in complete control of your handcraft. The fact that you are reading material of this kind is evidence of interest in doing something with your work besides just making it for display or giving it away. By reading on and applying the suggestions presented, you might be able to bask one day in the joys of successful entrepreneurship.

People have various reasons for wanting to market and sell the things they make. Some view the venture as a way of supplementing family income through spare-time work; others seek enough income to fully support a family while dropping out of the nine-to-five routine and the hassle sometimes associated with it; and still others simply want to make a few dollars from a sideline business. Even the hobbyist who pursues a craft in on-and-off fashion must find an outlet for his or her work before storage around the house becomes a serious problem. Whatever the motivation may be, the fun of trying and the feeling of accomplishment that goes with selling your own creations in the marketplace can be extremely gratifying.

A MATTER OF ATTITUDE

Perhaps you have already decided—albeit a courageous decision—to plunge ahead. You feel your craft is of marketable quality, but you have very little knowledge of how to proceed. Look around you. You have lots of company. Very few craftspeople also have experience in marketing and selling. Such experience has to be acquired. The good news is that any uninitiated individual who will take time to study the principles and put forth the effort can readily learn how to market and sell handcrafts.

Actually, there are not many reasons why an average adult cannot develop a successful practice. Matters of age, business education, ethnic background, financial status, and sex do not in and of themselves present formidable barriers. Neither are a product's type and composition major limitations. Woven rugs, needlepoint pictures, sculptures in clay, tooled leather purses, country decorations in wood, and a variety of other articles fashioned at home are marketable, as long as they are properly presented and of reasonably good quality.

The initial step for many handcrafters is to overcome their tendencies to offer excuses. Some will dismiss any interest in marketing and selling their work with comments such as "I can't do it," or "I don't know how." Such negative statements are too often given as a way of avoiding any effort to learn what could turn out to be a surprisingly easy extra step. A willingness to learn is a basic necessity. Undoubtedly, many people who have put forth the effort needed to master a craft are also capable of learning how to sell their work in the marketplace.

Confidence and Personality

A common barrier, and one that can seem most difficult to overcome, is a lack of confidence. A fear of failing seems to control all interest in attempting something new. People do not always realize they have the ability to master things unknown to them, and that is a disappointing fact. Virtually everyone has hidden potential, and as any competent psychologist or teacher knows, individuals seldom work and achieve to the limits of their capability. The tragedy is not that people have no talent, but that they do not use what they do have. If you lack confidence, finding ways to release your inner potential is an important beginning.

By way of contrast, you also must not be overly confident about what can be attained. For example, assuming a crafts business in the home can become a means of getting rich quickly is a serious misconception. If you expect such results, you would be better off in another, more lucrative line. A homecraft business is not likely to make anyone fabulously wealthy or rich overnight.

Another concern of many prospective entrepreneurs is that they don't have the personality to sell. Like it or not, selling is part of a handcrafts business, and selling means meeting and dealing with strangers. You don't need to have a charismatic personality, but you do need to have an ability to get along with people (and to like them). Fortunately, most people can learn to do so, if they don't already.

WHAT A HOME-BASED BUSINESS CAN DO FOR YOU

Homemakers, hobbyists, retirees, handicapped persons, and even those who work full-time jobs often pursue some kind of craft in the home. The crafts business then becomes a natural extension of the work started there. A business of this type, commonly referred to as a *cottage industry*, provides advantages not to be found in any other retail operation.

For one thing, a home-based business of your own could bring about a significant change in the quality of your life. In comparison to a regular job, for example, you would now be free to concentrate on something you like doing rather than on things someone else tells you to do. You could work according to your own plan, taking breaks, holidays, and vacations when you want to. You would also be free from the potentially stressful conditions of working in an office.

Lower cost is another advantage of working at home. The tax breaks from having a workshop and an office in your residence can be substantial. Furthermore, working at home can be particularly beneficial for a working mom or if there is a sick person or an invalid in the family. In other instances, you can enlist a member or two of your family to help in the business.

Personal feelings are especially important. As much as anything else, they may be the reason for embarking on a home-based venture. The sense of accomplishment, genuine enthusiasm, or exhilaration that can come from single-handedly developing and successfully running a business can be most heady.

While the possible advantages are many, there is always a negative side to consider. Isolation from peers or fellow workers is one concern. Also, at least in the beginning, you will probably need to work longer hours than before, including evenings and weekends. Although such conditions seem more detrimental to some people than to others, they should be acknowledged and thoroughly thought through at the outset.

The logical thing for you to do is to weigh all the disadvantages that might occur in relation to the potential advantages before going ahead. However, keep this in mind: The current trend in America is toward working regular jobs in the home. That fact alone strongly indicates there are substantial benefits involved.

THE POSITIVE APPROACH TO SELLING

Probably many more people would try to sell their crafts if they held a more positive impression of selling and salesmen. Most of us have had direct confrontations with high-pressure salesmen (some of whom will say practically anything, whether it is true or not) or have heard stories about con artists making a convincing sales pitch before absconding with sums of money. The unfortunate result is a bad name for an otherwise responsible, helpful, and essential occupation.

Despite the occasional negatives, selling has an established place in modern living. Practically everything manufactured today is made for sale, and someone has to sell it.

A preferred approach to selling is to make a presentation to customers who have warmed to the idea to the point of showing interest. In selling crafts, this is the best method to use. Techniques for using this positive approach are explained in chapters 8 and 9.

The most successful salespeople consistently approach their public and presentations in a positive manner. Their methods are worth emulating. They seem always to speak favorably about themselves, their product, and their clients.

You, as the one doing the selling, must first of all have something to sell of which you are proud, and you must be able to speak convincingly about the product. An appearance of sincere honesty in extolling the qualities of what you have to offer is equally important. You probably will not go far in this business by trying to fake that impression.

Secondly, remember that you are performing a service. You are making something available that might otherwise never become known or convenient for the customer to buy. Be concerned about being of service first and worry about increasing your bank account later. These factors in combination with the more positive, personal approach to selling mentioned are sure to convey a positive impression. By being of service and showing concern for the client's needs and feelings, you are likely to be surprised not only by how many customers you will have but by how many of them become friends.

A Prestigious Product

As a dispenser or purveyor of handcrafts, you will have a powerful public impression working in your favor. Handmade articles have individuality, uniqueness. and rarity (FIG. 1-1). Unlike the public's view of mass-produced products, handmade articles are expected to work as intended and to have an unlimited life. The shoddiness of construction and the planned obsolescence and failure of many items manufactured in large quantity today has negatively affected consumers everywhere. As a consequence, the general attitude toward mass-produced items has diminished while that toward handcrafts has been markedly enhanced. This is a matter of great importance to you because it means the public already has a positive feeling and acceptance for the type of product you have for sale.

The special appeal of handcrafted work is an undeniable plus. The public's acceptance and willingness to pay increasingly higher prices for artifacts fashioned before industry became mechanized is leading to a general interest in all things made by hand. The terms *artisanship* and *craftsmanship*, related as inherently to handwork as they are, contribute positively to the image. Their use helps make selling easier.

PROCEEDING ON YOUR OWN

Knowing the specifics of selling is essential for staying in business. Of equal importance is knowing how to set up your enterprise. The requisite

1-1 Handcrafted articles are in great demand. The quality of leatherwork this woman does is much of the reason why her business has been operating successfully for over 30 years.

for applying this knowledge is a strong desire to succeed. Without that desire, a business owner or operator is not likely to persist in reading literature relevant to the purpose nor to obtain results at the level of expectation possible.

Evaluate What You Know and Can Do

You should also consider your place pertinent to knowledge and skills. For example: What do you already know about operating a crafts business? What do you still need to know? What things do you do skillfully? By means of this analysis, you may come to realize that you have a substantial foundation for going forward.

You might already be in control of certain techniques and procedures of importance in the development of a small business. Perhaps you have previously gained experience in the complexities of filing taxes, have a source for borrowing capital, have studied marketing methods, have successfully sold something to the public, have an acquaintance in an agency of government who knows the legal requirements, or have contacted a member of the SBA about the procedures for starting out. Search your background, and you might find you have a substantial base of experience available to build on. But whatever has been personally acquired, chances are much remains to be learned.

Study and Practice

Once you have evaluated what you already know, you might identify a need to round out your experiences through additional study and practice. Like the body builder who exercises the parts of his anatomy that need to be brought up to the muscular equivalent of other well-developed parts, you will have to concentrate on adding to your strengths to increase important abilities over a broad range. Results may not be immediately apparent, nor should perfection be expected in all instances. Procedures once unknown become easier and easier to apply through repeated effort, with achievements in production, marketing, and selling eventually becoming routine and second nature.

That's where this book comes in. The information presented in the chapters that follow is a suitable guide for proceeding by yourself.

There is no guarantee of success in this business. Diligent study, hard work, and constancy of purpose will only lessen the probability of failure. If you add to these a bit of leg-work thoroughly carried out, you will achieve greater personal understanding and better results in the long run.

2
CHAPTER

Make It Easy On Yourself

THE DECISION TO GO INTO THE BUSINESS of selling handcrafts begins with desire. The requisite for success in such a venture is sincere commitment. Aspiration alone might bring on that first step, but only through unrelenting determination can the procedures that follow be carried out smoothly. Perhaps you have what it takes.

To start, you must be convinced the advantages outweigh the disadvantages. You might want to work when and how you see fit, but you will probably end up working longer hours and having less time to relax than before; you might cherish the freedom of doing your own thing, but you will likely be less secure than if you were holding a job with steady income and fringe benefits; and you might long to experience the self-fulfilling power of accomplishment, though you know that, historically, more businesses fail than survive. You have acknowledged these probabilities, yet you are not dissuaded. You have observed several people who have apparently succeeded on their own, and you feel sure you have as much on the ball as any of them. If these things are true, your conviction is impressive. It implies, among other things, a compulsion to succeed.

In addition to an unwavering will, you must possess a realistic awareness of what you need to be successful. You must analyze the requirements of the business in relation to your personal circumstances in order to gain a fair idea of whether or not you can measure up to the demands of the venture. Be cognizant of the risk involved, but prepare yourself for doing whatever is necessary to avoid adding to the statistics of failure.

DO YOUR THING AND ENJOY IT

There is a story of a young man who likes to take icy showers, so he says. When asked why he bathes in such cold water, he replies, "Because it feels so good when I get out."

While this masochistic practice is evidently tolerable and sufficiently gratifying for one person, periodic and prolonged involvement in practices seemingly negative or torturous will be avoided by most. And so it is with a business. Doing the many things that have to be done to start and operate a business should be basically enjoyable. To end each day feeling frustrated or sighing with relief that it's over is certainly not the way to build a successful operation nor a lasting peace of mind. Life is much too precious to waste doing work that seems distasteful, especially when the likely consequences are miserable performance and ultimate failure.

One way to achieve a measure of gratification in the workaday world is to direct your efforts toward producing results in a pleasurable way. Just as you can feel invigorated and clean by bathing in water at temperatures to your liking, so can you perform a large number of tasks in business by applying your own personal touch. Consider the working plan, for example. Some books on the subject would have you write an extensively large and thorough volume when a simpler, more concise, less time-consuming statement in several pages will suffice. The extraneous verbiage would add little to the goals and procedures set forth as essential in your type of operation.

The suggestions given here in no way negate the need to perform duties in an orderly, totally thorough manner. The things to be done before entering into business are no exception. There are important steps to take then as well as later.

Steps When Starting

Steps to observe when preparing to start a handcrafts business are listed below. Follow them, but alter the sequence if desired.

1. Define exactly what you want to do.
2. Learn what operating a business entails.
3. Evaluate your personal fitness and commitment.
4. Do the necessary research in several basic areas.
   a. The market—analysis of need and competition
   b. Zoning ordinances and limitations
   c. Labor laws or other legal restrictions
5. Decide if you have the wherewithal to go ahead.

The first step is basic to everything else. Once you have defined what you want to sell, settle on whether you will be manufacturing or buying the crafts to be sold. The location of the proposed business, your intended market area, and whether you expect to hire help are other essential considerations at this time. What you now have is a "wish" list. The feasibility of going ahead with the idea depends on your findings in steps 2 through 4.

As implied in the second step, some knowledge of business practices —at least a basic insight as to what operating a business entails—is essential if you are to proceed comfortably. This book helps foster that insight.

Experts commonly say that anyone who knows how to balance a checkbook can learn to operate a business successfully. They are probably correct. However, with over 70 percent of all new businesses terminating in failure, the need to study and understand fundamental procedures from the beginning becomes ever more evident. With adequate preparation, you might eventually find that managing a business is easier than you first thought possible.

Armed with an understanding of the operation's requirements, the next step is to evaluate your attitude toward the work and the strength of your commitment to succeed. Briefly, this step is an exercise in self-analysis, a determination of whether or not you are suited for the business. Questions about your work ethic, emotional stability, responsibility, persistence, and reliability are among those to be answered at this time.

Having drawn favorable conclusions to this point, you are now prepared to make an assessment of the proposed market. This involves determining who your competitors are, what methods they are using, and how successful they have been. Are there already too many of them? Evidence of overcrowding in the field is as beneficial to you as knowing why attempts by others in your line have failed. Perhaps the need for a business exists, but with a new product line. The more evidence you can generate about need—perhaps by observation, by means of questionnaires, or by trial sales to market segments—the better you will be prepared to make decisions about the market.

Research the law, too. Zoning ordinances and labor laws could alter your plans relative to the business's location and employment. Some preferences might turn out to be legally prohibited, but, as will become clear, there are ways to avoid some regulations and still achieve what you have set out to do. Their use is entirely legal, workable, and effective.

Setting Up the Business

After completing the preliminary analysis, consider what needs to be done to set up the business. The steps below are a guide. Those not fully covered here are explained in detail in later chapters.

1. Prepare a comprehensive working/financial plan (chapter 3).
2. Finalize the location and consider using a P.O. box (chapter 5).
3. Define the business's legal structure (chapter 4).
4. Choose a business name; register it if fictitious (chapter 4).
5. Obtain a license to operate (chapter 4).
6. Obtain a permit to sell (chapter 4).
7. Open a separate bank account (chapter 11).
8. Install a business phone—*optional* (chapter 5).
9. Borrow start-up money, if needed (chapter 10).
10. Obtain IRS forms and filing information (chapter 5).
11. Organize the office, workplace, and record books (chapters 5 and 11).

You will find that many of the preliminary activities listed above are easily completed and will not take much time. Nevertheless, they are important and must not be bypassed. Upon completing them, you are ready to proceed with a full-fledged business.

MINIMIZE THE RISKS

Success in business depends primarily, if not almost exclusively, on knowledge of effective procedures. It necessarily follows that the more thoroughly studied and practiced the procedure, the easier becomes the application. Given information on finding the best solutions to problems, learning to think positively, setting goals and objectives in measurable terms, designing a business plan for achieving success, and making use of worthwhile sources of information and assistance, a conscientious person will profit materially. If you persistently study and practice the various techniques involved, even the difficult procedures will soon seem routine.

Much of what you need to know to keep matters of ownership and management from becoming unduly complex is covered in this chapter. If you don't have a business background, you should certainly read the topics carefully before beginning a venture on your own. Knowledge of these processes will turn the odds in your favor.

Read other literature on the subject, also. The more you read about the subject, the more comfortable you will feel about entering into an entrepreneurial venture.

First Steps

There are a number of possible steps to be taken for avoiding or reducing the risks involved in starting and developing a crafts business. Some of the major ones are included in the following list. While you might need to modify some of these suggestions to suit your own needs—as, for instance, when moving quickly or with urgency into a vacant retail store—the points listed here are widely applicable and deserve the full consideration of anyone who does not have a solid grounding in business methods.

- Start small and gradually—perhaps part-time.
- Learn about the business by reading.
- Enroll in classes on entrepreneurship.
- Consult or join relevant associations.
- Have a financial cushion to fall back on.
- Observe what the competitors are doing.
- Plan thoroughly and with measurable components.
- Keep personal problems out of the business.
- Get professional help, if needed.

Moonlighting

Undoubtedly, one of the best ways to avoid failure in a handcrafts business is to start it as a sideline. No published statistics are available to verify this point, but the matter seems easily concluded by means of logic. Investments of time, money, and material need only be very minimal when starting out part-time, as smallness and moonlighting go hand in hand. Only the uninhibited stockpiling of products without having first tested their salability might cause great difficulty. With sensible planning and the customary restraint of a sideline practice, the handcrafting of products subsequently found lacking in sales appeal can be terminated with little loss.

A crafts business planned as a moonlighting operation is naturally started in the home. This practice has the distinct advantage of slow pacing, for there is no inherent need to shift into high speed. Only a compelling, personal urgency might lead to a decision to do otherwise. You can usually implement both the production and selling phases of the practice gradually, and you will probably find it easier to work out any bugs at this pace. In addition, you can undertake trial-and-error experimentation with very minimal loss. This gradual approach imparts, in effect, a protective factor of safety.

Study and Learn

Set a goal of learning as much as you can about the crafts business. The more you know about it the better you will do it and the more you will enjoy it. Become as knowledgeable and proficient as you can, and the result will be increased pride, public and personal, in your accomplishments.

While urgencies sometimes occur that cut short the learning period, the need to know the business will always be present. For most people this means studying. Although you occasionally hear reports of people blundering into paying propositions, "dumb luck" success is extremely rare in business. Comparatively few businesses that have not been based on the soundness of acquired knowledge and planning will ultimately succeed.

Read all you can. Your local library might have what you need. Books, magazines, and pamphlets relating to various aspects of business and crafts are generally available there free of charge, and a public library of any consequence will borrow books for you if it doesn't already have on hand what you want to read. The libraries of local high schools or universities might be other sources available to you. With a little searching, you could find written material at no cost and of a quality well worth reading. In the absence of a convenient local library, consider purchasing a good reference through a bookstore and/or subscribing to a magazine.

While learning by reading can be effective, learning by attending classes can be extraordinarily beneficial. Classes provide the advantage of expert consultation and teaching in addition to selected reading material.

Community colleges, vocational schools, and high schools regularly offer courses for adults. Topics as broad as small business ownership and as narrow as depreciating property for income-tax purposes are presented. The courses are usually offered at low cost.

If you intend to become truly proficient in business methods and practices, you should not overlook an opportunity to enroll in such course work. Evening and weekend classes are generally scheduled on popular demand, so do not hesitate to inform the school's officials of your desires. They are constantly on the lookout for topics of interest to the public. Those in the adult continuing-education division will be specific in their attempts to implement your suggestions.

Seek Assistance

The conferences, workshops, and training sessions offered by the Small Business Administration (SBA) are especially helpful. They cover a wide variety of subjects of use to home-business operators, including beginners. The offerings are distributed by time and geographic location, and the price is reasonable.

Because the knowledge you acquire directly correlates to your business performance, you should consider every available source of information and advice when starting out. Practitioners experienced in the same or similar business can be very helpful. A vehicle for becoming acquainted with successful entrepreneurs and their work is a professional association of people involved in homecrafts businesses. Conventions and similar gatherings of those organizations make it possible to meet peers and learn from them in face-to-face discussions, to say little of the practical, procedural suggestions covered by different speakers. Literature distributed to members of an association is an additional source of helpful information. Periodic newsletters, "how-to" manuals, directories, advertising mailers, show schedules, and notices of important legislation typify this service.

Nearly every city and town has some form of business organization operating for the benefit of its members and the community. These vary in composition from an informal gathering of a few business owners to the more formally organized chamber of commerce. It would be wise to join a local group of business people, if such is conveniently available in your area.

The Finances

The choice between operating full-time and part-time frequently hinges on matters of financial well-being. The comparatively minimal demand for money when beginning part-time while earning another income points to the method's safety. Starting full-time, on the other hand, can also be done safely if you have adequate financial reserves and a strong responsibility in money management. Freedom from burdensome bills and enough money in reserve to cover expenses for awhile are the customary essentials.

Obviously, then, people who are heavily in debt would not be the best candidates to take on the extra financial burden of starting a business. Further, those who owe money that hasn't yet been earned have no cushion of funds to pay expenses during rough times—and such times are very likely to occur when beginning. People who use credit cards uncontrollably or indiscriminately are among those whose chances of failing increase dramatically. Simply put, there is little room at any point in business for compulsive spenders. Spendaholics do not have enough control over their purchasing habit to exercise consistently sound judgment and to conserve needed capital. Their lifestyle seems to be dominated by indebtedness rather than by a propensity to prepare for financial contingencies.

Borrowing is a frequently used alternative among entrepreneurs who lack start-up capital, and you should consider it only if you are reasonably confident about your ability to make and to manage money. Whether you borrow from a friend or relative or from a lending institution is irrelevant. If you are in any way conscientious, you will not want to betray the trust placed in you by your lender, and you certainly would not want to alienate a friend or family member in the event of being unable to make your business a success. By borrowing money to start a business that cannot be paid back, not only do you adversely affect your own and your family's financial security, but you might also be subjected to legal penalties for failing to make payments on time. All things considered, you will probably be better off by starting part-time and small, especially if you have any doubt about your ability to repay a loan for the business.

Observe and Prepare

One means of obtaining valuable information is to observe people engaged in businesses similar to yours. Get to know those individuals personally, if possible, but don't be discouraged if you can't find somebody in your vicinity doing exactly what you intend to do. In fact, such a finding might simply indicate that the area is wide open for your business.

Make an effort to observe others in your field by attending a crafts show. There you will see a variety of products on display, and, if you watch very closely, you might be able to tell which items are selling best. Your observations might produce several valuable ideas, including an indication of which kinds of crafts are likely to be marketed more profitably by some other method. The ideas you are sure to glean regarding product design, pricing, and displaying could by themselves be worth the trip.

Craft and gift shops, bazaars, and flea markets are also fertile sources of ideas. They should be included in a schedule of places to visit.

The object of all this is for you to get a general notion of which articles and types of crafts are most in demand by the public. You can then adjust the emphasis in design and production accordingly, while judiciously avoiding the copying of designs. Some popular items are copyrighted and might not be legally reproduced for commercial purposes. But even when the merchandise is not under copyright, as generally holds for home-crafted pieces, articles you prepare for selling should be done in your individualistic style, not as someone else has created them.

A Timetable

Trivial though the idea might seem at first, preparing ahead and delaying your start-up until you are ready to go into business can markedly increase your chances of success. Entering a business unprepared is almost certain to end in failure. By the same token, attempting to reach perfection in each and every undertaking could easily result in a lost opportunity. It is practically impossible to *simultaneously* accomplish the many things you will want to do to prepare for starting your business. For this reason, I recommend you set up and use a timetable.

A timetable specifies when the activities mentioned will be started and finished, and it will assist in pacing if it contains no more activities than can be accomplished at a time. It has the further advantage of setting out activities in small, individually manageable bits. When religiously applied, each item noted in the table will build upon the others until a complete system of objectives has been accomplished.

An example of how a timetable might be drawn up is given in FIG. 2-1. Both the time frame and the activities might vary from those shown, so you should develop a schedule according to your own special needs.

Each dot in the timetable represents an approximate point in time, and each line represents a period of days or weeks within which to complete an activity. Exact timing is not always important as, for instance, when determining the restrictions regarding zoning. The important thing is that you review ordinances and initiate any alternate arrangements near the outset.

Individual characteristics, circumstances, and plans enter into the making of a timetable. A particularly enthusiastic and energetic person might want to condense the time period, and another might adjust the schedule so that the first sales presentation occurs in time for the Christmas holiday season—the time of year when sales are likely to be easiest to come by. In any event, you must think through your schedule carefully so you won't rush unprepared into the marketplace. Impulsive actions can easily lead to failure over the long pull.

You can add other activities to your timetable, but some things, by their nature, should be left unlisted. The support of one's family is a case in point. While such backing should always be obtained, it is not properly listed on the schedule. It is a variable that should be settled before becoming deeply involved in planning.

ACTIVITIES SCHEDULE

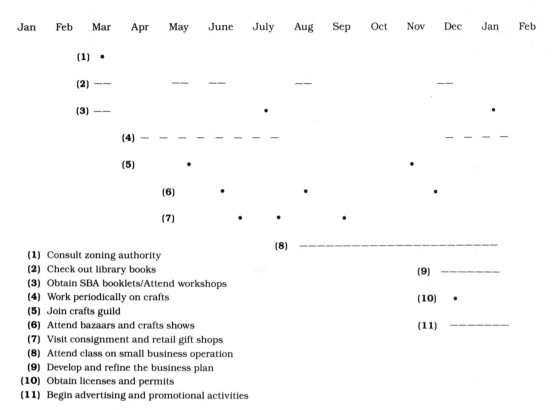

	Jan	Feb	Mar	Apr	May	June	July	Aug	Sep	Oct	Nov	Dec	Jan	Feb

(1) Consult zoning authority
(2) Check out library books
(3) Obtain SBA booklets/Attend workshops
(4) Work periodically on crafts
(5) Join crafts guild
(6) Attend bazaars and crafts shows
(7) Visit consignment and retail gift shops
(8) Attend class on small business operation
(9) Develop and refine the business plan
(10) Obtain licenses and permits
(11) Begin advertising and promotional activities

2-1 This schedule of activities shows some of the items that might be included in timetable in preparation for a home-based crafts business.

IRS REQUIREMENTS

Certain restrictions of the Internal Revenue Service (IRS) are important to recognize at this point. Many of the preparatory activities listed in the timetable are legally deductible as part of the business operation. Unfortunately, the IRS enforces a system which, while intended to forestall cheating, has made procedures unnecessarily complicated for the many honest, average citizens who would boost the economy by starting small businesses.

By way of illustration, the IRS requires the capitalization of costs incurred relative to preparing for a business. Deductions must then occur over time or when the business is sold or dissolved. Business costs may be deducted as expenses in the year they occur *only after operations have begun*, and a business is considered to have started with its first sale. The question then becomes one of how to bring about a compromise between requirements of the IRS and one's personal inclinations.

Several solutions are possible. The easiest of all, though not generally recommended, is simply to eliminate most preparatory activities. Preplanning expenses are then strictly limited to licensing and a few related costs. This practice has initial advantages, but it might seriously affect your state of readiness. Other, more preferable possibilities include:

- Complete all preparations considered necessary, but neither record the details nor make any claim for deduction when filing the business tax forms. The problem is that this practice means more tax will be paid than owed, although the amount will not be great in all instances.

- Prepare as necessary, incurring start-up costs as you do, and capitalize the entire amount. Some capitalized costs add to the basis for the business and cannot be recovered until the business is terminated. Expenditures for capital assets can generally be recovered through depreciation deductions over time. However, you can elect to amortize certain start-up costs. Doing so will allow you to deduct the amortizable costs in equal amounts over a period of 60 months or more. For most, the total amount of paperwork involved will be considerable for what will likely be a relatively small tax saving.

- Make an early sale. In other words, sell an item or two near the beginning of the scheduled period. Collect any sales tax due and record the sale. Many of the things you will do thereafter by way of preparation are legally deductible as business expenses in the year when they occur. This is true even if you make only occasional sales after that initial one. If you have sold a few of your crafts to friends before deciding to enlarge the operation, you might already have made a qualifying sale. The advantages are noteworthy: paperwork can be kept to a minimum while most initial costs become immediately deductible expenses.

  The result of this practice could be a loss during the first year, but it could also result in a legally permissible reduction of taxes. A profit needs to be shown for your crafts business in three (any three) of the first five years.

Some combination of the several alternatives noted above could be used, as well. In any case, keep a complete and accurate record if a tax deduction is intended. The information on tax requirements in chapter 4 covers related points, while emphasizing the need to consult IRS literature for complete and current details on business tax procedures.

KEEPING A POSITIVE ATTITUDE

Success in working closely with the public depends on the personal attitude you carry forth. The evidence is very much apparent to anyone who has ever been waited on by a sourpuss sales clerk or waitress. Some unrelated, negative occurrence seems too often to result in sarcasm, complaining, and grumbling. Those expressions never please customers, nor do they stimulate repeat business. To win friends, people dealing directly with the public must think and act positively. This is a business in which a morally supportive family can be extremely beneficial; acting as if the burdens of a disagreeable home life are dominant could make the difference between continuing and getting out of the business.

How you view the routines of production, record keeping, advertising, and so forth is equally critical. Some people view their work as barely tolerable, and some take it more positively in stride. For others, work is absolutely exhilarating.

What makes the difference? Part of the answer is in having worthwhile goals and control over how to achieve them. Another substantial part lies in controlling powerful mental processes. Fortunately, being in complete control is within the power of many who seriously try.

Repeated, conscious efforts to replace negative feelings with positive thinking is a step in the right direction. A positive outlook comes to those who learn to minimize periods of gloom, misery, and despair, displacing them with thoughts of delightful, pleasurable, and cheerful experiences. Favorable results are within the grasp of those who put forth the effort.

Success in the endeavor involves a will to change. Habitual smokers who have quit the habit completely and abruptly by virtue of the will to do so know how powerful the force of mind over matter can be. Strong-willed persons, in particular, should have no difficulty learning to direct their thoughts to pleasant events at moments when worry or unpleasant feelings seem about to dominate. Chronic worrying and negative thinking are nonproductive and antithetic to success.

The gist of all of this is to place emphasis on the positive aspects of things. Make a concerted effort not to dwell on past failures. Try and try again. If you need more information on how to make this work for you, consider reading some of the books (available in most public libraries) that extensively cover the benefits and techniques of positive thinking.

Accomplishments

A comment once made by the late Rosalind Russell bears repeating. "Success," she said, "is a public affair. Failure is a private funeral."

Although you might never bask in the limelight to the extent Rosalind enjoyed it, you might be surprised to learn how eager others are to hear about your achievements. Being asked to share something in which you take great pride is a compliment of the highest order. Moreover, by making your accomplishments known, you will discover that people from many walks of life and locations have similar interests. A whole new area of sharing, association, and support thereby opens up for you.

GOALS AND OBJECTIVES

Goals and objectives form the basis for directing a business. The terms are often used synonymously. Each, as is done here, commonly refers to the achievement of results, the aims, or the end toward which effort is directed. Unless goal-directed statements are formulated to guide the business in areas of general and specific endeavor, the operation could be analogous to going on a trip without first deciding where you are going or how you will get there. Undisciplined aimlessness could be expected, to say the least.

Measurable Terms

While most people recognize the need to set out statements defining their business goals, few people observe the best way to write them. Consider the phrase "to make money." It could be a fundamental goal for the owner of a crafts business, but, while its purpose seems obvious and noble enough, the statement lacks the kind of specificity required to be measurable. It tells no one how much money is to be made, how it is to be made, or the time period in which it is to be made. In that sense, the operator is on safe ground. The objective could be accomplished by merely earning a dollar, say, over a couple of years. As a practical guide, the statement is almost worthless.

The point of this example is to show the need for writing objectives in measurable terms. *Measurable objectives* are statements of expectation that communicate the standards and conditions for observing and evaluating accomplishments. They have three basic components:

1. A statement of *expected results* (the outcomes and accomplishments being sought)
2. A definition of *conditions* (the parameters of performance, usually elements of time relative to the attainment and evaluation of results)
3. A description of *standards* (the levels of performance, the quantities, or the qualities of results being sought that define acceptable levels of attainment)

For an objective to be truly measurable, all three of the above components must be present. Consider this statement: "During the fourth quarter of the year, income due to sales activity shall increase by 15% over that of the previous quarter." The expected result is increased gross income from sales, the condition is that this increase be accomplished in the final three-month period of the current year, and the standard by which success will be measured is a 15% increase in sales income over the amount realized in the third quarter.

Besides defining expectations in precisely measurable terms, the statement must indicate, explicitly or implicitly, who is responsible for performance. In the objective given, responsibility for the activity rests by implication with the person in charge of sales. That person would be the owner in a one-person operation.

Accountability

When writing objectives, observe how activities and accountability for results become difficult to define if you are not explicit. If, in the previous statement, the words *due to sales activity* were dropped, an indication of how the 15% increase is to be obtained and who holds responsibility for doing it would not be completely evident. Then, the desired increase in income could conceivably be attained by increasing sales price or sales volume. Either one or both become viable activities. When more than one way to achieve an end is intended, a separate, measurable statement for each would be clearer.

As a guide to writing measurable objectives, ask yourself these questions: What, as owner, do I want to accomplish this year? This quarter? In five years? Your answers might be directed toward income, profits, volume of sales, quantity of pieces produced, quality of products, customer complaints, hours worked, numbers of sales presentations, or some similar goals. Both the results desired and the time limits for achieving them are established at this point.

Next, pose questions about the effectiveness of results. In other words, define standards of performance for each goal. Ask questions such as: How much? How well? By what percentage? At what cost? Or, as compared to what?

Carefully constructed, measurable objectives pay greatest dividends during the completion of activities. A clear-cut guide then exists. Effectively drawn objectives also make evaluation easy at the time of performance appraisal.

Being Realistic

Failure in business can result from failing to achieve goals or from never defining what the goals are. Another danger is failure from setting aims too low. Goals must be realistic and attainable, although if they are set so low as to do no more than maintain the status quo, the exercise could prove to be useless. The best statements seek improvement because of the commitment required for their fulfillment.

Routine goals fail to obtain the level of commitment needed. Simply repeating the same expectations year after year does little to challenge an operator. Most surviving businesses begin with only marginal success their first year. They need to be directed toward better returns as time goes by.

Another point of significance in writing goals is to base them on appropriate time frames. Goals are short-term and long-term. The former cover time periods up to a year or two; the latter cover anywhere from three to ten years. Short-term goals control day-to-day operations more closely than the latter with their overall, strategic orientation. Both types have a place in a well-defined business plan.

A PRACTICAL BUSINESS PLAN

A business plan is important in operating a profit-oriented organization, whether under sole ownership or held in conjunction with others. It is a guide for managing the business in all of its aspects. Matters of legal organization, marketing, pricing, profit, financing, and cash flow are among the topics covered. Specific goals for each are set out in written form.

The plan for the first year of operation is the most critical and difficult to write. The reason is that the business has no established history on which to base future goals. All projections are, at best, educated guesses. How realistic they eventually prove to be depends on the nature of the planning and the effort directed to achieving the results predicted.

Simplicity and Directness

The best plans are simply written. An analogy is found in engineering. There, the simpler the design for accomplishing a task the stronger will be the preference for the result. The reason is fewer things can go wrong with a device of simple design, to say little of the lower initial cost. Although a business document has no mechanical parts to wear out, it can be so cluttered with minute detail that the reader loses sight of the important points. A few important goals stated and accomplished for each major area of concern are far more beneficial for the business than numerous goals listed but not achieved.

Accounting school graduates, in particular, are inclined to make the business plan overly complex. They sometimes view the small business as a microcosm of a large corporate enterprise, with the plan being cast in the same mold. One highly educated person suggests the following for the financial part, alone, of a small business plan: a detailed profit-and-loss statement, balance sheet, cash flow analysis (a monthly statement showing uses of funds), long-term debt statement, break-even analysis, personal financial record, and a list of credit sources. Such an extensive array of documents might be necessary when borrowing large sums of money to establish a business, but much of it is unnecessary for the average craftsperson. No wonder some plans cover as many as 50 to 100 pages when eight or nine will do.

The financial section of a small business plan can usually be adequately covered by a carefully thought-out budget. The document will show projected income, expenditures, and cash flow on a monthly basis for the year (the same 12 months used in tax reporting). A more elaborate listing of financial projections would often take away time that could be devoted otherwise to achieving the organization's goals. How to write a simple plan, including the basic budget, is covered in chapter 3.

ORDER AND ORGANIZATION

If you can write coherent goals, you can put other aspects of your business in order. Keeping a tidy and orderly place of work, maintaining records in a systematic manner, and scheduling and coordinating activities for optimum results are practices within the reach of any who truly try. Regardless of the situation, an effectively organized operation comes about through concerted effort and conscientious performance.

A Best Foot Forward

Being well organized personally is prerequisite to developing a functionally sound business. The reasons pertain to matters of public image and the management of internal affairs. First of all, anybody dealing directly with customers—as often occurs in this form of retailing—must do whatever is necessary to put a best foot forward. The perception of being organized and in control is essential. An appearance of being disorderly, unkempt, untidy, and in general disarray will not create the kind of impression needed for selling crafts or any other goods. Inconsistency of facts in a sales presentation will not help matters, either.

A second consideration involves an individual's ability to establish practices astutely and to carry out their performance with sufficient stringency. For example, can we expect someone who detests the use of work calendars and time budgeting techniques to manage time effectively? What about the person who is nearly always late to appointments, or the one who puts things off until the last minute? Would either be likely to set and follow a schedule closely? Bad personal habits, unfortunately, will probably find similar expression in the affairs of the business.

To compound problems, the operator of a home-based business is subject to all sorts of disruptive occurrences. Efforts to establish routines and adhere to good work patterns tend to dissipate because of interruptions by unexpected visitors, private telephone calls, critical family problems, unplanned shortages of material, and even the disturbing antics of house pets. You can overcome these problems only to an extent. By disciplining yourself and establishing control, you can alleviate some of the difficulties and keep operations in reasonably smooth order.

The Workplace

Begin by organizing the workplace. Avoid clutter and the inefficiency that goes with it. Keep frequently used items within easy reach, and arrange them so you can avoid digging through stacks of material. Organize both the office and the workshop. Remember the adage: *A place for everything and everything in its place.* It has merit here.

Learn to file letters, canceled checks, bills, and receipts according to how you will need to access them later. Instead of tossing the papers into a cardboard box or an empty drawer, promptly record important data and file the originals for possible retrieval. Imagine having to search time after time through unsorted papers in order to gather data for filing taxes, to say nothing of the need to know ongoing financial balances. If, as sometimes occurs, you cannot respond promptly to correspondence or record data daily, place the papers in a *tickler file*—a file containing items to be attended to by a specified date or as soon as convenient. Try not to let such matters go unattended beyond the weekend. Bad habits are easily formed but difficult to correct.

In the workshop, schedule operations to maximize efficiency in production. Whenever possible, cut out duplicates or machine multiple pieces at once, rather than completing operations from beginning to end on individual pieces. Moving unnecessarily from station to station or from operation to operation is wasteful. It is equally important to have machines placed in proximity and sequential order according to their use.

Something similar can be said of storing materials and accessories. By positioning items close by and in the order in which you will use them in production, you can attain an orderly progression of operations regardless of whether they are performed by hand or machine. Place things within arm's reach. You can save much time that way. In industry, efficiency experts base many of their recommendations on this very principle.

Scheduling

A daily planner is an indispensable tool for organizing your daily activities, both as related to your craft and to the routines of living. Use a planner to schedule everything you need to accomplish during the day, from ordering office supplies to shopping for groceries. Also, record starting times for the different activities. Not only does this practice help you coordinate your schedule with other people involved, but it also forces completion of the tasks within the times allotted. When well planned, a schedule serves as an excellent guide for managing time.

In addition to its potential as a time saver, daily scheduling helps you identify and prioritize activities. When planning a day's activities, you should first consider things you need to do, followed by things you want to do. You can logically work around established necessities, such as dinner time, so as to avoid conflict. Then set your schedule in some order of preferred accomplishment and time allotment. Enter items of low priority last so you can use them as fillers when you complete major tasks quicker than anticipated. Finish the schedule by reviewing it for oversight and entering any previously uncompleted activities.

Although many tasks lend themselves to a daily routine, some are more properly put into schedules of longer duration. A weekly, monthly, or yearly timing will better accommodate some repetitive activities. Common sense tells us what to do when. The sorting of mail logically takes place at about the same time each weekday, while the writing of paychecks might be done weekly, the balancing of a checkbook monthly, and the payment of certain taxes quarterly or annually. Paying bills, on the other hand, occurs less routinely. The object there is to schedule payments to take advantage of any discounts offered and, above all, to avoid paying a late penalty.

Without a doubt, scheduling is a worthwhile practice. The variety and frequency of activities in the ordinary conduct of business make it virtually indispensable. People who are chronically late to meetings and who fail to complete tasks on time might, indeed, disdain having to build schedules on a day-to-day basis. The best advice for them, though abrupt it might seem, is either to learn how to schedule activities and be timely in their completion or to find a line of work where the consequences will be less severe.

Keeping Organized

Proprietors sometimes have more of a problem keeping their operations organized than putting them in order initially. Time-wasting disruptions are part of the reason, especially for those who work alone. To eliminate or counteract such problems in your operation, install an answering machine to avoid telephone interruptions, instruct friends and customers about your business hours, and enlist your family's assistance in controlling potential distractions in an effort to remain free to do your work. Regardless of the effectiveness of these measures, unexpected impositions on your time will still occur. Such is the nature of business.

BRAINSTORMING

Why is it that some people become successful entrepreneurs while others of seemingly equal ability fail miserably in the attempt? The answer lies, in part, in knowing how to solve problems. Fortunately for many, problem-solving abilities can be improved with practice. One way is by brainstorming.

Brainstorming enables the practitioner to generate workable ideas and solutions to problems within a limited time period. Its use is especially helpful during the early stages of business when solutions are most needed and time and knowledge are least abundant. Nevertheless, deliberate and persistent application will prove beneficial throughout the entire life of a business.

Repeated research studies have revealed several significant observations that apply to the general needs of people. For one thing, repeated use of brainstorming results in nearly a doubling of imaginative power—that is, the ability of the individual to think up unique and useful ideas in a limited time. Interestingly, proportionately equal gains occur among people of low and high initial creative ability and among those having low and high levels of intelligence. Age makes no significant difference, either. Additionally, improvements due to repeated application of the method transfer directly into later work.

Brainstorming also produces results effectively and efficiently. In other words, it leads intentionally to the best solutions conceivable in a minimum of time. Both outcomes have a place in the business world.

By and large, people do their most productive work as they approach fixed deadlines. The closer to the end of a planning period, the greater becomes the number and quality of the ideas generated. Experiments involving shorter planning periods have shown no substantial effect on results. The exception occurs when the periods are too radically restricted. Apparently, there is much truth to the contention that man will take as much time to complete a task as is available to use. The lesson this suggests for the entrepreneur is to carefully limit periods of ideation and planning and to adhere strictly to the bounds of time.

Three Phases

The process of brainstorming has three distinct phases: problem identification, ideation, and problem resolution.

Problem identification, the first of these stages, entails identifying, stating, delineating, and scrutinizing the problem so as to completely understand it. The usual thrust is to view the problem through direct analysis. A different approach is to attack the underlying concept. For example, the problem of how to word a poster might shift from that more or less precise idea to a broader thought, such as communicating visually with a particular group. When circumstances do not indicate which approach to apply, there is no apparent harm in doing both.

The second major phase of a brainstorming session, ideation (or idea-forming), has the objective of producing as many ideas as possible in the time set aside for the purpose. Quantity leads to quality. The evidence shows that an increase in the number of ideas results in an increase in the number of good ideas.

During this period of ideation, direct your efforts to the freewheeling production of ideas. Complete open-mindedness is the rule. The statements you come up with may be radical or conservative, original or commonplace, related or unrelated. Try to defer critical judgment until later so you will be completely free to create thoughts by combining, associating, and contrasting ideas one with another in piggyback fashion.

The third principal phase of the process, choosing the best idea or solution, involves judicious evaluation of all the thoughts listed. At times, several possibilities will appear to have equal merit; after all, there is "more than one way to skin a cat." In such instances, make a choice based on the relative costs, time, personnel, and any other related factor. If you still have possibilities that seem equally valuable, choose intuitively or by hunch. For example, consider the selection of a name for your business. You can easily brainstorm 20 to 30 possibilities in less than an hour, with several on your list seeming better than others. Suppose further investigation indicates none of the top selections duplicates existing names, so all of them would be acceptable to register in your state. The one you finally decide to use comes down to a matter of personal preference. You might even be surprised to realize that you had not thought of the name before you began your brainstorming session.

Sleep on It

Always try to make a decision far enough ahead to allow time to sleep on it. You can make this practice work in one of two ways. One way is to put your subconscious mind to work at night. The key is to think about your decision before going to sleep. With proper concentration right before sleep takes hold, you might discover, upon considering your choice sometime during the following day, that a solution becomes much clearer than before. Proponents of this technique claim the subconscious mind actively works during the sleep-filled hours, producing remarkable powers of recall and problem solving. Only you can tell whether it works for you. In all likelihood, the technique is more productive for some than others.

The second procedure, a variation of the first, is to put your topic aside and return to it some days later. Within a few days (or as long as it takes to completely forget the subject), you will be able to analyze or review your decision with a fresh outlook. Artists, writers, designers, and other professionals commonly use this technique to advantage. With very little effort, you can apply it when solving the problems normally encountered in your business.

Although neither of the aforementioned practices is strictly part of the brainstorming process, each adds another dimension to the decision-making process. At least one of them will probably work effectively for you.

Alone or Together

One of the beautiful aspects of the brainstorming process is that it can be done alone, in pairs, or by a group. Brainstorming by yourself can be very productive, but the combined input of several experienced people will sometimes be best. The amount of preparation by the participants makes a difference, though. Not much is gained by involving a person who has very little knowledge of the business or has no interest in it. In view of the possibilities, the limits of time for each session should be adjusted to accommodate the numbers of participants, their experience with the method, and their understanding of the problem.

The complexity of a problem also affects the choice of time. Ordinarily, sessions vary in duration from about 15 minutes to several hours. Knowing the participants' experience with the method helps when determining what time limit to set.

WHERE TO GET HELP

Everyone needs help at some point. Successful business operators usually begin by learning a great deal of all they need to know by reading and attending workshops or classes. Many also enlist the assistance of experts. Some hire professionals when starting out; others do so later to keep their businesses functioning effectively. The various needs, whether for self-help or paid assistance, are readily fulfilled from the extensive selection of services available.

Professional Services

Depending on the amount and quality of your preparation, you might at some point find the advice of a specialist to be helpful, if not essential. You can hire a specialized expert to help solve any legal, financial, managerial, or other type of problem that could place your operation at risk. Because the fees of such professionals will vary substantially, and because some have highly specialized practices, always do a bit of comparative shopping before entering into an agreement. Find out what service you will receive from several professionals in the line of work under consideration. Then check out their qualifications and reputations. Contact three or four clients or former customers of each professional. Word-of-mouth assessments obtained are often very enlightening, although sometimes contradictory.

National and regional organizations of professionals, such as the American Bar Association and its affiliates, generally restrict their comments about individuals to matters of membership. For that reason, they do not shed much light on the specific qualifications of an individual practitioner.

Lawyers, accountants, bankers, and insurance agents represent the professional types most frequently used in business, although consultants will be employed on occasion. The first four of the five mentioned have offices in most communities. Professional consultants are likely to be located only in large cities. All normally charge for consultation services except, perhaps, the bankers and insurance agents. Generally, officers in banking institutions give advice on loans and other monetary services as part of their duties. Insurance agents customarily consider advice to be part of their business function, too.

You would be wise to proceed cautiously when employing professionals. Learn enough about the individuals and their firms or agencies to make an intelligent choice when hiring one, and study your situation thoroughly enough beforehand to be able to tell what needs doing.

Bear in mind, individuals who charge for their services intend to make money. It is to your advantage, therefore, to make an intelligent selection before entering into a contract. Here are the points to raise with any consultant, attorney, or accountant you are seriously considering. You should ask:

- What percentage of his or her practice is devoted to small businesses and home-based operations
- What regulations cover your business in your state and in your locality
- If he or she has written or spoken on the subject
- How many small businesses he or she has helped initiate or advised in the last four years
- About his or her familiarity with tax regulations for small businesses like yours
- About charges or fees and what, specifically, would be done in return
- For a list of references (clients) recently counseled on small business matters

Tell the professional you will get back with a decision in due time. Evaluate the responses carefully. Look elsewhere if the person refuses to answer a request, seems unfamiliar with your kind of problem, or leaves you feeling uncomfortable in any way.

Remember, too, most of what you need to know is obtainable through other sources. The free and inexpensive advice offered by agencies of government is a good place to start.

Government Resources

Contacts with local, state, and federal agencies of government might save you from unnecessarily spending large sums of money. The wealth of information at your disposal is close to astonishing, and by utilizing this source, you might find you need an attorney or accountant only for very complex problems or for those procedures for which you want the convenience of having someone else do the work. Face-to-face consulting, workshops, institutes, and literature are the types of help available from various governments. Direct charges to the public for these services are ordinarily low.

Local and state offices Make your first contacts with local officials. Bring matters of zoning, licensing, taxing, and registration to their attention. If you don't know which city or county offices to visit or call, simply ask one of the secretaries or receptionists in a municipal building for assistance. Some local auditor's offices, in the course of advising what needs to be done, will give you all the information required to satisfy state as well as local regulations on sales taxes and business registration.

When you are first starting out, a good source to contact is the office in charge of economic development for your state. Consult your telephone directory for the phone number. If the number is not listed in your directory, consult the one for the state's capital or dial directory assistance.

Small Business Administration As users of this service know, the SBA has extensive benefits. Its current role as an independent agency of the federal government seems not to have diminished its services. Individual counseling, guaranteeing loans, small business institutes, business development centers, courses, conferences, workshops, and publications cover the array of approaches to assisting new and established business owners. The services are offered throughout the United States.

Call the number of the nearest SBA office, or write to the address below. Request information on institutes and workshops. If new to business, ask for the "Business Start-Up Kit." It is free for the asking.

U.S. Small Business Administration
1441 L Street, N.W.
Washington, DC 20416

Also, obtain information about the course offerings in your state. The "Start Right Workshop" and the "Home Based Business Seminar," each variously requiring a day or an evening to complete, are among the many instructional sessions generally made available to the public. Some of the topics frequently included cover the pros and cons of starting at home, record keeping requirements, licenses, permits, zoning, insurance, taxes, marketing, advertising, and pricing. The sessions are helpful in determining if a handcrafts business is really for you. Additionally, they provide expert advice to take into account if you decide to go ahead.

You can also request, free of charge, a directory of publications and videotapes for starting and managing a small business. All items in this series carry a charge. The topics covered fall under the headings of planning, marketing, financial management, personnel management, and controlling crime in the business setting. Each videotape is accompanied by a workbook.

Counseling and instruction by SBA is provided through the Service Corps of Retired Executives (SCORE), a cadre of over 13,000 volunteers. SCORE helps owners of small businesses solve problems through a well-developed system of training sessions, besides one-on-one counseling in the regional offices and limited consulting at places of business. A $20 to $30 fee is now charged for the workshops. Counseling and consulting remain free, except for traveling expenses.

Other federal sources Business-related publications are available from various federal agencies. Request those applicable to your operation. By all means, obtain literature distributed by the IRS. The number to call for ordering IRS forms and publications is listed in your telephone directory. Ask for the "Business Tax Kit." It contains the kind of information every business operator needs for obtaining an employer's identification number and for filing federal taxes.

A second source, the Department of Labor, makes available literature that covers a variety of aspects of employment and work standards. Explanations are given about the law on minimum wage, overtime compensation, wage garnishment, equal employment opportunity, affirmative action, small business regulations, job safety and health, unemployment insurance, and employment of youth and student learners. Obviously, these publications are most useful to employers and those about to hire workers of one kind or another. A free booklet, *Publications of the U.S. Department of Labor,* lists the printed matter, prices (if any), and sources of availability. Request it from:

U.S. Department of Labor
Office of Information and Public Affairs
Washington, DC 20210

The final source I want to suggest is the federal government's Consumer Information Center. Available are quarterly mailings of the "Consumer Information Catalog," a catalog of free and low-cost federal publications, and the "Consumer's Resource Handbook." Both contain information of use to the entrepreneur. Write to:

Consumer Information Center
Pueblo, Colorado 81009

If you have never before searched for information at the federal level, you will soon discover how eager most government employees are to help. In fact, the agencies are so structured as to honor citizens' requests as positively as possible. In the event you want information but don't know the source, call one of the Federal Information Centers (FICs). The assistants in your congressman's local office will usually be very helpful, also.

Independent Business Associations

Duly constituted associations offer still more services and information for small business owners in the home-business industry. Several associations worth considering are listed below. They vary in numbers of members from several thousand to over half a million. Membership in the associations listed includes people who work in their homes, either producing merchandise, providing a service, or using the site for flexible work time. Because certain organizations direct their efforts toward specific populations, you should read the promotional literature before choosing among the organizations.

As to the services provided, most distribute newsletters, magazines, and a booklet or two, and most dwell on solving problems related to small business. Another common feature is the planning of annual conferences and shows. A few of the associations buy office equipment and supplies in quantity in order to sell them to members at discounted prices.

Literature might be requested by post card. Write to:

MOTHERS' HOME BUSINESS NETWORK
P.O. Box 423
East Meadow, NY 11554

NATIONAL ASSOCIATION OF HOME-BASED BUSINESSES
P.O. Box 30220
Baltimore, MD 21270

NATIONAL ASSOCIATION OF WOMEN BUSINESS OWNERS
600 S. Federal St., Suite 400
Chicago, IL 60605

NATIONAL FEDERATION OF INDEPENDENT BUSINESS
600 Maryland Avenue, S.W.
Suite 700
Washington, DC 20024

Not to be overlooked in the search for information is your local chamber of commerce. You might already know some of the members, and others will become friends when you join. With a little effort, you are certain to find someone in the organization who will give you sound procedural advice.

Considering the many associations, governing bodies, and professional firms involved today, it is apparent that information and assistance on any aspect of small business can be found somewhere. It is also apparent that this extensive involvement is due to business management being an art rather than an exact science. Infallible sets of rules simply do not exist. Thus, the reasons for drawing widely from among the various sources become ever more apparent. Each entrepreneur can consolidate the facts and bits of advice to suit his or her purposes.

MAKE THE MOST OF IT

The production (or purchasing) of articles to sell, the marketing of products, and the selling of the goods are major parts of an ongoing function. Your business begins, technically, with the first sale. As previously explained, you can begin selling early in the process. It is a way of simplifying bookkeeping requirements.

Joy comes to those who know what to do and how to do it well. There is no magic wand to wave. Establish goals and work hard. Learn all you can, then do the work in the way you find most fitting. The important thing is not always how something is done but that the outcome is effective. The IRS will tell you very much the same thing with regard to keeping tax records. Results are more important than methods.

In your own business, in contrast to many other areas of work, you are free to develop your own individual style. Structure it to your benefit. Learn to be creative. Utilize the hidden potential you possess, and strive for efficient solutions as you progress. Refer occasionally to the several methods explained in this chapter for bringing forth those unrealized powers. Apply them. The sense of fulfillment that derives from personal accomplishment and from unleashing unused abilities could be the spark you need to keep working toward a major goal.

3
CHAPTER

Develop a Sound Working Plan

A BUSINESS DEVELOPS FROM AN IDEA—a thought about making extra money, creating an outlet for a hobby, finding something to do in your spare time. That idea, in turn, must be transformed into a working plan. The result is essentially a road map that shows the way to a prescribed destination by the most efficient route.

The plan should be carefully written. The details appropriate for a thoroughly developed plan of action are far too important to depend on memory for their recollection. Goals for the business, market considerations, production organization, sales procedures, and profit expectations are several of the basic subjects to be thought through and set down in clear, measurable statements.

ESSENTIAL BENEFITS

Business plans are written basically for internal management, although some of them are slanted for purposes of borrowing capital. The management function is ordinarily the sole concern of handcrafters. Not only does a plan so written provide direction for the entire organization and its different components, it also gives the business owner standards by which to assess the operation's strengths, weaknesses, and successes. The document should contain statements that represent targets toward which to direct effort over the life of the plan. In short, an effectively drawn plan turns goals into action-oriented tasks.

One of the main benefits of writing a detailed business plan is the thinking involved. In the process, you can anticipate accomplishments and avoid errors. Thus, it is a means of avoiding some of the difficulties you can expect to encounter in the absence of sound planning.

Another benefit is improved managerial competence. The planner develops a guide for decision making, a plan for taking actions essential for running the business, a set of goals and standards for judging operational performance, a timetable for making things happen, and an aid for identifying and obtaining resources. Sound planning gives an owner practice in thinking and figuring out problems about competitive conditions, promotional opportunities, and situations that are potentially good or bad for the operation. The process sharpens important managerial skills and, at the same time, improves prospects for the business.

According to experts in the field of small business, poor planning and financial shortfall are among the main reasons for business failure. Both subjects are covered in the business plan. A well-developed instrument will at least avoid failure due to neglect.

THE WORKING DOCUMENT

Your primary interest is to put together a plan containing the kind of information needed to keep the operation on course and effectively functioning. Write it in simple, straightforward language, and include only those goals basic to the conduct of business. Be concerned about the accuracy of content rather than drawing up a show piece. The essential thing is to produce a document that will serve as an easy-to-follow, concisely stated working guide.

Defining the Contents

At the initial point of planning, seek answers to some basic questions about the business. In other words, determine the *why*, *what*, *how*, *where*, *when* and *who* of it. Ask:

Why are you going into business? The answer you give will define a purpose. Perhaps you want a better living, or maybe you are more interested in seeing people respond favorably about your work than in making a profit from it. The purpose you choose, if precisely stated, will determine which goals and objectives for the business are of highest priority.

Be advised at this point that if you are going into business with the dream of becoming extremely wealthy, you will probably join the ranks of the many who have overestimated their potential for profits. Circumstances would have to be highly unusual for a huge income to flow from a handcrafts business. Be prepared to earn modest returns at the outset, and you will be headed down a much more realistic path.

What do you intend to do? Be specific. To say you'll sell crafts is not enough. Elaborate sufficiently so that the thought behind your main goal comes clear. An explicit conclusion might indicate that you plan to operate a sole proprietorship selling stuffed country animals as a sideline to your regular job. You would then have a sufficiently defined basis for identifying operational procedures.

You might also want to further define what you will sell, whether only things you make or crafts fashioned by others. Perhaps you will do both. A decision must be made up front, but remain flexible enough to change your objective as the business progresses.

How will you accomplish this goal? In other words, what steps will you take, or what activities will you perform to do what you intend to do? The response at this juncture might produce an extensive number of ideas. Listed first might be the major components of the business, such as producing, marketing, financing, and selling, followed by the exact actions to be undertaken in each area. The different components and activities identified will comprise the bulk of the working plan. They should be stated as objectives, and they should be written in measurable terms.

Where will you perform these activities? An analysis of everything you need to do will result in conclusions about the locations of your office, the workshop, the market area, and the places where the goods will be sold. It will also raise serious questions about the reasons for your choices. That is good. Location should always be based on critical analysis.

When will each activity be started, completed, and evaluated? Unless you spell out time limits fully, you won't know when to perform various tasks or how to benefit from completing important steps efficiently and effectively. Timeliness, diligence, and industriousness are the fruits of observing intelligently set time restrictions. Ordinarily, the short-term portion of the plan covers a one-year time period. The calendar months covered in your federal income tax report are the usual basis.

Who will perform the various tasks? Will the owner be both dreamer and doer? What about using members of the family, a retired relative, or an unrelated person? If someone is to be employed for certain operations, how will the division of labor and matters of pay, taxes, and fringe benefits be defined? Your answers are fundamental in forming a preliminary picture of all that goes into the finished plan.

Although the content as briefly outlined here should be covered fully, the format of the plan might vary according to individual preference and the nature of the business. The information contained therein, rather than the titles and subheadings, is most important. When developing the document, bear in mind that a plan intended for your own use might be somewhat different from one planned for borrowing money from a financial institution.

Size

As plans vary in format and content, so do they vary in length. The range is from several pages to several dozen in number. The size and complexity of the organization makes a difference. For a small, one-person, handcrafts business, no more than ten pages will be adequate in many instances. Nevertheless, an individual who feels comfortable with a large amount of detail and structure should lengthen the document somewhat, but never to the extent that the plan takes on more importance than the operation.

Outline

The writing of a plan begins with an outline. Set down the major headings. These might be directed primarily to the major subjects to be addressed in the process of developing and operating the business. An example is given below.

PART I. GENERAL: A description of the business—its type, purpose, and structure. Also matters of legal authority and scope of the plan.

PART II. FINANCIAL CONSIDERATIONS: The finances needed to start, earnings, profits, percentage for promotion, handling of sales taxes, payment of bills, purchasing, and re-investment. A monthly budget of projected revenues, expenditures, and cash flow is a major part of this section.

PART III. FACILITIES/EQUIPMENT: Locations of office, workshop, and storage spaces; planned improvements or construction needs, utilities costs, transportation, and depreciation.

PART IV. PRODUCT/SUPPLIES: Quantities of material for shop and office, kinds and quantities of products, quantity production techniques, inventory, display props, cost factors and pricing.

PART V. MARKETING: Geographic area to cover, whom to contact, involvement of competitors, promotion techniques, advertising, publicity, acquiring leads, repeat business, displaying.

PART VI. SALES: Open-house procedures, party-plan techniques, presentation requirements, use of promotional items, hostess selection, sales by individual order, taking orders, service and follow-up.

PART VII. RECORDS: Method of keeping financial data, monthly and yearly accounting, recording fixed costs and variable expenses, data on sales and buyers, correspondence, tax data and reporting.

PART VIII. LABOR: Who will do the craftwork and the selling, keeping and compensating for time, quality of workmanship expected, and fringe benefits, if any. Division of labor in a partnership arrangement would be included here.

PART IX. EVALUATION: Assessment timetable, determining areas of strength and weakness, target for updating the plan.

The outline as presented indicates only the scope of the considerations to be included in a soundly planned working document. Numerous other factors could be detailed that do not show. For instance, a decision to accept credit-card purchasing would lead to additional work to make buying by this means possible. The plan should include something about it, if that is to be done.

ACTION-ORIENTED GOALS

For purposes of analysis, portions of a plan for a crafts business are presented in FIGS. 3-1 and 3-2. The two illustrations show one way to present details effectively. This format will suffice when recording the goals and activities for your own handcrafts business.

The first of the illustrations shows how the introductory portion might be written. It defines the type, purpose, location, and scope of the business. The second illustration shows several objectives and activities, the arrangement of which carries typically throughout the document. Notice that, taken together, each statement of related objectives and activities makes a precisely measurable unit. This practice accomplishes all that

---

Business Plan
for
CREATIVE COUNTRY CRAFTS
P.O. Box 00
Anyplace, USA
Jane Doe, Owner

GENERAL

Type of business: This is a home-based sole proprietorship for making and selling stuffed and wooden creations in country style on a part-time basis. Employment will be restricted, initially, to members of the family.

Purpose: To supplement family income by selling handcrafted products directly, locally, and at a reasonable profit.

Location and authority: The business will be operated from the residence at 123 Country Lane, using the business P.O. 00. The above listed business name has been registered, an operating license has been obtained, and a permit for operating from the home as currently zoned has been received. Restrictions pertaining to a home occupation in Somewhere Township apply.

Scope of the plan: This plan contains goals, objectives, and activities for the business for three years, with emphasis on the initial year of operation, 19__.

3-1 The introductory page of a plan for a small business should contain brief explanations of basic information.

V. MARKETING:

Goals

5-1. Promote the business and maintain a positive image of it within the tri-county area.

5-2. Increase the frequency of sales leads and follow-up with contacts each year.

Objectives and Activities

5-1-1. Prepare image building material for distribution
   a. Design and print 1,000 business cards (1st month)
   b. Print letterhead and envelopes, 250 (1st month)
   c. Print 2,000 one-page flyers (3rd month)
   d. Print single-fold hand-lettered price catalogs, 500 (5th month)

5-1-2. Advertise locally
   a. Place 1-inch ads in the "for sale" section of daily newspaper—6 weeks the first year
   b. Place 4-inch display ad in daily newspaper for 3 weeks, beginning one week before Thanksgiving
   c. Place 10 30-second spot ads on the local radio station weekly—4 times first year

5-1-3. Obtain newspaper publicity
   a. Have reporter write a personal-interest story about my venture in "Local Life" section
   b. Submit news releases of my speeches to local civic clubs—2 annually

5-2-1. Obtain leads for prospects from local newspapers
   a. Identify and contact one person per week the first year; $1\frac{1}{2}$ average, second year; 2, third year

5-2-2. Increase leads from customers annually

3-2 This part of the plan shows one way to list goals and divide them into specific objectives and measurable activities.

the measurable objectives of the previous chapter are intended to do, only in a different format.

Not shown, but entirely acceptable, is a place for recording the actual performance achieved after completing each activity. You have merely to add another column for this purpose or, otherwise, to use a separate sheet.

The ability to compare achievements with initial expectations is important for measuring progress and setting future goals.

Close analysis of FIG. 3-2 reveals that many of the activities listed have far-reaching ramifications. That time and costs are inherently related is apparent. Be sure to take those factors into account when writing your objectives. Failure to do that carefully could result in a highly unrealistic plan, one going well beyond the limits of personal capability and financial resources.

As another word of caution, do not aim too high when preparing a plan. The common tendency is to list excessively large numbers of activities and levels of profits. The demands on individual performance are too great as a consequence, with the eventual result being not only a failure to measure up to the standards set but also the possible loss of interest in trying. However, from a practical point of view, overstatements of intentions are not nearly as serious as failing to record the goals in the first place.

THE FINANCIAL PLAN

Practically all commercial organizations exist for profit. The motivational value is undeniable. Money for expansion of the business, to support favorite charities, and to bring about a more comfortable life for the owner's and employees' families are several of the commendable incentives.

Yet the accumulation of money can become a woefully ungratifying experience. The one thing worse is not making enough of it. After all, businesses seldom close when showing a profit. It is when the financial aspects of business get out of control or are not taken seriously enough that difficulties begin to develop. A well-written plan helps keep the operator focused on a sound financial target.

A complete business plan contains information about financial needs, problems, and expectations. It serves as a mechanism of control for such things as profit taking, start-up capital, business expansion, accumulation of fixed assets, and product pricing. One of its main purposes is to assure a positive flow of cash. Negative cash flow is often the first indication of trouble for the business. The balance of funds flowing into and out of the business represents a topic of indispensable concern for planning and managing the operation, especially during the initial stages of development.

Budgeting

A term used to describe financial planning is *budgeting.* Its basic purpose is widely understood, for the idea has been literally drummed into the minds of parents and heads of households everywhere. It is used here to describe an essential part of the business plan.

Budgeting is estimating. Income and expenditures are projected as they are expected to occur throughout a set period of time. The period usually selected covers the same year (fiscal or calendar) used for reporting income taxes. Budgets of longer duration are similarly based on units of the tax year.

The newer the organization, the less certain will be the projections that make up details of the budget. The absence, initially, of past profit and loss statements makes estimating with a high degree of accuracy much more difficult than it will eventually become. Hindsight is always easier because there are precedents to rely upon. In view of this fact, the need to estimate conservatively when beginning and to make frequent comparisons of budgeted and actual results during the initial year of operation becomes evident.

A budget contains projected revenues, expenditures, and balances. In bookkeeper's parlance, this is a *pro forma cash flow sheet*. A form with 13 columns (12 for the months and one for yearly totals) is a good format for recording the figures. (The forms are available in office-supply stores.) The left side of such forms has a column for descriptive headings of rows of figures. These headings are mainly subdivisions of the revenue and expenditure categories. The columnar pads generally on the market are lined for about 40 rows of data.

Income

Begin budgeting by listing the sources of revenue. Revenue accrues basically from sales of things made or purchased for resale. On occasion, you might sell some capital item (a piece of machinery or facility) or receive rental income from subletting part of the business facility. Be sure to record those things, too, along with any interest earned from reinvesting cash receipts. In addition, devote a row to listing the cash on hand at the beginning of each month. Prepare a form much like that in FIG. 3-3.

For a new business, the first balance you list will represent any investment in the business as start-up money. Thereafter, you will list that amount of cash carried over from the previous month. Whether the money is kept partly in petty cash or primarily in an interest bearing investment makes no difference as regards the amount for forwarding, as long as the money is readily retrievable for use in the business. A separate checking account for the business, particularly one that bears interest, is highly recommended for at least a portion of the cash on hand. Such an account for handling the cash satisfies several purposes: easy access and availability, increase in revenue through reinvestment, and compliance with IRS requirements for not commingling business and personal funds.

Be aware that the method of budgeting recommended and explained here is based strictly on the cash system. In this system, any merchandise sold on account is not recorded until the money is actually received, and cash payments are recorded when received. When the merchandise is

BUDGET

Year: _____	Jan.	Feb.	Dec.	Total
1. Balance forwarded				
2. Revenue				
Sales income				
Interest earned				
Other –				
3. Cash available (1+2)				
4. Expenses				
Advertising				
Auto Expenses				
Depreciation				
Dues/Subscriptions				
Electricity				
Employee benefits				
Freight/Postage				
Heat				
Insurance				
Interest payments				
Material/Supplies				
Merchandise				
Legal & Prof. services				
Licenses/Permits				
Office expenses				
Rent				
Repairs & maintenance				
Tax, owner's				
Tax, Sales				
Telephone				
Travel/Meals				
Wages & commissions				
Other –				
5. Total expenses				
6. Personal draw				
7. Balance [3 – (5 and 6)]				

3-3 Headings on an annual budget should generally follow allowable entries for tax purposes. The use of a 13-column sheet is convenient for making monthly estimates.

ordered and delivered makes no difference in this system. Additionally, a payment by check is recorded on the date received even if days or weeks go by before cashing it.

Recognize, also, not all money received is income for the business. Money for personal purposes is thereby excluded, including some intended for the business. Money received from a life insurance policy, investment in stocks, or interest on a personal checking account represent several kinds of inapplicable personal income. Nontaxable funds received in the form of a loan from a bank are not to be included as ordinary business income, either.

Expenditures

The expenditures portion of the form contains both direct and indirect costs of doing business. *Direct costs* pertain to outlays for things related solely and strictly to the business. Examples of direct costs are material and supplies, equipment purchases, wages and benefits, advertising, legal and professional services, repairs and maintenance, licenses, and any other costs fully and totally related to the business.

Indirect costs are legitimate costs that relate to things partly assignable to areas of personal use and to those that support the business but not directly in the production or selling of merchandise. These include such expenditures as the additional cost of insurance, utilities, maintenance of the workshop, use of family car in the business, and other costs shared with normal operation of the home. Only the portion of expenditures allowed by law might be allocated to the business for tax purposes. Thus, the area of an office in the home (only if it is used solely and exclusively in the business) is legally used in determining the proportion of total area in the home and the part legally depreciable and deductible when computing taxes. The proportionate use of light, heat, and power is similarly determined when figuring the amounts deductible as business expenses.

In general, three requirements must be met for deciding whether an outlay is a deductible expense for tax purposes:

1. The expenditure must be incurred in a business conducted by the taxpayer

2. It, with some exceptions, must not be for a permanent asset (capital item) to be used in the business more than one year

3. It must be an ordinary and necessary expense of operation.

Always consult publications of the IRS to be sure the deductions are legitimate business expenses.

There is little sense in listing items other than those allowed for income tax purposes. Two important exceptions, however, are the expenditure of business funds for the retirement of a loan and the amount of owner's federal income tax for the business. Both of these are costs to the business, but not deductible calculations for income taxation. Then, too, a home business will sometimes involve regulations unlike those applicable to a commercial business operated outside the home. The use of a telephone illustrates this point very emphatically. Currently, the only deduction permitted for using a home phone in a home business is for related long-distance calls, while a separately installed line for a business phone in the home will qualify for full deductions if used strictly for conducting business. A cellular telephone or similar telecommunications equipment is subject to still other restrictions. If special equipment of that kind is not used more than 50 percent for qualified business purposes during the tax year, the deduction of operating expenses is not allowable and depreciation deductions are limited. The point to remember is to estimate the deductions and list the amounts much as they would be reported on the year-end tax report.

The Balance

After listing the expenditures, add the amounts and subtract the total from the sum of the revenues and balance on hand at the beginning of the month. Hopefully, this final balance will provide enough funds (the cash flow) to cover any amount you need to withdraw, as well as a cushion for forwarding to the next month of the budget.

The amount the owner plans to withdraw will depend on individual circumstances. Complete dependence on the business for full family support could place a serious drain on the business, while partial dependence on income from the business, as would probably be true for a retiree, a married person, or a part-time entrepreneur, would be less likely to cause a serious problem of cash flow. Logically, the plan should call for smaller withdrawals early in the business as compared to amounts taken out for personal use when the operation is established and ongoing.

BUDGET ENTRIES

Some common entries are included in the budget form in FIG. 3-3. Brief descriptions of the headings follow.

Balance Forwarded and Revenue

Item 3 on the form, the amount of cash available for doing business, is a combination of the balance from the previous month (or the initial investment) and the revenue brought into the organization through sales, interest, and other earnings. In order to fill in amounts for each of the 12 months and the totals, it will be necessary to have planned special sales events. Because some periods of the year have greater potential than others, uniform monthly sales are extremely unlikely. The projections must necessarily be based on a complete plan reflecting the highs and lows of marketing and selling throughout the year. They must also be based on pricing determinations. Furthermore, any sales tax that must be collected should be listed as income. This tax is later deducted as an expense.

Deductible Expenses

Expenses, too, must be planned individually and as they are expected to occur throughout the year. Some expenses, such as utilities, will be registered monthly, while others will be experienced less frequently, if at all. Advertising is one that could lead to either regular or irregular listing, depending, again, on how you choose to advertise.

Advertising   Include in this row of the form estimates of the costs of promoting the business, such as printing, mailing of circulars, promotional giveaways, and newspaper and radio ads.

Auto expenses   Project the cost of operating a car for business purposes. The use of a family car might best be figured for the budget on an estimate of the miles to be driven for business purposes, but actual business expenditures and depreciation, as explained later, are allowed as tax deductions. Keep an accurate log.

Depreciation/deduction   Enter on this line amounts planned for purchasing certain property as capitalized and depreciated or taken as a deduction, subject to limitations of the IRS tax code. Up to $10,000 might be deducted if qualifications are met.

Dues and subscriptions   Record monies to be spent for membership in business associations and for magazine subscriptions relevant to the business.

Electricity   Include only charges anticipated for using electrical current in the business. Compute the proportional usage if a qualified workshop and office are supplied under one billing for the entire home.

Employee benefits   List the dollar value of purchasing fringe benefits for the year for wage earners, if any.

Freight/postage   Show expected freight, express, and mailing charges for deliveries and on merchandise purchased.

Heat   Include expenses likely for heating the business premises, computed as for other utilities.

Insurance   Deduct only premiums for the business. A homeowner's policy is deductible only to the extent of the extra coverage provided to cover the business operation. The owner's personal insurance is not deductible.

Interest payments Deduct any interest on business indebtedness, as for a loan. Interest on personal loans is not deductible here. Penalties for late payment of bills are not interest and are not deductible, either.

Material/supplies This includes all raw material to be consumed in the construction of articles for sale.

Merchandise List the cost of any finished crafts to be bought for resale.

Legal and professional services Record here allocations for accountants, attorneys, and consultants to be employed for the business. Do not include allocations for any non-business purposes.

Licenses/permits Show the annual expenses for all licenses necessary for the conduct of your business.

Office expenses Include here all expenses expected for operating the office, except for utilities and maintenance.

Rent Record any rent for business facilities. Part of the rental charges for a home when part of it is used in the business might qualify as a tax expense under the exclusive use rule.

Repairs and maintenance Enter in this row amounts for repairs and painting of equipment, machinery, or facilities to be used in the business. Include such things as brooms, mops, soaps, disinfectants, and other cleaning supplies.

Tax, owner's List the amounts for self-employment tax, real estate tax (proportionate for a home business), and federal, state, and local income taxes. Although federal income tax resulting from the business is not deductible as a business expense when filing federal tax returns, it is often a substantial cost and should be included in the budget.

Tax, sales Enter all sales tax to be collected and included in receipts.

Telephone List the charges to be incurred for business telephone services. As previously mentioned, a separate line added to a home phone might qualify for deduction; otherwise only the long distance charges for business purposes might be deducted for home phone use.

Travel/meals Expenses such as car fare (rental cars and taxis, not your own car expenses), plane fare, lodging, and tips on qualified business trips and conventions might be deducted. Meals taken on business away from home are deductible at the 80% level. Estimate the amount, and keep an accurate record of such expenses as they occur.

Wages and commissions Wages for employees, including amounts to be deducted for taxes, are entered here. Money drawn by the proprietor or partner.

Other Identify and record any miscellaneous business expenses to be incurred during the course of the year.

Monthly and Yearly Balances

The last deduction I will cover here is the amount to be taken monthly from the business as a personal withdrawal. This amount represents a drain on the business, and it is not deductible for income tax purposes. It might be applied to living or family expenses, including withdrawals by the owner for personal use, insurance on the dwelling or owner's life, or payment for food, clothing, servants, medical care, and the upkeep of pleasure vehicles. Of course, the amount of money to be taken from the business can be a serious problem when the total cash left for business purposes is inadequate. It follows, then, that a substantial financial cushion will help offset or completely eliminate problems in this area.

The bottom line of the budget should be your best estimate of how much money will be left each month and at the end of the year. Whether expenses and payments to yourself will actually leave as much as you project can only be discovered as each month goes by. If the balance, your profit, is practically nil, your business will be earning little to hold in reserve for unexpected hard times or for expanding operations. The obvious need before you, therefore, is to budget intelligently and to work diligently to keep the balance from falling short of the amounts projected.

A complete financial plan contains objectives and activities in addition to the filled-in budget form of FIG. 3-3. The limitation of the form to a one-year period is a major reason for this. Include any reference to long-range objectives, such as "to double profits in three years," as a separate notation in the financial section of the business plan. Product pricing, investment practices, and insurance coverage are other factors warranting separate notation.

A carefully prepared, reliably accurate financial plan will obviously make management of the business less of a chancy proposition. It is helpful to use tax guides when setting up the budget. Precisely accurate projections are not required, nor do you have to budget only those expenditures that are legitimate tax exemptions. Federal income tax payments and amounts to be withdrawn for personal use do not qualify as tax deductions, but they do represent important expenses to consider when budgeting for the operation. The idea of having most expense items recorded as they will be used when filing taxes establishes an operating pattern of value later.

THE BUSINESS STRUCTURE

There are many legal details to be taken into account during the planning phase of business development. Whether to structure your business for managing it alone or in conjunction with other people is a basic one.

Sometime early in the planning process you will have to decide whether to organize your business as a sole proprietorship, a partnership, or a corporation. In most situations, the choice will have to be made before filing for a license or vendor's permit, registering the business's name, and putting together the business plan. Each type of structure has its purposes, limitations, and advantages.

Choosing a Structure

The majority of the 20-million-plus small businesses operating in the United States are sole proprietorships. Partnerships are next in line. Home businesses, too, operate predominantly under the traditional form of one-person ownership. This is a telling fact. There must be good reasons for it. The main point is that a sole proprietorship does not encumber an owner with many of the complexities of the other forms.

What considerations should be taken into account when making a decision about your business's structure? Here are some basic ones:

- The kind of business—its product
- The need for operating capital
- The number of people needed
- The tax advantages and disadvantages
- The legal restrictions and complexities
- The potential for lawsuits
- The division of responsibilities and earnings
- The matter of business dissolution or perpetuation

By way of a brief analysis, consider two of the several ways of selling handcrafts. One is through the party plan to homemakers and the other is through a retail gift shop. The first of these could be readily operated as a one-owner business, while the latter would likely profit best under a more elaborate partnership or corporate structure. The reasons are clear. A retail store has to be in operation many more hours than required for making household sales, and it requires more workers, takes more capital to start, and is subject to more traffic and potentially more legal responsibility than the party-plan business. Payroll-tax withholding and reporting can be avoided altogether by following the simpler, party-plan method. An owner working alone can handle a party-oriented operation comfortably, and he or she will have none of the problems of dividing duties and earnings that often arise through shared ownership.

The Sole Proprietorship

This form of business is the simplest of all. It is the easiest to start, to operate, and to stop. The owner has complete, undivided control and full responsibility for the operation's successes and failures. Results fall squarely on his or her shoulders. There are no partners or shareholders with whom to divide profits or debts. Yearly gains add to any personal income the individual owner earns, and losses might be used to offset personal income on the tax form. Although the tax laws seem excessively restrictive in many respects, the regulations of government are generally least restrictive on this type of structure.

Implementation involves nothing extraordinary. The licenses, permits, and name registration (for some names) are ordinary requirements regardless of the business's structure. In many localities, zoning ordinances will actually permit operations under a sole owner where other business organizations are disallowed.

Termination of sole proprietorship can be extremely simple. If there are no unmanageable outstanding debts, you need only liquidate assets, pay off bills, and forget it all (that is, until filing the final income tax report).

In the eyes of the law, sole ownership and personal responsibilities are inseparable. Damages from a lawsuit against the business extend to the owner's personal assets. Both the business and one's personal belongings could be lost. *Unlimited liability* accompanies this structure. As a consequence, some proprietors seek greater protection by incorporating. Gross negligence is not protected by the business's structure, however.

As to the fear of being sued in this litigious society of ours, you should analyze aspects of the business likely to fall subject to litigation. Physical injury in a place of business, failure to observe all features of a contract, and the unfulfilled or untimely delivery of goods are several possibilities. A business that sells a product—even a fairly safe one—could fall subject to damages due to whatever unusual circumstance of use or misuse might occur. Having the protection of an insurance policy to cover such contingencies is strongly recommended, no matter what the structure.

Termination of a business upon death or interruption of operations upon incapacitation are sometimes other serious concerns for the sole proprietor. Either condition could be extremely crucial when income from the business is the only means of personal or family support. A small business operated part-time or as a sideline would probably not have the same importance. If, for whatever reason, continuity of operation is necessary or desired, you would be wise to train a friend or a member of the family to take over the operation in case of illness or death.

All in all, the sole proprietorship form of operation is the best for most people who intend to establish a small business. Prospective owners so inclined who are confident of their abilities to handle affairs and who have enough cash to get under way effectively should proceed by themselves. The psychological rewards alone can be exceptional. An individual's freedom to experiment with different methods of production and marketing is without equal, and the person who pursues such a course of action with a modicum of intelligence will not incur operating losses beyond the means to cover them. This individualistic approach to business, with its potential for personal gratification, is a natural extension of handcrafting that many have successfully developed on their own.

The Partnership

Partnerships are of two basic kinds: general and limited. General partners usually share ownership on a 50/50 basis, but other divisions are sometimes agreed to if responsibilities and investments are not equal. Ordinarily, two people of unequal skill, managerial ability, energy, and money will form an agreement to do business on equal footing—thereby achieving better managerial balance than either could provide alone.

A limited partner is an investor only. Such a person is often a friend or relative. Unlike the general partner, the limited partner has little say in management. This person should not be confused with the venture capitalist who is not restricted from delving into the managerial affairs of the company. A limited partner's liability is limited to the amount of the investment. The sole purpose of obtaining a limited partner is financial backing, preferably at a low rate of interest.

Despite the advantages, partnership arrangements have serious drawbacks. A few are: shared decision-making, shared profits, more paperwork, and the potential for deteriorating personal relations. Perhaps the most serious drawback of all is the legal consequence of each partner being held responsible for the debts and obligations of the other. Liabilities taken on by one in the name of the partnership are the responsibility of both. One could be left holding the bag as a result of the other's disinterest, dishonesty, or death.

By all means, draw up an agreement spelling out the various details before entering into a partnership. Include in it the division of duties, the initial input, procedures for withdrawing profits, provisions for keeping business and personal activities separate, how to continue the business in case of the other's departure, and the conditions for dissolving the partnership. Considering the short-lived history of dual ownership (which, according to a member of SCORE, is a little over a year on the average), written stipulation of exact details for discontinuing the arrangement becomes of utmost importance. The agreement need not be written by an attorney to be legal, but it should be signed by the principals and witnesses. Never be so naive as to proceed on the basis of a smile and a handshake. Doing so could soon result in making an enemy of a person who was once a close friend.

Incorporation

One of the main reasons for a small-business person to incorporate is to protect personal assets from litigants and creditors. A regular corporation, which the IRS labels as a C corporation, has profits taxed twice: once as corporate income and again when distributed and reported as income to the owners and any other shareholders. For that reason, some will set up an S corporation. This form is not taxed as a corporation, but income passes through to the owners as in a partnership. All corporations are required to hold meetings, keep written minutes, and have officers. Interestingly, a corporation must name officers no matter how many people are in the organization.

Fees, also, are a reason for concern. Whereas the fee for incorporating a business in many states is as much as $2000 or more, the costs for licensing other structures will often be less than $100. Fees for an attorney's assistance could be considerable, as well. Add to these costs the extra work of incorporating and you have the main reason why small operators prefer to begin with the simpler, sole proprietorship. Incorporation becomes more realistic as the business gains the viability of an ongoing operation.

The choice of a particular business structure has other legal ramifications. The additional considerations are covered in chapter 4.

4
CHAPTER

Know the Legal Requirements

THE TENTACLES OF GOVERNMENT are far-reaching. You might be unaware of how intrusive they are until you begin to establish a business. Virtually every phase of your operation, from the structure of the business to the selling of merchandise, will be regulated by one official body or another.

Zoning, licensing, and tax collecting are just a few of the controls. Other regulations apply just as surely. Among these are restrictions on hiring, minimum wages, tax withholding of several kinds, owner reporting, limitations on manufacturing, where and how certain goods may be sold, the name of the business, and on and on. All levels of government—federal, state, county, city, and township—have something to say about the conduct of business.

Undoubtedly, some people pursue other occupations in order to avoid the bewildering maze confronting the prospective entrepreneur. You could not be faulted for wondering whether it is worth the bother to start a business of your own, considering all the regulations with which to comply. You, after all, probably want nothing more than a small, easily managed operation. The unfortunate fact is you will have to deal with almost as many regulations to set up a small operation as a large, complex one. Compliance might even seem downright stifling at times.

Don't be discouraged. Many people of only average ability have plunged ahead successfully. Adopt an attitude that you, too, can find a way past the barriers encountered along the path. The material in this chapter will help steer the course, pointing in the direction you need to go to succeed.

A WORD OF WARNING!

In chapter 2, I referred to requirements of the IRS and your need to meet applicable rules of taxation. This need is reiterated here. Always be sure of the regulations as they are currently written, whether by the IRS or another agency of government.

Agencies of government promulgate rules, so we are told, not to trap people but to keep them out of trouble. Perhaps they do. But the complexity of certain regulations sometimes brings on an inordinate amount of head scratching in amazement. Much of what is produced for business people generally seems only to make life difficult for the little operator while fattening the wallets of lawyers and accountants. (The federal government's well-intentioned Paperwork Reduction Act of 1980 seems not to have made much difference, either.)

A book such as this can only take the regulations as they exist and discuss their applicability in the broad context. To deal specifically with each individual situation is impossible. Some readers will encounter circumstances that cannot be anticipated or addressed completely and precisely in a general overview, and some of the regulations that apply this year might be changed year after year thereafter. Such changes are not at all uncommon.

Prepare yourself by obtaining copies of the latest laws and rules, and follow this advice strictly: Read and follow the legal requirements and regulations of government as they are currently written. Hire a professional if you find that necessary or desirable, but recognize that not all practitioners are completely knowledgeable in legal matters of immediate concern to you. Be prepared to pay the price in any case.

NAMING YOUR BUSINESS

Early in the development of your business, you must choose a name for its identification. The name will be needed for preparing a business plan and for obtaining the necessary operating licenses and permits. Visit your local library. The librarian can steer you to directories that list businesses registered by county of residence. By reviewing such resources, you can avoid selecting a name already in use or one too similar in sound to others.

Do not undertake name selection lightly. Try to select one indicative of activities as first begun and as they will eventually be. Most businesses do change with time. A thoroughly thought-through name will cover both new and altered activities without need for revision later. A change in name can affect a business's identity and image.

Image

The name selected for your company should be memorable but not too cute. It should be simple rather than exotic, descriptive but not hobby-like and, certainly, short and pronounceable. Try to keep it businesslike. You must build credibility with your customers. A name relevant to the business's activities will tend to stimulate identification through association.

A clear indicator of what the business is about will help in marketing by attracting the attention of people specifically interested in the merchandise identified. Simply put, a name can be made to advertise. One such as "The Corner Cove" tells little, while "Cindy's Country Crafts" is more explicit.

Is the use of one's name, as in the previous example, a good idea? While a surname or nickname in your company's name is not essential, there are advantages at times in using one. A personal name will impart an individualistic style and make duplication of the company's title less likely. In addition, an individual's name used as part of a title can be of considerable help in selling throughout an area where the person is known and respected. People seem most willing to accept personal names that are easily pronounced. As an added bonus in some states, no registration fee is charged if one's name has been included in the business's title.

Registration

You are free to use virtually any title you want for your business, as long as it does not infringe on one already registered, contain a vulgarity, or is not otherwise misleading. The primary purpose of registration is to assure exclusivity. An unregistered business, though perfectly legal in many states, has no such protection. Any other owner could file registration papers with the same title used to identify your unprotected company, and you could be required to select another title—perhaps, experiencing adverse consequences in the marketplace in the process. For this reason, some owners will choose to register their company's name regardless of whether or not registration could be legally avoided. Others will not bother to go through the registration and renewal processes, although those are relatively simple procedures. A company's limited size, its restricted area of operation, a perceived unimportance in protecting the name, or the limited likelihood of the name being duplicated are reasons for making a decision to avoid filing. In some states, the exemption is achieved only by including a person's surname in the title. The small registration fee generally charged seems unlikely to be a major consideration when weighing the merits of registration pro and con.

Always check with the authorities in your state to be sure the name you have selected is not in current use and to complete registration if desired or necessary. Although the laws and practices vary among the states, the usual place to apply is your secretary of state's office. You might also check with authorities in your county seat to ascertain the procedures to follow in the place where you will operate. Be aware, additionally, registration (and licensing) in several states might be required if you intend to do business across state lines.

Some states require publication by a registrant. A common requirement is to have a notice of intention of doing business under a certain name published in a local newspaper for four consecutive issues, followed by the county clerk's verification. This practice furthers name recognition among the buying public, but it also might alert competitors to possible infringement and any existent creditors to the potential for redress. It also adds to the preparatory costs.

Trade Name

An example will help show how registration works. In Ohio, an owner who wishes to assert a right to a name's exclusive use registers the business under a trade name. Application is filed on a one-page document. The form contains places for stipulating the true name being registered, the address (prohibiting use of a P.O. Box for cities over 2,000 population), the name of the registrant, the type of business structure, and the nature of the business. A fee of $20 is charged for filing, with renewal required every five years at a cost of $10 each.

Many of these details are shown on a copy of Ohio's registration form in FIG. 4-1. The reverse side of the form contains general instructions and descriptions of limitations in filing, such as a warning to show the date of first using the trade name as preceding the date of registration.

Fictitious Name

A fictitious company name, that is, an assumed name, is frequently referred to as a ''DBA'' (doing business as). In general, it might be used in lieu of a trade name but does not carry the same degree of protection. Ohio's form for reporting a DBA is also a single-page document. It must be filed within 30 days of the name's first use. The initial fee is $10, and five-year renewals cost $10.

While a DBA in Ohio is reported rather than registered, legal action to protect the name might be taken by the owner or company's representative. Also, a change of address must be reported in writing at the time of occurrence. The fee is $3.

LICENSES AND PERMITS

A license provides official permission to practice a certain business activity. A *vendor's license*, or seller's permit, is a customary requirement for selling a product, and it becomes an unavoidable essential where taxable sales are to be made. The state's taxing authority or a county auditor will provide the information and forms needed.

Taxable Sales

In some states, three forms are available to a person applying for a vendor's license. One is for making taxable sales at a fixed location, another seeks a transient vendor's license for making retail sales and collecting

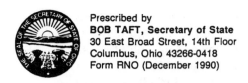

Prescribed by
BOB TAFT, Secretary of State
30 East Broad Street, 14th Floor
Columbus, Ohio 43266-0418
Form RNO (December 1990)

Approved_____
Date_____
Fee $20.00

TRADE NAME REGISTRATION

1. The exact Trade Name being registered is_____

_____ .

(SEE INSTRUCTION # 1 ON REVERSE)

2. The registrant is: (check appropriate box)

☐   an individual
☐   a General Partnership
☐   a Limited Partnership; County in **OHIO**
where certificate or application of limited
partnership is filed is_____

☐   an Ohio corporation, charter no._____
☐   a foreign corporation incorporated in the
state   of_____
holding Ohio license no._____
(SEE INSTRUCTION # 2 ON REVERSE)
☐   an unincorporated association

3. The name of the registrant designated in item 2 is:_____

_____

NOTE: Where the registrant is a partnership, the name of the partnership must appear on this line.

4. The business address of the registrant is:_____
(Street Address)

_____,_____County, _____ _____.
(City, Village or Township)   (State)   (Zip Code)
NOTE: P.O. Box addresses are not acceptable for cities with populations over 2,000.

5. Complete only if registrant is a partnership:
NAMES OF ALL GENERAL PARTNERS   **COMPLETE RESIDENCE ADDRESS**

_____   _____

_____   _____

_____   _____

_____   _____

6. The nature of business conducted by the registrant under the trade name is:

_____ .

7. The registrant has been using this trade name since:_____/_____/_____
(SEE INSTRUCTION # 3 ON REVERSE)   month / day / year

**This document is signed by a corporate officer, general
partner, association member or officer, or the individual
registrant.**

By: _____

4-1   Businesses in Ohio use this form for name registration in lieu of reporting a DBA.

applicable sales taxes throughout a county where the company has no fixed place of business, and the third is for selling and collecting taxes at temporary locations such as at occasional trade shows. Any one of these licenses could be useful in the business of selling handcrafts.

The fees for the licenses vary. In Ohio, a regular vendor's license will cost $25, with a $10 annual renewal fee, while a transient vendor's license will cost $100 initially. Its renewal fee is $40 each year. A license for temporary sales costs $25, as does an annual renewal. An application for a license to make taxable sales in a fixed location in any county of Ohio is shown in FIG. 4-2.

Permissible Tax Exemption

Upon receiving a permit to collect sales taxes, you will have acquired evidence of what is considered in some places to be verification that you need not pay sales taxes on goods bought for resale. This exemption applies to the purchasing of raw materials and finished products, as long as they will be used in your retail business. Items intended for personal use are not exempted, and it would be a violation of law to evade paying the tax by making a false claim. The apparent purpose of the law is to avoid double taxation through collecting from both supplier and retailer.

Always inquire about any special conditions that apply. For instance, some state laws authorize local officials to prescribe less-than-the-usual monthly submission of the sales taxes collected, provided the owner expects low-volume sales for the business. Furthermore, some are permitted to give a discount to vendors who promptly turn over the taxes at specified times. An allowance for bad debts is another possibility. The auditor's or treasurer's office in the local county seat might be the most conveniently available place to do the inquiring.

ZONING ORDINANCES

Zoning regulations are adopted by local politicians in cities, towns, and townships under authority granted by state law. The purpose is to restrict and limit the location and use of buildings, structures, and land according to the use intended. The underlying concern is the interest and general welfare of the public.

As with licensing, acquiring knowledge of the zoning regulations in your area is not something to be put off until after your business has begun to take in money. Make sure the location selected will conform to local ordinances when doing the preliminary planning. To proceed without taking this precautionary step could lead to costly and embarrassing problems, including the expense of relocating or being forced to discontinue operations entirely. Ignorance of official rules and regulations, like attempts to evade them, is legally inexcusable. While ignorance might also be blissful at times, it is not an effective substitute for the peace of mind that goes with knowledge and compliance.

STATE OF OHIO
DEPARTMENT OF TAXATION

APPLICATION FOR VENDOR'S LICENSE
TO MAKE TAXABLE SALES

PRESCRIBED
SALES TAX FORM
NO. ST 1 (Rev. 7-87)

**LICENSE NUMBER ASSIGNED
BY COUNTY AUDITOR**

NON - TRANSFERABLE

TO THE AUDITOR OF _____ COUNTY   DATE _____

Pursuant to Section 5739.17 Revised Code of Ohio, I/we herewith make application for a license to make taxable sales at the following location: For sole owner, print individual's name; for partnership, print full names of all partners; for corporation, print corporation's name and Ohio corporation charter number. If a foreign corporation, print certificate number issued by Secretary of State authorizing transaction of business in Ohio. Section 1703.01 O.R.C.

_____ # _____
NAME   CORPORATION CHARTER

_____
TRADE NAME OR DBA, IF OTHER THAN ABOVE

_____
BUSINESS ADDRESS

_____   _____   _____   _____
CITY   STATE   ZIP CODE   TELEPHONE NO.

_____   CODE NUMBER
KIND OF BUSINESS

_____, County Auditor   By _____ Deputy

NOTE: The County Auditor shall not issue vendor's license until all questions pertaining to the applicant on this application are answered. For kind of business and code number classification and further instructions, see reverse side of this form.
APPLICATION AND PAYMENT OF THE $25.00 APPLICATION FEE IS TO BE FORWARDED TO THE AUDITOR OF THE COUNTY IN WHICH THE SALES ARE TO BE MADE.

1. MAILING ADDRESS (IF OTHER THAN ABOVE)

_____   _____   _____   _____
(STREET ADDRESS)   (CITY, TOWN, VILLAGE)   (STATE)   (ZIP CODE)

2. RESIDENCE ADDRESS OF VENDOR OR HOME OFFICE OF CORPORATION

_____   _____   _____   _____
(STREET ADDRESS)   (CITY, TOWN, VILLAGE)   (STATE)   (ZIP CODE)

3. FEDERAL EMPLOYER IDENTIFICATION NUMBER OR IF NONE ASSIGNED FOR RE— PORTING FEDERAL TAXES PLEASE ENTER YOUR SOCIAL SECURITY NUMBER.

1 - FEDERAL IDENTIFICATION NO.	0 - SOCIAL SECURITY NO.

4. CHECK TYPE OF OWNERSHIP   0. ☐ CORPORATION   1. ☐ SOLE OWNER
   2. ☐ PARTNERSHIP   3. ☐ FIDUCIARY   4. ☐ ASSOCIATION   5. ☐ OR BUSINESS TRUST

5. If vendor is a corporation, show officers names and addresses below.

President _____
          Name   Street   City and State

Vice-Pres. _____
          Name   Street   City and State

Secy/Treas. _____
          Name   Street   City and State

6. When did or will you start making taxable sales at this location? _____

7. _____
   Name   Address   Vendor's license number of previous owner

8. Will you be selling beer, wine or liquor at this location?   YES ____ NO ____ . If a holder of permit(s) issued by the Department of Liquor Control, state permit class _____ and number _____ (see "E" on reverse side)

9. Approximately how much sales tax do you expect to collect each month? _____

10. If two or more stores are operated and you file returns under cumulative return authority, what is your Master Number?

_____

I HEREBY DECLARE THE ABOVE TO BE TRUE AND CORRECT TO THE BEST OF MY KNOWLEDGE AND BELIEF.

_____
(signature of vendor or agent)

4-2   This form, one of three application forms for a vendor's license in Ohio, permits sales and the collecting of sales taxes from a fixed business location.

Know the Area

You must have a fairly good idea of where you will conduct your business when obtaining a set of official zoning regulations. This will enable you to identify a specific political subdivision and the districts specified within it. Your final choice of location might be determined as much on the basis of what you are able to do as by what you would like to do. The less restrictive, more lenient ordinances are likely to be encountered in rural or sparsely populated localities.

Obtain the regulations that apply to your area, and review them carefully. Some governing entities provide single copies without charge, but others require a payment of $10 or more. The higher costs occur in cities where a document might be several hundred pages in length. You can avoid paying the full charge by knowing where you will locate and by purchasing only those sections of the publication that apply to your situation. Maps showing the divisions of districts within the political subdivision are readily available for inspection in the office of the zoning authority.

Zoning regulations usually include the following districts of concern to handcrafters: agricultural, residential, commercial, and industrial. Most regulations further divide those districts according to the concentrations of population within. Divisions of low, medium, and high density are especially common in residential areas, with the restrictions that apply varying accordingly. Requests for exceptions to the different regulations are commonplace.

Variance and Rezoning

Local officials are inclined to look unfavorably on requests for variances and changes in zoning. The greater the number of people affected, the fewer are the chances a regulating board will want to make an exception or change an ordinance. Public boards are normally disinclined to rule in opposition to potentially numerous objections and the interests of large numbers. Nevertheless, stand up for your rights. Seek a change when needed. Rather than assuming "you can't fight city hall," apply for a variance or request rezoning if the change will not adversely affect the surrounding community. Your chances of success will greatly improve if you can show how essential the chosen location is for your welfare. You will have a particularly good chance of getting your way with a zoning board or board of appeals if you have witnesses who can testify that the livelihood of your children depends on the change requested.

Don't rely on a single approach, however. Become knowledgeable about the board's method of operating and, to the extent feasible, become personally acquainted with the individuals in authority. Obtaining the visible support of several neighbors will also have a positive influence when making your appeal.

Commonly, there are prohibitions to consider regardless of type of district. Certain activities will be explicitly prohibited nearly everywhere.

Dangerous activities and those that create excessive traffic or a nuisance of some kind are among them, including businesses that would cause a form of environmental pollution or that could detrimentally affect your neighbor's health. Crafts businesses ordinarily do not fall into this general category, but here again read the zoning regulations so that you will know exactly what applies. An ordinance in one municipality, to show how protective and detailed they can become, does not allow operating from a converted school bus—even if the vehicle has been completely covered over.

Home Occupations

Because crafts businesses are often started in the home, the regulations applicable to operating there will probably interest a large number of people who are planning to enter the business. Why does the home deserve such special consideration as a place to initiate operations? For one thing, a person's dwelling is a convenient and economical place to work. The selling of handcrafts from that location requires little more effort or investment than when handcrafting strictly as a hobby. Moreover, home-based enterprises of various kinds are often permitted in areas zoned residential and agricultural—areas not generally open to other types of commercial businesses. In places where home businesses are disallowed completely, the intent is to have all retailing and wholesaling done in areas specially set aside for commercial work.

The restrictions for carrying out an occupation in the home can be extensive. The nine criteria below are the kinds of requirements frequently addressed.

1. Only members of the family residing on the premises shall be engaged in the occupation.
2. The use shall be clearly incidental and subordinate to its residential purpose.
3. Not more than 25 percent of the floor area shall be used in the conduct of the home occupation.
4. No change in outside appearance shall result, except for a sign of one square-foot area, non-illuminated and mounted flat on an outside wall.
5. No home occupation shall be conducted in any accessory building.
6. No traffic shall be permitted beyond that normally expected in a residential neighborhood.
7. Any need for parking generated by the conduct of the home occupation shall be met off the street and not in the front yard.
8. No equipment or process shall create noise, vibration, glare, fumes, odors, or electrical interference detectable off the lot.
9. No electrical interference in any television or radio receivers or fluctuation in line voltage shall be detectable off the premises.

Without a doubt, once permission to engage in an occupation from your home has been granted (perhaps by means of a low-cost zoning certificate) someone in authority will check to see that your operation complies with the regulations in effect. Your neighbors could be very instrumental in the evaluation. The best policy is to establish friendly relations with them and to do nothing that might cause a change in their attitude. The mere perception of a nuisance occurring because of the business could give an adversary the argument needed to bring about the termination of your business activities. The cost of continuing to operate as before when found guilty of an infraction is as much as $100 per day.

Concern for the Neighborhood

Some home occupations can be conducted in a way that the neighbors do not know of their existence. The advantage involved might be apparent. Authorities ordinarily become concerned about home-based businesses only upon receiving complaints from residents in the area. In fact, officials will sometimes overlook minor infractions that are not apparent externally.

An increase in traffic to the home could be the tip-off that something unusual is going on. To avoid raising suspicion of a possible zoning or other legal infraction, home-based entrepreneurs can maintain a low profile by obtaining a post office box. Its use eliminates excessive traveling in a residential area by customers and mail carriers. Any decision to follow this practice should be undertaken in the light of potential disadvantages from not publicizing your home address.

For the person renting living quarters or residing in a condominium, a check of the lease or the association's rules should be made even before investigating the zoning regulations. Anyone in either of these situations might have already agreed not to conduct a home business at that particular location, but such restrictions, like zoning ordinances, are written by people and can be changed by people. When attempts to change a restrictive regulation fail, the prospective entrepreneur has no choice other than to seek a different place of operation or to give up the idea entirely.

OTHER REQUIREMENTS

In addition to the requirements and restrictions already discussed, be aware of other local, state, and federal regulations and laws on the books that apply to different handcraft businesses. Whether or not they will apply to your situation depends on individual circumstances and the nature of your organization. Check with local and state authorities concerned with business development, such as an economic development council. Determine from them what applies to your business locally, and consult a federal agency for advice about regulations of national origin. In the absence of appropriate sources in your telephone directory, contact your state or national legislative representative, as appropriate, for assistance.

Local and State Levels

Locally, your business might be required to conform to the building code in effect. Any remodeling outside and building anew will most certainly be subject to prevailing restrictions. Be prepared to pay a fee to cover the cost of the permit and on-site inspection after submitting a duly prepared plan for such work.

Home occupations and handcrafts are not widely restricted among the states. An exception occurs whereby federal regulations are extended to cover workers employed in the business. Some states require use of an employee's handbook for this purpose. Another requirement enforced in some places regards the registration of trademarks and the labeling of items made of precious metal. The purpose of these laws is to assure that standards of employment and the content of certain consumer goods are being met.

Municipalities and states vary in the way they tax businesses. To determine what taxes apply locally, contact the auditor's or treasurer's office in your city or county. For information and forms on taxes in your state, direct your inquiries to the department of taxation or revenue in the statehouse.

Federal Laws

There are federal laws about which nearly every proprietor should have an awareness, if not specific knowledge. Two particularly important pieces of legislation come to mind: the Child Protection and Toy Safety Act and the subsequently passed Consumer Products Safety Act. The former bans harmful or dangerous toys from the marketplace, and the latter prohibits selling a harmful product. Failure to observe the technicalities involved could be disastrous for any owner who sells something tangible. Nobody can predict or control how consumers will use or misuse whatever they buy. As a precaution, the craftworker would be wise to eliminate pointed corners, sharp edges, easily loosened parts, toxic finishes, etc., from his or her creations. Even then, you should consider purchasing the protection of product liability insurance.

Debt collection The collection of debts can be another source of legal concern for business people. Aside from the cost of collection and recovery, the tactics used to bring about a positive response from a debtor can be subject to litigation and, in the process of presenting a defense, be very costly. The Fair Debt Collection Practices Act bans all forms of harassment and other unreasonable tactics in attempts to collect past-due accounts. The best practice for the small-business operator is to avoid debts. The recommended way to do this is to accept no credit on account; insist that all purchases be made in cash or by credit card. While this practice might not be completely foolproof, normal procedures of collecting for an occasional bounced check or depleted credit-card account are reasonable and fairly persuasive.

Labeling   Another miscellaneous, but important, federal law of concern to some craftspeople pertains to labeling. One law stipulates exactly the information to be placed on labels attached to products made of wool. Another covers the packaging and labeling of flammable fabrics and hazardous substances.

Mailing   People selling by mail order are obligated to observe the special regulations in that area. Delivery by mail order should take place within either the time stated or 30 days of the receipt of the order. Otherwise, the supplier must inform the buyer in writing of any expected delay and extend an offer to cancel the order cost free. The Federal Trade Commission promulgates rules on the matter, as it does for the licensing of businesses engaged in interstate commerce.

Advertising   Still another law seeks truth in advertising. The honest entrepreneur can easily avoid difficulty in this area by making only truthful and supportable claims.

SELF-EMPLOYMENT AND TAXES

A very extensive area of legislation at the federal level pertains to employment. Few of the laws apply to self-employed, independent business people, because much of the legislation regulates industrial work and strives to eliminate sweat-shop conditions for employees engaged in home work. The business owner who employs one or more workers must be sufficiently knowledgeable to comply with the federal requirements. These are discussed in the next section of this chapter. Most handcrafters, especially when beginning, are more immediately concerned about the regulations affecting self-employment.

Your personal status with regard to employment will depend on specific circumstances. As an owner, you are generally considered to be self-employed. If engaged in an incorporated business, however, the federal government takes a different point of view.

The IRS classifies you as self-employed (working for yourself) if you are a sole proprietor, an independent contractor, or a member of a partnership. Whether you work full- or part-time is immaterial.

As a self-employed person, you will not be required to pay federal unemployment taxes. Estimated and annual income taxes (local, state, and federal), federal self-employment (social security) tax, and unemployment tax in a few states are among the personal levies to be concerned about. Sales taxes and the additional payments of "head" taxes on employees are covered elsewhere in this chapter.

Social Security

The self-employment tax is a FICA tax on individuals who work for themselves. You could be liable for it even if you are now fully insured under social-security law and are receiving benefits. If you are not covered, operating your own business would be one way to work toward qualifying for coverage and the benefits of this form of insurance. If, on the other hand, you already qualify but your spouse does not, consider putting the business under the nonqualifying mate's name so that he or she can accumulate the necessary credits toward retirement. This decision must be based on further determinations, such as which one is fully employed elsewhere and which is most involved in the operation.

Currently, a self-employed person must pay self-employment tax on annual earnings of $400 or more. Business income and other wages are included. The amount of tax is figured for 1992 at the rate of 15.3% of net earnings (12.4% of earnings up to a maximum of $55,500 for social security and 2.9% of $130,200 maximum for Medicare). One-half of this amount is deductible. It is reported when filing income tax forms. Both spouses must pay self-employment tax if both are self-employed, but one might be exempted when working under a sole proprietorship held in the name of the other.

Pension Plans

Another advantage of self-employment, and possibly the determination of which spouse should be so classified, is the permission legally granted for establishing a pension plan. A self-employed person might be covered by a Keogh (HR-10) plan or a simplified employee pension (SEP). The plan selected must be made available to all employees. Contributions to the plan are invested, and no taxes are paid on the contributions or earnings until they are withdrawn. A business deduction might be taken for contributing to the plan for oneself as owner, based on the income received from the business alone. Depending on certain specifics in the IRS regulations, up to the smaller of $30,000 or 15% (20% on occasion) of net compensation might be contributed and deducted yearly from the business's income for tax purposes. Employees you hire are treated similarly, with special rules of capitalization and deduction applying.

EMPLOYMENT PRACTICES AND LAWS

Before hiring employees to do your work, carefully weigh the benefits and disadvantages. Taking on a single employee will increase your paperwork dramatically. Add to this workload the demands of managing and supervising that one person and you will soon realize a significant increase in income is needed to make the venture profitable. The increased paperwork, the employer's expenses mandated by government, and the fringe benefits you provide will raise the cost of employment at least 25 percent over the wages paid.

Having employees might necessitate compliance with costly regulations at all levels of government. At the federal level, you must withhold income and social security taxes on each employee, pay the employer's share of social security and unemployment taxes, and do the mandatory record keeping and periodic reporting. Many states and some localities also require income-tax withholding and reporting. Another common state-legislated expense is workers' compensation insurance for occupational disability and death. Nothing should be overlooked at any level of taxation. The penalties can be severe.

When you need only one or a few employees, you might be able to put your spouse and minor children to work without all the hassle and tax liability of employment. Another alternative is to use independent contractors.

Independent Contractors

The IRS makes a strict distinction between contractors and employees. The determination depends not on what you call a person but on the type and manner of work done. The general rule is that you are employing an independent contractor when you have the right to control only the result of the work and not the procedures for accomplishing the result. A salesman to whom you pay 20% of the retail price for each item sold, without having stipulated precise methods of sale, is an independent contractor. A craftsman you pay by the hour to produce items in your shop by your methods is an employee.

You do not have to withhold taxes or pay taxes on payments you make to independent contractors. People so classified are, with some exceptions, in business for themselves. They must file taxes accordingly. Nonetheless, for each one paid $600 or more during the year, you must file a form with the federal government indicating the amount, to whom it was paid, and the recipient's social security number.

Be careful when reading the IRS regulations on this subject not to be tripped up by what seems to be unnecessary and inconsequential detail. How you advise a person engaged in your business might not be readily substantiated in the absence of a simple, clear-cut requirement. To illustrate, a salesman can be defined as an independent contractor for income tax purposes but be either an employee or a contractor for filing social security tax. The same distinction holds true for unemployment tax purposes. Of course, an owner's tax liabilities and reporting obligations depend on which of the various combinations apply. Again, read the regulations carefully when planning to contract for work in your business to be certain you know which rules apply to your situation.

Employee Management

Some businesses will naturally have to hire employees in order to operate effectively, and others will choose to operate on a grander scale than possible in a one-person operation. A good personnel-management plan could be the key to success in the undertaking. It is an essential ingredient not only for achieving the maximum effectiveness and efficiency among employees but also for assuring compliance with various labor laws and avoiding infringement on personal rights.

The legal and extra-legal effects of employment mentioned here will become clearer by studying the comprehensive plan in TABLE 4-1. When reviewing the plan, notice that many legal aspects of management are not identified—despite their involvement. It simply is not possible to set up a plan for controlling human conduct without giving thought to matters of nondiscrimination, safety standards, and the numerous other regulations affecting employers covered in the broad field of labor and civil rights legislation. Similarly, the demands of employment on administrative time are merely implied in the plan.

Seven major areas of concern in the management of personnel are shown in TABLE 4-1. They range in scope from the broad concepts of planning to the specifics of supervising and evaluating. The idea of a manager

Table 4-1
Employee Management Plan

Topics	Activities
Personnel Administration	Job needs analyses, personnel policies, goals, cost control, job descriptions, labor law and legal compliance (OSHA, EIN)
Staffing	Recruitment, selection, orientation, and turnover
Training & Development	Program planning, scheduling, and group and individual training sessions
Wage Administration	Pay surveys, compensation, fringe benefits, retirement plan, tax withholding and filing, and plan review and revision
Employee Welfare	Health and safety standards, work improvement suggestions, leave and vacation policies, and grievance adjudication
Supervision & Evaluation	Work observation, performance evaluation, promotions, work incentive, discipline, absence, and firing
Record Keeping	Employee files, financial and productivity records, time and overtime cards, tax data, etc.

merely explaining to an employee what needs doing and writing out a check at the end of each week for work well done represents a grossly unrealistic understanding of personnel management. Those several tasks are necessary but represent only a small portion of everything to be done in an effectively managed operation.

Employer's Identification Number

One of the first things to be done after deciding to hire help for your proprietorship is to file for an Employer's Identification Number (EIN). Do this before the actual hiring or if you are setting up a pension plan. (If you don't hire employees, you will use your social security number for tax identification.) If you obtain an EIN but for some reason do not develop a need for it, use the number on your business tax form and write next to it "for identification only." The IRS will then not send employer's withholding forms to you.

The EIN is mandatory for all partnerships and corporations, including S corporations. Those organizations do not enjoy the simplicity of operation accorded the sole proprietorship.

When acquiring an EIN, prepare policies according to the personnel-management plan and determine which IRS rules apply and how to comply with them. Withholding and reporting taxes on employees for social security, unemployment compensation, and wages can be a complex process, and with deducting and reporting payments for pensions and other benefits adding to the complexity. The penalties for not complying properly can be severe. Besides, you must devote a considerable amount of time to keeping abreast of the frequent changes that occur in tax law. For those reasons, many entrepreneurs who decide to put someone on the payroll often seek the assistance of a tax specialist.

Labor Legislation

The need to comply with labor legislation falls as squarely on the shoulders of the small business employer as it does on those of the corporate executive. The difference is that the corporate executive can more easily obtain adequate legal advice. The employer in a small business must often rely on occasional reading, common sense, and infrequent legal consultation. Major pieces of legislation to be observed by employers, without regard to their economic or other business status, are outlined in TABLE 4-2.

A cursory review of the different legal requirements related to employment leads to the conclusion that few business operators are likely to be completely versed in this broad area. Not many devote the time necessary to study and remain up-to-date on all the applicable details. Instead, they will direct much of their effort to the many other important aspects of developing and operating a business. Established, wealthy, large-scale operators have a relatively easy time of it. They can hire legal and account-

Table 4-2
Federal Labor Legislation

Laws	Purposes
Age Discrimination in Employment Act	To bar discrimination against 45- to 70-year-old persons in interstate commerce
Civil Rights Act	Prohibit discrimination on basis of race, religion, sex, or national origin in hiring, compensation, or promotion
Equal Pay Act	Prohibit differential pay based on sex
Fair Labor Standards Act	Regulate hours, minimum wage, overtime pay, and child labor
Mandatory Retirement Act	Eliminate the requirement of compulsory retirement at age 65
National Labor Relations Act	Give employees the right to organize and engage in collective bargaining
Occupational Safety and Health Act	(OSHA) Require compliance with safety and health standards, keeping records, and being open to inspection
Vocational Rehabilitation Act	Outlaw discrimination in employment against handicapped persons

ing specialists (whole teams of them, at times) who have devoted years to learning their subjects.

How, then, do small-scale operators proceed? It is to your advantage, especially when starting with limited funds, to put off hiring help until you are ready to expand operations—thereby concentrating on giving the business a solid foundation while gaining time to become familiar with IRS-employment and labor-law requirements. A work force consisting of independent contractors and family members will often be adequate for a time.

Some operators, such as retail-store owners, will usually have to employ help from the start. Those who do might save money by consulting an accountant or attorney. If yours is such a case, consult a qualified person willing to work on an hourly basis, and be prepared to limit your questions to things you need to know and do to stay out of trouble legally. The more you have learned, the easier and less costly it will be for you to deal with a specialist in that way. Keeping a tax or law specialist on a retainer fee is ordinarily more appropriate for a large, ongoing concern.

PUTTING YOUR FAMILY TO WORK

After reviewing the requirements of employment, perhaps you are now ready to look compellingly to your family for help. A spouse and minor children can save you money in taxes and time in paperwork. That they are and will remain psychologically supportive of your business is the first requirement. The second need is to be sure you are complying with standards of the IRS.

Initial Advantage

Your spouse and dependent children can work in your solely owned business but not be on the payroll or be officially included in any way. This practice is perfectly legal. There will be no payroll tax, no social security tax, no unemployment tax, and no extra paperwork for you on behalf of your spouse and children. Your business is taxed as if no wages are earned, and none may be deducted as expenses. The disadvantage to those helpers is that no credit will be earned toward social security, a pension plan, or other fringe benefits.

Observe the Law

Be cognizant of intricacies in the regulations. The wages earned by your child in your handcrafts business are not subject to social security tax if the child is under the age of 18, nor are such wages subject to federal unemployment tax if the child is under 21. The exemptions do not hold universally. Wages for services performed by a dependent child (and your spouse) are taxable for purposes of federal unemployment, social security, and income tax withholding if your crafts business is incorporated. The same conditions apply if your business is a partnership, excepting instances when, for the child's purposes, both parents are partners.

Income paid to qualified family members but not treated and taxed as employees' wages are free only of some costs. You, the sole owner, pay income tax on your working spouse by virtue of reporting all income with no deduction for wages and at the rate determined when filing your federal tax return. You also pay social security and Medicare taxes on money paid that is not deducted as wages. When compared to other arrangements (specifically to ownership or employer-employee arrangements whereby you and your spouse file separate returns), you might realize a savings if the combined (total) income is beyond certain taxable limits. You can avoid paying the employer's share of social security tax (now 6.2% of $55,500 maximum pay), Medicare tax (now 1.45% of $130,200 maximum), and federal unemployment tax (currently 6.2% minus your state's rate on the first $7,000), by not putting your spouse on the payroll. Any higher income tax rate realized would probably be offset by the larger deductions permitted through joint filing.

Remember, you have an option as sole proprietor regarding your spouse and minor children. It will probably be to your advantage to treat them as employees only after the business has become firmly established.

DO YOU NEED INSURANCE?

Theories about insurance coverage abound. One extreme holds that no-body ever has enough, and an opposing point of view credits much of the wealth among insurance companies to the public's habit of buying more than needed. Convincing arguments can be advanced in support of either position. It follows, of course, that failure of a company due to carrying too little insurance can be as serious as failure due to the financial burden of being too extravagant.

Despite the arguments pro and con, insurance is widely acknowl-edged as a means of spreading the risk. Premiums paid by large numbers of people help pay for the frequent or unusually costly incidents be-leaguering the few. Seldom can an entrepreneur predict whether or not certain coverage will be needed, but having it available when catastrophe strikes can truly be a business-saver.

Government Programs

Our government, too, recognizes the need for insurance. The mandate to comply with the social security and unemployment programs at the fed-eral level clearly exemplifies the general interest in insuring workers. Any-one unsure of how those laws apply to business and self-employment should request literature on the subject or seek information by calling the nearest office of the IRS.

At the state level, worker's compensation provides insurance relative to disability and death. All states require it for employees. In some, self-employed people are given the option of electing coverage and paying the tax. Be sure to check with the appropriate office in your state about this possibility. You might be able to obtain some valuable coverage for yourself at a relatively low cost.

Private Coverage

How much private insurance coverage should a small business have? The answer depends on individual circumstances. Need, not desires—and cer-tainly not available funds—should be the determining factor. Consider, again, two different crafts businesses. One retails entirely from a store; the other utilizes the party-plan method with only an office in the home. The retail outlet will have customers on the premises who could claim injury from slipping or having merchandise fall upon them. Something similar could occur in a party-plan presentation, but the likelihood of such occur-rences in a house and among acquaintances is greatly diminished. The amount of liability insurance needed will vary accordingly. Additionally, the number and types of vehicles used in the businesses will lead to differ-ences in property damage and personal liability vehicular insurance. The costs of fire insurance will be substantially different for the two business properties, as well.

When setting up a business in the home, the first thing you should do is determine that your operation will in no way negate any part of your existing homeowner's policy. If possible, have the policy extended to cover all aspects of the business you plan to conduct on the premises. Ask your agent about an *umbrella clause*. One that applies to liability claims of customers who might be injured at the home site could be a very economical way to acquire a high level of extra protection.

Use some common sense when you buy insurance for your business. Take out policies with deductibles as large as you can afford, but don't overlook the need to insure against losses of personal property. By following this practice, you will keep costs down while being on the safe side. A loss of personal property can be as catastrophic for a sole proprietor as losing part of the business.

Types of Insurance

Besides protecting your personal and business property against losses due to fire and accident, you would be wise to take out a policy on product liability. Being in the business of selling crafts, you are vulnerable to lawsuits due to all sorts of uses and misuses—many unforeseen and most unexpected—in the way the products you have sold are handled. How careful you are to produce a safe product makes a difference. By taking precautions to eliminate all potentially dangerous features, you will at least reduce the probability of negligence. You could still be so charged, of course, and you might have to go to the trouble and expense of defending yourself in court.

You must face this area of concern squarely. The propensity of Americans to litigate is well publicized. Even the slightest injury will sometimes bring on a search for someone else to blame. The high level of charges among lawyers, a court system that favors representation by one or more attorneys, and the trend among juries to make exorbitant awards are other matters you should recognize. The cost of defending against a product-liability suit in this legal arena can be horrendous. An adequate insurance policy could be a blessing. If, however, you are found negligent in creating and distributing an unsafe product, only you will be called upon to serve the term of incarceration should you be involved in the rare situation where one is imposed by the court. The insurance company cannot serve time for you.

Depending on the nature of your business, insurance against losses resulting from *unintended interruption or termination* and from *errors of omission* are other types worth considering. The first of these mentioned here will help offset losses of income when, for some reason, production and sales cannot proceed normally. Insurance to compensate for loss of income becomes most important if you are the sole breadwinner in the family and no one has been trained to carry on the work for you. Insurance against errors of omission is most needed when doing business under contract, as in commission work. This type of insurance, like several others mentioned here, is a deductible business expense.

LEGAL BUSINESS DEDUCTIONS

The costs of doing business are taken into account when filing income tax returns. The IRS imposes a series of regulations that apply as equally to operators making only a few thousand dollars as to those taking in millions. Deductions for a handcrafts business are no exception. They must be made in accordance with the rules of uniform capitalization, while distinguishing among ordinary business expenses, the cost of goods sold, and regular capital deductions.

The overview below indicates the main regulations controlling allowable expenses. Although they are applicable to tax determinations, they are much like those you would follow when drawing up a budget.

General Requirements

To be deductible, an expense must be:

- Kept separate from personal expenses or be properly apportioned if business and personal expenses are combined
- Ordinary, i.e., common and accepted in this business
- Necessary, i.e., helpful and appropriate but not necessarily indispensable
- Kept separate from the cost of goods sold and regular capital expenses

Strict interpretations of these rules must be observed when filing income tax for the business. The income tax form currently in use for sole proprietorships, Schedule C, is included in the appendix, pages 223–229. Both sides of the schedule have been copied to show the list of deductions and the method of calculating the cost of goods sold. Notice that the method of accounting, whether cash, accrual, or hybrid, must be marked on the front of the sheet.

Cost of Goods Sold

Expenses incurred from selling products you produce or purchase for resale enter into the cost of goods sold during the year. Included are: the cost of raw materials and products in the inventory, the cost of shipping those things to you, storage costs for the products you sell, the cost of labor to produce the products, the depreciation on equipment used in production, and the production overhead expenses. In addition, the rules of uniform capitalization require that all indirect expenses due to production and resale must be accounted for in this category.

Indirect costs include rent, interest, taxes, storage, purchasing, processing, packaging, handling, and general administration to the extent each is chargeable to production and inventory. Now for a little break. The reporting of indirect costs under "Costs of Goods Sold" does not apply to crafts you obtain for *resale*, provided your average gross receipts for the preceding three tax years does not exceed $10 million. Why a similar exemption could not have been made on items you *produce for sale* defies all logic.

If you remain confused about filing taxes after reading literature on the subject, contact an agent of the IRS by dialing the toll-free number made available to the public for that purpose. The response will be made courteously and cooperatively. Then, too, you can always employ a tax accountant to help sift through the details.

Capital Expenses

A crafts business typically has costs that are part of the investment in the business. These must be capitalized, that is, be recovered one part at a time over a number of years instead of being deducted fully in the year incurred. This is done by deducting a percentage each year by methods of depreciation or amortization. *Depreciation* is used to recover capital expenses for most of a business's tangible assets. *Amortization* is used to recover only certain kinds of capital expenses, such as start-up costs.

Under certain conditions, the IRS allows you to deduct in one tax year an amount up to and including $10,000 spent for tangible property in your business. In other words, you might elect to treat all or part of the cost of qualifying property as an expense rather than a capital expenditure. You are not allowed to use any such deduction to increase or create a net operating loss, but that part not deductible in one tax year due to this limit might be carried to the next year.

Deductible Expenses

In general, business costs not computed as costs of goods sold nor defined as capital expenses might be subtracted from income in the year when they occur. Amounts incurred for marketing, advertising, selling, and distributing goods are among these. Consult the IRS documents for complete listings and for distinguishing among the several categories of expenses.

Tax deductibility should be a consideration when you set up your business. There are instances when an early decision will work to your advantage. The use of the telephone is an example. Only long distance business calls might be taken as an expense if you use your personal phone, while you might write off the entire cost of having a second line installed if it is used exclusively for the business.

The use of an automobile is another important example. You have the choice of using the standard mileage deduction or of deducting actual business expenses for operating the vehicle. Keep accurate records in any case. You might also want to think about purchasing and using a "business" vehicle so as to take advantage of the benefits of depreciation.

Finally, there is the use of your home in business. It, too, can result in valuable tax advantages. This topic is covered at length in the next chapter.

5
CHAPTER

Profit from the Home Advantage

Y<small>OU SHOULD SERIOUSLY CONSIDER</small> using your home as a place to conduct your crafts business. It might not be ideal, but it could be the best of the alternatives available. Whether you rent or own your residence and have little or much space, the use of a spare room or corner of the garage could lead to substantial savings in effort, time, and money. The expense of setting up business and operating elsewhere, if not beyond your means, could be much beyond the potential for the kind of business you have selected.

Homemakers, moonlighters, and retirees are among the millions profiting from home-based businesses. They are devoting areas of their living quarters to both the production and marketing of goods. Some begin very meagerly, starting out by using the kitchen table as an office and cardboard boxes in a corner for storage. They learn to tolerate such disadvantages for the benefit of going it alone.

ADVANTAGES

What are the advantages? Several pertain to the business end; others are more personal.

Compared to different locations and types of facilities, the home is without equal in many respects for setting up and operating a crafts business. The risk is minimal. Start-up costs, overhead costs, commuting expenses, and the financial backing and reserves needed are probably as low as can be expected. Tipping the scale further are the tax advantages, convenience of work areas, flexibility of work scheduling, and managerial independence. Concomitant values of being close to family, away from the stress and problems of a regular workplace, having the visible, direct support of friends and relatives, and experiencing the psychological effect of being solely responsible, productive, and in charge are among the additional benefits of potentially great significance. The home is also a place where a retiree or moonlighter can conveniently parlay a skill or hobby into a business.

POTENTIAL PROBLEMS

Now for the downside. Interference is a distinct possibility. Friends, neighbors, and customers will sometimes visit in person or call by telephone at the most inconvenient times, and members of the family might make bothersome demands when you are trying to get out a rush order. The need to interrupt production to attend to overdue chores, the supervision of an assistant, or the repositioning of materials in the shop because of inadequate storage can add to frustrations in the workplace.

The residential location of the home, itself, can be a source of difficulty. Problems might arise not only in directing customers and materials vendors to the home but also in keeping business travel within the restrictions imposed by a zoning ordinance. The use of a post-office box will avoid increasing traffic in a residential area, but it will make traveling to the post office a more frequent occurrence. In addition, some customers might assume that your use of a P.O. box means you have something to hide.

Being at home and alone when working presents another potentially serious problem. In fact, some people simply can't handle it. They seem to need constant companionship.

In addition to being able to work hour after hour in isolation from peers and acquaintances, there is the matter of having the self-discipline to keep busy without a boss to give you directions. Chronic procrastinators, as well as people who can't work alone, could have an extremely difficult time trying to function as homecrafters.

MINIMIZE THE PROBLEMS

While the psychological and human hurdles might be formidable, you can make technical changes to minimize or completely eliminate many of the other difficulties involved in working at home. Some problems can even be turned to your advantage. The procedures are worth implementing.

Avoid Interruptions

Because interruptions are bound to occur, you can only attempt to minimize them in order to keep the workplace functioning smoothly. Two extremely helpful practices for doing that are establishing work boundaries and using an answering machine or service.

Establish work boundaries by setting aside an area or areas you can call your own, and define the limits of your work periods. Do these things from the very beginning, making sure that people close to you are aware of the times and limitations you have set up. Although small children will have to be kept under supervision, close friends, neighbors, and family will generally try to accommodate your schedule and not interfere. Inform customers, too, but be flexible so you don't discourage any. You need them.

The use of an answering machine or service can be very beneficial during periods of work and absence, and it is practically essential as a means of avoiding frequent interruptions and not having callers become discouraged when receiving no answer. The answering service is preferable because it is more personal than a machine. The problem with it is the expense.

If you use a machine, be sure the greeting is businesslike. Answering by beginning with the name of the business might seem odd to a personal caller, but the effect will probably be less costly than losing a customer due to a poorly developed, unprofessional response. For the same reason, do not have a young child answer the phone. A recorded response can at least be made to sound professional.

Establish Control

You can avoid problems to an extent by thinking ahead and taking control. Unless you learn to do those things, your life working at home can be less than desirable.

Take charge by scheduling visitations. Help your customers and yourself. Very likely, your crafts business will develop locally. Turn this knowledge to your advantage by having potential buyers who live within easy driving distance visit your home at predetermined times, thereby creating for yourself an occasional diversion from the routines of chores and regular production activities while increasing the opportunities for sales. Mail directions to customers you know, and display a neat, professional-looking sign in front of your house. Be selective and apportion the invitations mailed so you can both obtain maximum results and remain within any local restrictions that might exist regarding business traffic.

Often overlooked, but of considerable importance, is the need to relax. In order to help adjust to working consistently in the home, arrange your schedule so there will be time for yourself. Diversion and relaxation are necessary. Get out of the house frequently. Do some shopping and socializing. Your time at work will be much more enjoyable and enthusiastically spent if you maintain a balance among activities.

Think Twice Before Beginning

Probably the best advice to be given about working in and from the home is to consider carefully what you are about to get into before you start. To avoid pitfalls you must be aware of them. Awareness, in turn, is prelude to the understanding necessary for developing effective strategies.

The following are 10 fundamental questions to consider. You should be able to answer "yes" to each before starting a home-based business.

A Homecraft Business
10 Points to Consider Before Starting

1. Do you have a marketable craft? Whether you do the craftwork yourself or purchase items for resale, people must be willing to buy the finished crafts. Try selling a few pieces in your area. The opinions of friends alone might not be sufficient basis for proceeding in large-scale fashion.

2. Will local zoning ordinances allow a business in your home? If they are prohibitive or too restrictive, seek a variance. An alternative is to operate from a friend's or relative's house.

3. Is the home suitably located? Is the building in a safe neighborhood, easily found by customers, free from major parking problems, or otherwise within easy driving distance to your intended market?

4. Is your home adequate? A crafts business takes more space than a hobby. More storage will be necessary, and special areas for an office and for displaying crafts are likely additions. Remodeling and renovating can be costly.

5. Can your craft be easily displayed? Although not completely essential, a showroom in the home is helpful. Most small products can be displayed in your home, but large or very expensive items (e.g., handmade furniture and exquisite artwork), are preferably shown in stores and at exclusive shows.

6. Does your family support the idea? Your relationship with a spouse or others living with you will change. They must be willing to accept that and to actually help in the business when the need arises.

7. Will your neighbors accept the idea? Ask them. Assure them your business will be nuisance-free; then cultivate attitudes that will not deteriorate into vocal opposition.

8. Can you begin without making huge, initial purchases of equipment and furnishings? Unless you already have a furnished office and everything needed to function effectively, you should cost-out and schedule acquisitions so as to avoid a heavy financial burden.

9. Do you have enough money? A home-based operation usually costs less than other forms of business, but you do need a cushion for covering business expenses and living costs when starting. An eight- or nine-month reserve is recommended. Borrowing, of course, is an option.

10. Are you well enough informed? People starting at home are generally on their own. Advertising, legal requirements, scheduling, writing a business plan, knowing where to sell, how to sell, and where to get help are a few of the things you should try to understand at the outset.

Upon deciding to use your home, use it to greatest advantage. Make it both enjoyable and profitable. One helpful way is to keep a neat, orderly, and businesslike place in which to function. Another advantage results from knowledge of the financial angles on which to base decisions. Knowing how to use your home so you will pay no more taxes than you should is among the considerations.

THE TAX BREAKS

Your home can save you tax dollars. The operation of a business in your place of residence is a way to write off some of the costs of utilities, mortgage interest, and property depreciation. The IRS sets the guidelines.

To take a deduction for using part of your home, you must use that part *exclusively* and *regularly* as the *principal place* of your business or as a place to meet and deal with customers. If for business purposes you use a separate structure that is not connected to your house, it need not be your principal place of business. The amount of the deduction allowed under any of those conditions may not exceed the gross income resulting from the facility's business use.

Qualifications

Exclusive use means use for the business only. A spare room used as an office for the business and also for writing personal checks does not qualify. Either do all unrelated, personal work elsewhere or do not attempt to claim a deduction for the office. The same principle applies to a workshop area.

As might be expected, the IRS allows an exception—in this case an exception for storage. Expenses for that part of your home used to store inventory in your crafts business might be deducted if (1) you sell the products wholesale or retail, (2) your home is the only fixed location for the business, (3) the storage space is used regularly, and (4) the space is separately identifiable and suitable for storage. Suppose you use one-fourth of your basement for storing finished crafts. This you do over a period of months each year, and at other times you store personal items there. The expenses for the area are deductible even though it is not used exclusively for business purposes.

For applications other than storage, *regular use* means use on a continuing basis. Office or workshop spaces used occasionally or incidentally in the business and for no other purpose will not qualify. Although the IRS literature does not define "discontinuous use," the customary breaks taken on weekends, holidays, and vacation periods will not disqualify a claim.

Another special consideration applies when you use more than one place for the business. In order to deduct any of the expenses for use of your residence, you must determine that it is the main place of your business. The relative amount of income, the time spent working in each place, and the facilities used are among the factors to consider when making this determination.

Dividing Expenses

If your home qualifies for a business deduction, you must divide the expenses incurred in operating the home between business and personal uses. The computation might be made on the basis of floor area or on the basis of the number of rooms assignable to each function. Figure the percentage of business usage by dividing the floor area in square feet devoted to the business by the total square footage in the home or, if the rooms are about the same size, by dividing the number used for business by the total number in the home.

Expenses you pay to maintain your home might be either directly or indirectly related to the business, or not be related at all. You are permitted to deduct direct business expenses but only part of the indirect costs. Unrelated expenses, such as landscaping and repairs of personal areas, are not allowable deductions.

Direct expenses benefit only the business section of your home. They include painting and repairing of a specific area or room devoted to production, record keeping, or sales.

Indirect expenses are incurred for the entire home. They are incurred for both business and personal purposes, and they might be deducted as a business expense to the extent determined by applying the business percentage to the total. Included are: real estate taxes or rent, applicable mortgage interest, utilities, insurance, repairs, security systems, casualty losses, and property depreciation.

Consult the IRS publications for specific information on how to claim the various deductions. There are limits for the total claim, and the steps to be taken in determining certain deductions follow a specific order. Although the methods vary according to type of cost, the time invested in becoming acquainted with the procedures could be well worth the effort. Remember always to keep complete and accurate records of the details of home usage.

How worthwhile can it be? You must determine that for yourself on the basis of your particular situation. An example might help when deciding whether or not to claim any of the special exemptions associated with using your home.

Special Deductions

In this illustration, two deductions only will be considered. The first has to do with depreciating part of the home used for the business. Assume that a self-employed taxpayer's records show the cost of his home with permanent improvements over the years amounts to $85,000 and the area of the home devoted to business is 16%. He also determines the market value of his home to be $105,000. He multiplies the smaller of these two amounts, the *basis*, times the percentage of his home qualified for business deduction, thereby obtaining $13,600, which might be recovered over time. His home, being used in business, is classified as nonresidential real property and must be depreciated over 31.5 years using the straight line method of the Modified Accelerated Cost Recovery System (MACRS). Thus, in this simplified example, he would be able to deduct over $400 annually until the entire $13,600 is recovered. A situation involving part of a year or the partial capitalization of expenses would make the initial calculation a bit more complex than that, but after the initial determination is made, annual deductions merely require the recording of the calculated amount on the tax form.

Recognize that the deduction resulting from depreciation only defers the tax; it does not dismiss it. The entire amount depreciated is deducted from the home's basis and is taxed accordingly after the property is sold. The immediate advantage to the business should be apparent, nonetheless.

The second example illustrates the depreciation of a vehicle. While this is not a matter related exclusively to working at home, a homecrafter will still have to use a conveyance of some kind to work there. Whatever the situation might be, the allowable deductions will vary according to whether the vehicle's use is for business, personal purposes, or both.

Let's assume you purchase a new van, at a total cost of $12,000, for *exclusive use* in the business. The IRS classifies this vehicle as 5-year property, subject to MACRS by the double (200%) declining balance method. In this case, the entire cost might be recovered according to a table of changing values that, interestingly, begins with 20% of the total cost the first year ($2,660 maximum), 32% the second, and with decreasing amounts thereafter for a total of six deductions. An alternate, section 179 method, permitted if the mileage rate is not used for operating expenses, would produce a similar result in five deductions.

Simple arithmetic will soon show that the permissible deductions for home and vehicle can be substantial. Add to those amounts the other deductions I mentioned earlier and the result might be so significant that nobody in a crafts business can afford to ignore them.

AN EFFECTIVE WORKPLACE

Aside from an office devoted solely to communications and record keeping for your homecraft, you might allocate parts of your residence to storage, an area for craftwork, and a place to greet customers and make sales. Having all areas qualify for tax deductions is probably no less important to the business than using them effectively. Always keep in mind that the underlying motive in the physical arrangement and utilization of any part of the home for business purposes is the maximization of profit. Inefficient activities generally prove to be unprofitable. Learn to look for areas of improvement, and make changes as necessary.

Efficiency

Your shop, or wherever you construct your crafts, should be an efficient place in which to work. Just because you use the workshop in your home when and how you please does not mean that it need not be kept tidy. Give it a thorough cleaning occasionally. When the chore of dusting, sweeping, and rearranging materials becomes sheer drudgery, either force yourself to do it or do as master craftsmen did in the apprenticeship system: Enlist a young hand for the purpose. The result will impress any informed customer who happens to see it, but most importantly, the area will be more conducive to production.

The quality and arrangement of equipment and furnishings can make a big difference in output. Materials placed within easy reach, seating that is comfortable but not too restful, and equipment arranged in sequential order of use are fundamental considerations for any work environment. A simple program of periodic inspection and preventive maintenance can be especially useful in maintaining productivity, for nothing can be more disruptive of a schedule than having a piece of equipment fail while in use. By this same reasoning, the replacement of worn equipment with new pieces should be planned in advance of the time of need.

Environmental Factors

The environment in the workplace also affects productivity. Light, air, sound, and color have a tremendous impact on an individual's ability to produce. As a matter of substantiated fact, some of these qualities can affect one's health.

A well-lighted work area is a minimum. Natural light supplemented with artificial illumination of the right intensity is best. Working in a poorly lighted place could cause your eyesight to deteriorate and your production to decrease, in addition to being at risk from dangers such as would occur when working with power tools. The general rule is to provide incandescent or fluorescent lights of increasingly higher wattage as the closeness and precision of the work increases.

With all that is being said about pollution today, the need to keep the air in your work area clean needs little comment. Just don't overlook the need to protect yourself. Adding dust collectors to power woodworking machinery and vapor exhausts or collectors to spray booths will go far toward providing the level of protection desired in some workshops. In places where fine cloth fibers or other barely discernible pollutants are suspended, consider installing a static precipitator for continually cleaning the air you breathe. Give attention, too, to changing the filters regularly in the cooling and heating ducts of your home.

As to sound, the concern is the possible impairment of hearing and loss of concentration to operators, occupants, and neighbors. Loud noises emanating from heavy equipment or high-speed tools often cannot be dampened except by some external barrier. Operators can wear ear muffs, but the protection of others might involve isolating the work area. Half of a garage intended for use as a shop might be partitioned off with drywall over studs. Further absorption of noise could be achieved by covering the walls and ceiling with acoustical tile. When in doubt about the level of noise carrying beyond the workshop, check the intensity with a decibel meter or, if you don't have access to one, ask a member of the Environmental Protection Agency to check the amount for you. Fortunately for most craftworkers, expensive renovation of the home in order to control sound is seldom necessary.

The use of color is a matter of extensive concern, for all areas devoted to the business should be decorated. Some colors are known to be psychologically exciting and others, depressing. Bright hues make up the first of these and dark ones the latter. In view of these effects, use brilliant reds, oranges, and yellows sparingly. Apply the same rule to the use of black, brown, purple, and dark blue, as their overuse, too, can have an adverse impact.

Generally, cover walls in a neutral shade, and avoid the psychedelic effect of many clashing colors. Lacking an understanding of the technicalities of using harmonious and complementary colors, you might seek the advice of an interior decorator.

Decorate each area according to its use. In a room where customers come to view, for example, your country creations, paper the walls in a decor of the country style, but give the walls of your office a comparatively neutral color that will be restful to the eyes.

A FUNCTIONAL OFFICE

Your office can be a simple fold-up table that you move about when being put to use, or it can be a more elaborately furnished, permanent location. A fixed place is better because the supplies, furnishings, and records needed for conducting business conveniently and thoroughly are considerable.

Contents

The supplies and equipment listed below are practically indispensable in a home business. If you don't place all these items in your office, at least keep them close at hand.

Accounting/record forms	Desk chair, swivel type
Book rack or shelf	Desk lamp
Books, IRS and SBA manuals	Envelopes, large and small
Business cards	File folders
Calculator	File tabs/labels
Calendar	Filing cabinet
Correction fluid	Glue or rubber cement
Desk, one- or two-pedestal	In-and-out boxes

Index cards
Invoicing pads
Letter opener
Letterhead stationery
Letter tray
Magazine rack
Paper
Paper clips/fasteners
Paper weight
Pencil sharpener
Pens, pencils, erasers
Pen and pencil holder
Pin-up board
Postage scale
Postage stamps

Ring binders
Rubber bands
Rubber stamps, name and date
Ruler
Scissors
Stapler
Staples/staple remover
Tacks
Tape, invisible
Telephone/answering machine
Typewriter and stand
Typewriter ribbons
Wall decoration (pictures)
Wastebasket
Window drapes

Within this list, you might observe several items that are not necessary from a purely operational point of view. Some things (wall decorations, for example) are appropriate in virtually any office. A nicely decorated office might be exactly what is needed to impress a visiting customer.

Nice-to-Have Items

Depending on the nature and extent of your business, give thought to supplying several other pieces of equipment for the office. Either a personal computer or a word processor is a handy addition that might be justified for your operation, although you should be sure your business will continue at least for several more years if you make the purchase for business purposes alone. A check-writing machine and an office copier are useful, also, but these are not of utmost importance in a crafts business, particularly when the business is new. Of higher priority are a fireproof safe for money and records and a means of locking the office.

You might find a need to keep packing materials on hand if you will be shipping products by mail or packaging delicate items.

The development of your office should involve thoughtful planning and, when possible, enough lead time for making acquisitions over a period of time. The advantage is the money you could save by purchasing some of the new and second-hand furnishings that occasionally come on the market at bargain prices.

NOOK-AND-CRANNY STORAGE

When selecting a place to store supplies and finished products, make use of what you have. A corner of the spare room you converted into an office, a part of a waterproof basement, an easily accessed attic space, or one side of the garage are some of the places that might be used. Box the items to be stored and place them so that those used first or most frequently will be most accessible. Cardboard cartons of similar size serve well for storing and stacking small articles. For storing old files, select cartons of a width that will neatly accommodate the folders, and cut hand-sized slots into opposite ends of the boxes for ease in grasping, lifting, and carrying.

Products made ready for later showing must often be wrapped for protection and yet remain identifiable after tucking them away in containers. Labels marked and glued to the wrapping paper and a list of contents visibly showing in the same area of each carton will be helpful. Placing the filled cartons for ease in reading the list of contents is also important.

When storing raw materials in a shop, particularly lumber for making articles of wood, you can store the pieces on end or in horizontal racks built for the purpose. Build a special container for storing usable scraps. A shelf beneath the workbench makes a convenient location for a unit of this kind.

You might have to consider other factors, depending on the type of material used in your craft. Bright sunlight, excessive heat, and dry (or wet) air could seriously affect certain fabrics, dried flowers, and leather goods. Also, freezing can be damaging to jars and cans of paint. Whatever the material, any special needs for storage must be given adequate consideration.

An ingenious homeowner will have no difficulty finding a closet or some other reasonably convenient place to keep projects and materials. About the only place to be avoided is an area where visitors might see things stacked in disorderly array. A catchall should be hidden. Even things temporarily out of order should be kept out of view. You can't afford the risk of creating an unbusinesslike impression among customers. Keep those makeshift arrangements to yourself and close friends.

WHAT ABOUT CUSTOMERS?

Make your customers feel welcome. Both the physical arrangement of the place for greeting customers and the manner of greeting them can make a big difference in sales. An untidy yard, a soil-filled doormat, or a cluttered living room can turn a visitor off about as readily as a frown or negative expression. Any excuse made about being caught unawares or not being ready will only exacerbate the situation. Visitors become uneasy, though they might not say so, whenever they sense uneasiness due to a homeowner's failure to be prepared.

Greeting Visitors

When customers arrive at your home, treat them appropriately, and look upon those occasions as opportunities rather than interruptions. Even if no sale results, each period of conversation could be the moments of relief you need to keep from falling into a monotonous routine. At the very least, you will have an opportunity to hone your personal relations techniques.

Be sure that the door bell will be responded to promptly at the time of a customer's arrival. Wire the bell into your work area if necessary, and instruct members of your family as to how to properly welcome and introduce a client to you. Assume responsibility yourself for putting the visitors at ease.

Don't neglect this responsibility. Offer each visitor a place to sit, have coffee and tea available, and have the bathroom freshly cleaned and supplied beforehand. That you should be prepared to say pleasant and complimentary things seems obvious.

Your home is not an ordinary place of business, so make use of techniques that can't be accomplished very well in a show booth or retail store. Give each customer who visits the kind of undivided, individual attention not generally possible in a busy public setting. In addition to providing the amenities already mentioned, make sure your customers have had an easy time of locating the parking area and the proper door to enter. Small talk such as this can go a long way toward showing concern for the customer's welfare and can even reveal matters that need improvement for future visitors. Besides, you will have taken the time-proven step toward making a friend by asking for that person's advice.

The Showroom

Another opportunity not common to store or booth displays is the showing of goods in an actual home setting. Make your living area a showplace. Tastefully decorated with your crafts, it is a place where the customer can gain an idea or two that might make a sale. How the decorations are arranged depends on the type of craft and the imagination of the decorator.

Convenient locations for displaying, demonstrating, and wrapping articles are other important factors to consider in the layout. A display of articles tiered for visibility and accompanied by colored covers, ribbons, balloons, posters, branches, straw bales, or whatever will define a theme and make the display attractive is especially desirable. A small table placed near the display is a useful location for unpacking additional items brought from storage and for performing the various activities related to finalizing a sale.

Welcome Advice

Always remain alert. Keep your eyes, ears, and mind open for ideas that will work to your advantage. A customer's comments or subtle inflections will be highly revealing, perhaps, and might just be the clue to a profitable change that is within your power to make.

Further, look upon each visit as an opportunity for the future and not merely a means of making an immediate sale. When the customer is about to depart after your presentation, you can merely say "thank you" and "goodbye," or you can also invite her to return to your home with friends. Use the more positive occasions to build up a list of clientele for your annual open house and to recruit a hostess for a home demonstration. In place of this approach, you could ask your client for ideas that will help your new business grow. You might be surprised at how effective a display of friendship, confidence, and personal interest can be when generated in your own home setting. Anyone who has made a special effort to visit your residence to view what you have to offer should always leave feeling good, regardless if a sale was made or not.

STEPPING OUT

In addition to having the many advantages previously cited, your home location affords a measure of flexibility not likely to be experienced in other situations. You can come and go just about as you please. You need not hire help to man a booth or to keep a store open, and neither do you have to be concerned about the occasional customer who makes an unscheduled stop at your house when you're away. The person who plans with you beforehand is the one you want to be present to greet.

Don't completely disregard the possibility of someone arriving while you are gone, however. Leave a courteous, explanatory note in a visible spot at the entrance to your house, but be careful about giving a precise time when you will return so as not to entice an unwanted intruder who is out looking for an easy touch. A note pad for a message, name, and phone number attached to or near the door could further your interest in not neglecting a potentially profitable opportunity.

Security

How does the location of a business in your home tend to affect security, and what should be done about it? The answer to the first part is relatively clear in the minds of insurance agents. Their companies will definitely have a special charge for insuring against breaking, entry, and theft where a business is operated. Insurance beyond the traditional homeowner's policy provides only part of the answer, for the extra coverage helps to offset the loss but does little about prevention. A security system will help solve the problem. You can increase protection on your property and simultaneously lower your insurance premiums by installing a good one.

Internal alarms, exterior flood lights, wireless alert systems, and combinations of different detection and alert devices are on the market. Installation prices vary considerably, from less than $100 to well over $4000. What you need, and whether you should make a large investment, depends on how you publicize your operation, the nature of your neighborhood, and local restrictions. Consider these facts, for example:

- A home situated on a street ending in a cul-de-sac is relatively safe from burglary.

- Radio and newspaper ads reach a broader audience (including people inclined to thievery) than do invitations and announcements mailed to select individuals.
- Audible horns or outside security lights are totally prohibited in some communities.
- Signals from security systems that automatically alert local police carry a charge for each response by law officers in some communities—including responses to false alarms.

A further consideration centers on just how much risk you are willing to take. The presence of family around the clock makes a big difference, of course.

Flexibility

A home-based operation is uniquely flexible. Both business and pleasure trips can be arranged to suit your needs. By thoughtfully preparing and scheduling your work, you can take short excursions or lengthy vacations without jeopardizing the business. No other permanent place of business provides the same degree of flexibility.

By exercising a bit of common-sense management, the home-business operator remains free to attend some of the arts and crafts shows commonly held in localities throughout the country. Church bazaars, flea markets, holiday celebration shows, and even garage sales are among the opportunities open to craftworkers within most communities. The public shows scheduled in different regions are open to those who want to go there principally for ideas or to place their crafts on sale. These opportunities remain wide open for the home-based business person, and they constitute viable ways of marketing and selling on a supplementary basis.

A major advantage of starting a business in the home is the possibility of moving to another location with little loss of investment in the facility. As a practical matter, the home serves as a place for the entrepreneur to get established without creating a serious deterrent to expansion. Owners move operations for different reasons. Some move due to the need for larger facilities; others change locations because of services.

Business Incubators

More and more small business operators whose volume of work has become too much for one person to handle at home are turning to nearby business incubators. Business incubators, usually set up at a university with state financing, provide office, warehouse, some production space, and a variety of services not immediately available in the home. Both costs and services are shared with others. Typical support services include: telephone answering, secretarial and janitorial work, photo copying, and the use of computers and calculators. Usually, too, professional advising and consulting can be purchased on subjects ranging from financial planning to marketing techniques. Professors who specialize in accounting and law are among those who might be hired on a part-time, after-class schedule at a reasonable fee. A frugal business operator will investigate this possibility even if there is no incubator in place nearby.

The feasibility of a crafts business operating in an incubator would hinge on specifics regarding cost, income, and personal ability. The accessibility of an incubator, mainly due to its distance from home, could rule out this method of operation for the average craftsperson.

For many, the advantages of starting and operating a crafts business in the home are without equal. The home makes entry into the field of entrepreneurship possible for thousands of people who could not otherwise afford to do so. It is truly a low-risk place to begin, and as suggested in the next chapter, its value is further enhanced by having a product that is designed to sell.

6
CHAPTER

Produce for Selling

HANDMADE QUILTS, stuffed fabric toys, hooked or woven rugs, decoratively painted gourds, leather wallets and purses, ceramic vases, jewelry with polished stone inserts, vine and pine-bough wreaths, floral arrangements, hand-lettered mottos, welded-metal figurines, and wooden lawn ornaments are among the many different things crafted in the home for which a buying public will pay cash. But being involved in some kind of craftwork is one thing; making it pay is another. You will have no business unless you can sell what you make, nor will you be able to pursue a business interest for long if your product lacks qualities of saleable goods.

The articles you intend to sell must appeal to a significant segment of the population. If the perceived intrinsic value is practically nonexistent, you will have a difficult time convincing enough people to purchase the merchandise. The things you intend to sell must satisfy individual wants and needs. In the absence of either of these motivating factors, no manner of super salesmanship will compensate sufficiently to save your operation from failure.

Whether your products are intended to fulfill a decorative function or some other useful purpose, you must take into account matters of workmanship, style, design, and price. Try to build desirable qualities into your products and fashion them according to your customer's preferences. This chapter tells you what is often expected in the marketplace and how to meet those expectations.

WHAT CONSUMERS WANT

You should produce your articles for sale according to certain basic rules, each of which can affect how the consumer will look upon your product. The first of these is to enjoy the work. If that can't be done, let someone else do it. Your attitude toward the work will ultimately show in the quality of the finished pieces. Furthermore, life is too precious to spend doing things you do not like to do.

The second important rule is to make articles of which you can be proud. Shoddily made pieces sometimes are the result of cutting corners to keep prices down, but such work has no place in a crafts business. Make your product at the level of quality appropriate for the handcraft, and always do your best to make ownership truly a benefit to the customer. Most certainly, what is sold is more important than the way it is sold. A product usually displays evidence of the workmanship long after details of the sale have faded away (FIG. 6-1).

As a final point, don't delegate handcrafting operations completely to others as your business expands and the workload increases. Keep a hand in manufacturing. In that way you will have some direct control over a major part of the business. You maintain full knowledge and responsibility for the styling and workmanship involved, and you can readily adjust or alter procedures and products to suit changing conditions. Although you

6-1 Faceted plastic beads and safety pins, cleverly fashioned into interesting and attractive assemblies, sell readily when quality is evident in the craftwork.

might be inclined to produce things only as you and your assistants like them, your overview of the business will enable you to take into account the concerns of groups to whom you market the goods.

Benefits

Generally, consumers are looking for benefits. Their satisfaction or dissatisfaction with a product will affect not only immediate but also subsequent behavior. Those who are pleased with a purchase relative to its price, quality, style, features, and safety will often become positive spokespersons for similar purchases. However, if the product is perceived as providing no real advantage in ownership, the finished articles and methods of production will have to be promptly changed or abandoned.

Talking a person into buying something that has not generated a positive feeling can be as detrimental to the reputation of the business as trying to push items that are overpriced, unsafe, or fall apart from lack of quality. For this reason, it is to your advantage to obtain the reactions of friends and other members of the public before going into quantity production. Seek evaluations of each of the major points of concern to consumers.

Consumer's Concerns

In the broad field of merchandising tangible goods, consumers complain mostly about high prices, poor quality, inadequate service for breakage, and the marketing of dangerous products—much in that order. The action sometimes taken deserves the attention of every entrepreneur. Some consumers stop buying and quietly warn friends. Others act more forcefully, seeking restitution by directly confronting the manufacturer, by reporting to a government agency, or by taking legal action. Well-known are the cases where groups have worked to have unsafe toys and goods removed from stores and to have mandatory laws passed. The mere possibility of creating adversarial reactions among consumers has to be a matter of serious concern.

People in a locally oriented crafts business must be especially careful to do what they can to avoid complaints and to rectify problems when they occur. Word-of-mouth assessments will travel like wildfire throughout an area if a product has been found seriously deficient in one way or another. As a precaution, you should promptly seek feedback from new customers.

LEARN WHAT SELLS BEST

Feedback from people who buy your crafts can be extremely helpful. Asking questions such as, "How does it (the product) look to your friends and neighbors?" or "What changes do you think they would want?" can help you obtain important product-related information. A personal follow-up call a few days after a purchase has been made is an effective way to gather such information.

The General Perception

Knowledge of your craft's image, that is, the public's perception of the work, can be helpful in giving your business the direction sought. The general perception might be positive, negative, or in between. Individual references might extend throughout an entire range of descriptors, including "high-priced," "shoddy," "beautiful," "well made," or any of many other terms. Make a special effort to find out what your customers are saying about your work, and make any adjustments that seem necessary to create the desired image. Your business's reputation is at stake. It can make you or break you.

Unquestionably, the person who has been selling his or her crafts for some time has an advantage over one who is just beginning. Production can then be based on sales, not merely on hope. An alert operator soon knows not only if a class of products sells readily but also which items within the group sell best.

Not having the benefit of experiencing actual results, the beginner must rely primarily on personal analyses and assumptions or the observations of others. The idea is to eliminate as much guesswork as possible. One's repertoire of indicators enlarges as the evidence from selling accumulates.

Be Observant

A significant indicator of what to make for sale remains constantly available to all handcrafters. Avail yourself of this wealth of information by taking a little time to observe the kinds of items people in businesses similar to yours are selling. Go to craft shows, bazaars, and variety or hobby stores, and see exactly what is happening. Observe what people are buying, not just what fills the shelves. Be careful, of course, not to brand an article as being bad or inadequate when poor salesmanship or improper displaying is to blame. Also, be leery of any cheaply made imitations and large-quantity imports that lack quality. Query the vendor, if conditions permit, about what items of interest to you are the top sellers.

You can further your knowledge in this area by going to a public library. Search through the books and magazines on display. The current issues often provide clues to the popularity of different handcrafted products.

Don't be reluctant to gather ideas from others by the techniques mentioned. Profit from what you learn, but don't copy a single item. Design and make things your own way. You will notice that similarities are rampant among manufactured articles that sell profitably.

Be alert, too, to seasonal or other occurrences that can make a particular item or style of item popular. Everyone recalls the proliferation of specially styled products that crowd the shelves for the holidays. Thanksgiving decorations, Christmas ornaments, and Halloween designs are indicative of the kinds of things sold each year. They could be a source of inspiration for a special product design or two of your own. Other opportunities might come your way, such as happened with the surge of nationalism that followed Desert Storm and the Gulf War, bringing on sales of flags made of cloth, paper, wood, metal, and whatever other material a craftsman was working with at the time.

Judgment and Purpose

Observation will not always provide all the information you need to begin production with an eye to making sales. Some judgment is usually required. Oftentimes no product like yours will be found elsewhere, or you will find something similar but with an apparent flaw in design, construction, or pricing. In those instances, you must decide whether or not to proceed with a few pieces developed and priced as you think best.

When in doubt, proceed with caution. Design your product with simple, honest lines, and hold your price to a reasonable minimum. Excessive ornateness is both inartistic and expensive to produce. Know your market as precisely as possible. What you will be able to sell, say, to an upper-income group in terms of quality and price will contrast with things saleable to people of more limited means.

Purpose is another consideration. You will probably reach a larger clientele by making available articles that have different functions. A handcraft that is strictly decorative will often have broad appeal, but one that is both useful and decorative will generally capture the interest of additional buyers. Here, again, you must be somewhat analytical of your market segments and remain flexible enough to adapt your product line to meet the needs of those you serve.

THE APPEAL OF HANDMADE

Handcrafts gain much of their appeal because they are handmade. No two pieces are exactly alike. If not exclusive in design, they are distinguishable by differences in the traces of hand tooling. The finished pieces might be highly finished or crude, simple in design or complex. The work is seldom as rigid in form as pieces manufactured en masse.

Unique Features

It is an article's uniqueness that creates much of the interest today in owning handcrafts. There is definitely a nostalgic affection for things from years past. "Early American" signifies something special. Evidence of its broad appeal can be observed in the growing demand for and the escalating prices of antiques on the market. Artifacts from the pre-Industrial (machine-manufacturing) era are most sought after, although the scarcity of handmade antiques is leading to interest in machine-made articles of early vintage.

Another factor that motivates interest in handmade articles, old and new, is a sense of relationship with the craftsperson. Feelings of a sort of acquaintanceship, affinity, and comradeship emerge. Mass-produced articles lack that individualistic, personal involvement. There is no practical reason for identifying who designed a modern machine-produced part or who made it. Therein lies an advantage for the handcrafter. The significance of this point has become apparent to several companies now manufacturing craft-like items in mass quantities; they do a bit of hand finishing and attach a neat little card explaining the design and production features, especially emphasizing the handwork involved.

Given the fact that the public is generally educated to appreciate things handmade, you can profit by structuring your product accordingly. If appropriate, base some items on artifacts in museums. The copies need not be exactly like the originals, but customers will find interest in knowing the source of inspiration. The continuing popularity of traditionally styled crafts and primitives is evidence of the worth of this approach.

Practical Construction

Although you will want to maintain the handcrafted feature in your work, do not be led to believe everything must be made exactly as old-time craftsmen made them. To use crude tools and hand-shape each and every part would be ludicrous, to say the least, for many tools and methods are available today that can save time and keep prices within reach. And, yet, there is no perceived loss. For example, a person who works with wood would not hesitate to use a board planed smooth as it comes from the mill, rather than saw and plane a log by hand to the thickness desired as in the old days. Furthermore, people will still think of such an article as being made by hand, even if hand-operated power tools are used throughout all subsequent steps of construction. It is the individualized process, as in FIG. 6-2, that merits the title "handmade."

VARIETY AND QUANTITY

There is no such thing as an ideal product that will satisfy all customers equally relative to price, quality, function, style, and form. In light of this, you would be well advised to produce and make available a product mix.

Observe the big boys. General Motors produces both Chevies and Cadillacs as a means of offering a wide range in price and quality, and the company doesn't stop there. Numerous models are manufactured within each class to further increase options and potential sales. Campbell's, with its large line of soups, also illustrates how a veteran firm produces to reach a broad segment of the population.

6-2 A skilled craftworker will use time-saving tools and methods that do not detract from the individual qualities of the creations.

Develop a Broad Line

The lesson to be learned by those self-employed in a crafts business is to make a variety of articles available to the public. A person in the business of making quilts would restrict sales considerably by producing only one size of bedspread, since beds are made for children and adults in several common sizes. Additional choices should be provided for by making each size in a variety of decorative patterns. Obviously, you can apply similar logic to other kinds of craftwork done in the home.

The need for variety I just described is a functional one, but there are other reasons to give the public a choice. Differences in emotional, esthetic, psychological, and physical composure will result in different selections by customers when the opportunity exists.

Make the most of this fact by producing a complete product line with optional colors and decorative features. As a way of keeping production and inventory under control while striving for variety, produce only limited quantities of certain types of articles. A single representative piece might be adequate in some groups. Give the customers' needs full consideration at the time of selling by offering to make additional pieces to specifications.

Color and Decoration

As much as is practical, produce a quantity of unfinished articles and let the customers decide how they want the finishing done. Allow them to select colors and accessories. The former is feasible when making items to which paint or glaze is applied, while the latter might be possible if you are customizing purses or wallets from leather. Think of the possibilities along these lines for your particular craft. Encourage color selections, add-ons, and complete customization—but make the buyer aware of the additional charge.

Keep color samples on hand by finishing a few display items in different color schemes. Every craft uses color, whether in the form of paint, dye, glaze, or stain to be applied or as a natural part of the wood, metal, fabric, leather, or ceramic material. Attractive colors make effective visual aids. An alert craftsperson will visit department stores and study professional ads in search of useful ideas in this area.

Judiciously selected and carefully applied, color can have a positive impact on the viewer. This is as true in product design as it is for decorating the walls of a showroom. Gold, silver, bronze, and royal blue seem to create a sense of luxuriousness; the blues and greens, coolness and tranquility; the oranges, reds, and yellows, a feeling of warmth and excitement; the pastels, femininity. A point of relevance to construction is to observe and study these differences. How different, for example, are the paints on children's toys as opposed to the colors on the more sophisticated styles of women's jewelry boxes? The more you learn about this area, the more likely your work will be finished in ways attractive to a broad segment of the market.

A finished line should certainly include articles that are basically of high quality and essentially different from anything available elsewhere. Unless you can produce that aspect of uniqueness, you have little in the way of product design to offer.

ORGANIZE FOR PRODUCTION

The viability of your business is inextricably tied to costs of production. Thus, make your product as inexpensively as possible without adversely affecting quality. Take steps to control the costs of materials, equipment, production time, and overhead.

In general, there are four ways to reduce or to hold costs to a minimum while maintaining the desired level of workmanship and product quality. They are:

1. Maximize working speed
2. Organize the work area
3. Reduce the number of operations
4. Improve purchasing practices

Maximize Working Speed

Increased speed in production comes about with experience and a conscious effort to do more than before. Begin by setting quotas. Then strive to meet them. If you have a habit of dawdling on the job, you might have the most to gain from some method of disciplined pacing. Through proper organization, scheduling, and practice, your work becomes more rhythmic, systematic, and time-saving. Reduce the time spent making an item, and you will cut costs in operations and overhead many times over.

Organize the Work Area

Just as you should think through the steps for constructing an item to arrive at the most efficient procedure, you should analyze the workplace in terms of the effectiveness of its arrangement. Your primary objective is to obtain the maximum in efficiency feasible under the circumstances. Where more than one station is involved, arrange them in sequential order according to use, keeping the distances for walking and reaching to a practical minimum. Use similar logic when storing raw materials. Store the materials near the work area, and arrange them in a manner that will negate repetitive handling and rearranging each time a selection is made.

Give attention to comfort when organizing the workplace. Shopwork is safest when done comfortably. The concern is not only for preventing accidents but also for avoiding the insidious injuries that result from stressful, repetitive body motions. Constantly holding tools and performing operations that stress parts of the body can, over time, lead to serious hand, neck, and back injuries. Employ counteractive measures. Occasionally change procedures and the position of your body.

For reasons of efficiency, limit the frequency of walking from one place to another and from operation to operation. Employees and family, when helping in the shop, can be situated in assembly-line fashion as a way of economizing motion and time. Make the work move, but have the workers remain in place. Doing the work in batches is helpful, also.

Reduce the Number of Operations

Batching is a particularly good way to trim construction time. Instead of carrying a single article through the entire process by itself, step by step, you can perform different operations on quantities of like parts. A woodworker, leathercrafter, or quilt-maker, for instance, might stack sheets of material, draw an outline on the top one, and in one operation cut out numerous pieces to the same shape. The need to coordinate the batching of quantities of items with marketing can be crucial in planning.

When making articles that are to be painted, complete all operations except the painting on a large number of the pieces. By following that practice, you will be able to apply each color to more than a single item at each sitting. The cleaning of brushes will be simplified, and you will find the finishing process to be generally less wasteful. A separate, dust-free area for this work is essential, as is a special means of holding small pieces while drying. The use of clothespins or bent paper clips attached to a taut line works exceptionally well for holding some pieces.

Make use of the latest technology in your work. Many a craft can be made easier by utilizing a small, electrically driven apparatus of one kind or another in place of an older, hand-operated tool.

Reusable jigs, fixtures, and templates are other time savers. The different pieces when made from hardwood or metal will serve substantially under repeated use. This practice can be used to advantage in any craft where patterns and duplicate sizes occur.

Improve Purchasing Practices

The reduction of costs through purchasing can be accomplished in three ways: by buying materials in large quantities, by purchasing cheaper substitutes, and by avoiding shortages. The purchasing of raw materials in quantity necessitates planning ahead and having enough capital available, and with a little shopping and comparative pricing, it is a cost-effective way to do business. Wholesalers are inclined to make special deals if they know you are likely to need more materials later and if they are paid in full at the time of placing the first order.

Substituting one material for another is a different matter entirely. Sometimes a cheaper material can be used in place of an expensive one without jeopardizing appearance, strength, or performance. Pine wood, when stained, will take the place of the more expensive black walnut wood as a means of economizing in certain applications. A wooden country figure is an example where that very thing can be done effectively. If, on the other hand, the cheaper substitute has a detrimental effect on the product and the image you want to project, avoid using it and look for another means of reducing costs.

When preparing to order materials, plan far enough ahead so the items will be delivered in sufficient quantities to avoid shortages. Having to stop production due to a shortage of material could be costly, especially if an extra trip to the supplier becomes necessary. You can't always avoid interruptions of this kind, but if it happens repeatedly something is radically wrong and needs changing.

QUALITY, PRICE, AND PROFIT

Quality, for the most part, is an unregulated variable. Laws impose safety standards for the protection of consumers, and some states have specialized legal requirements controlling the content of articles made of precious metals, but businesses are generally free to set virtually any level of quality desired. Some companies distribute products of average quality, some stress the exclusivity of their high-quality products, and others seek broad market penetration by concentrating on matters other than quality. As one would expect, cost and price vary accordingly.

Materials and Workmanship

The prices asked for finished products generally increase with the costs of materials and production, and those costs increase with each higher level of product quality. Price is related to demand, also. This relationship is inverse, so that the higher the price the fewer the buyers and, conversely, the lower the price the greater the number of buyers. The place of quality in this equation is an important consideration for the craftsperson.

What level of quality should you strive for in your craft? That depends on your craft and personal capability. Cases are on record of a metal sculptor commanding $8,000 or more for a small assembly and of a wood carver who obtains tens of thousands of dollars for each of his creations. Of course, these are rarities. The skill and artistry involved are exceptional. Like rare and expensive paintings, the works of those outstanding artisans will naturally be limited in number. Therein lies much of the desirability.

More commonly, the style, design, and type of product are such that no manner of quality in materials and workmanship will lead to exceptionally high pricing and relentless demand. Most crafts fall into this category. Relatively few crafts can be exclusively produced and consistently sold at the upper end of the price range.

Since you will probably market your craft on more of a personal basis than do large, nationwide distributors, you will not want to become known as one whose workmanship and product are deficient in quality. The public expects handcrafted items to be somewhat unique and top-line, "if they are any good." Cheapness is widely thought of as attendant to articles flooding the market in mass quantities. Personally, what would you think of an individually handcrafted couch pillow that was so loosely stitched the threads dangled from it? The public, in all probability, will not buy a handcrafted pillow that lacks the quality of one more cheaply manufactured.

Price Levels

Most people who have achieved a reasonably high state of design and construction in their craft will have to expand their product line to include some low or moderately priced articles. Variety in production, as previously explained, is more likely to result in a profit-making business than single-item construction. The display in FIG. 6-3 meets this criterion. A technique to consider is to stretch or expand the product line, extending it upward or downward, as interest and activity in the marketplace dictate.

The bulk of what you produce must sell profitably, but there is no harm in carrying an item at the top of the line with an asking price that is likely to be accepted only in extremely rare instances. You might be surprised at the result. Even if it doesn't sell, placing evidence before the public that you can do work at an exceptional level could work in your favor.

6-3 Variety in a product line, as with these cast and hand-painted concrete figures, is essential for reaching a broad spectrum of the public through price and style differentiation.

Market Pricing

Because price is the amount of money customers must pay to obtain a product, it has to be in line with the perceived value of the offer. This means price must be taken into account when designing the product and be revised when necessary to capitalize on changes in the market or inflationary conditions. Price should not be strictly cost-oriented nor be based entirely on what the public will bear. It should be close to what your competitors are charging, however.

What about discriminatory pricing? In other words, should you charge one flat rate for all buyers, or should you treat the clientele differently, such as according to ability to pay? In general, you should offer one price to all buyers within your market area. Some slight increase in price might be justified because of increased transportation or advertising costs when selling to a different segment of the market.

The setting of one price for all buyers is an idea now widely accepted. The practice was given impetus by large-scale retailers at the end of the nineteenth century, replacing the earlier practice of negotiating on an individual basis. Woolworth's and Wanamaker's were among those establishing the practice and promoting the idea so extensively that the public has come to prefer it to the vagaries, uncertainties, and sometimes unfairness of the negotiated deal. An expectation of one price for everyone extends similarly into the area of handcrafting.

Ethics and Price

The question of ethics in pricing must be addressed as well. While it is true that value is in the mind of the buyer and there is usually nothing illegal about a seller trying to get as much for a product as practically possible, there is a common-sense relationship between the worth of a product and the price asked. The example of the pharmaceutical firm charging over $500 for a single quantity of a drug that cost only a few dollars shows how ruthlessly a firm can treat some needy people in the absence of competition. This firm's explanation seemed to reflect an element of sheer greed. "That's what the market will bear," was the response when asked. Concern for an underlying moral obligation seemed to be missing.

Fortunately, legal prohibitions protect consumers from most of such monopolistic activities. The same is true for collusion in price fixing. People in the business of making and marketing crafts, while subject to the same restrictions as other businessmen or women, are not likely to be in violation of laws regulating collusion or monopolies.

The Bottom Line

Profit, the amount of money left after paying expenses must be at least enough to stay in business. A beginner looking to establish a business might have to settle for a low profit with the hope of increasing amounts over time. Two problems, setting the margin of profit too high and not putting enough capital back into the business for improvement or expansion, are common errors among beginning entrepreneurs, according to a member of the Small Business Administration's SCORE.

Markup over costs varies in the business world from a few percentage points to around 100 percent. Established commercial firms usually operate in the lower half of that range. In an individualized operation, as in a small handcrafting business, the margin of profit will have to be larger than when mass-producing pieces, but the amount of markup will have to be such that the asking price remains competitive in the marketplace.

ESTABLISHING A FAIR PRICE

The prices competitors charge are a useful guide, especially in the absence of other data about the market. The price finally established for an article will be between one that is too low to produce a profit and one too high to create a demand. Costs set the floor for prices; market demand sets the ceiling.

Cost Factors

Costs are the expenses incurred in making and selling the craftwork. They include both fixed and variable amounts. *Fixed costs* are often referred to as "overhead" and include proportionate amounts for light, heat, air conditioning, water, and rent or other facilities costs. A rule of thumb for estimating overhead is to use one-third the cost of either materials or labor, whichever is larger. *Variable costs* include materials, wages, and fringe benefits—things directly related to the rate of production, distribution, and selling. The sum of these expenses gives the total cost. The use of this calculation as the sole basis for determining price and profit, as is sometimes done in practice, ignores both market demand and competitors' pricing.

Market Demand

A market orientation in setting price takes into account consumers' perceptions of price and value. People want to feel they're getting their money's worth. Large companies will often assess this perception by means of distributing samples of new products and accompanying each with a returnable survey form. Another practice involves selling in selected test areas, a way of offering the product on a trial basis and evaluating results.

You need to combine some creative judgment with an awareness of buyers' motivations in order to arrive at a final figure using a market approach. While you may draw a few preliminary generalizations you can learn how consumers will respond in a given area at a given time only by making an effort to sell the product then and there. For practical reasons, consider the costs involved and the prices others are charging as the bases for setting price before placing a product on the market. Be prepared to modify prices as the market subsequently dictates.

A BASIC EQUATION

The procedure suggested for pricing crafts fairly and profitably begins with a cost-oriented equation, followed by adjustments according to competitors' prices and market-oriented pricing strategies. An equation for setting the price of an item, with cost as the basis, follows:

$$\text{Price} = \text{fixed costs} + \text{variable costs} + \text{profit}$$

Fixed costs, the overhead, must sometimes be figured on the proportionate use for business in comparison to the total billing for a period. Thus, monthly rental or mortgage payments on one's home will have to be divided into the part applicable to the business and the part that is not. The use of gas, electricity, and water will usually have to be treated in a similar way. However, such expenses as long-distance telephone calls, insurance, and office supplies, might easily be determined directly for a period before being divided by the number of items produced to obtain an average cost per unit.

The determination of overhead costs for each unit can be a bit involved initially, but once the basic units are calculated, later determinations will be easier. A good way to make the calculations is to use time as a basic factor. For example, if the cost of insurance for your moonlighting business comes to $35 for a 6-month period in which you worked a total of 585 hours, and you spent $2^{1/2}$ hours making an article, the cost for insurance would be nearly 6¢ per hour worked and 15¢ for that one article. Although a shorter time span might be more helpful at first, the longer the period on which to base calculations, the more accurate they are likely to be.

After calculating and combining all fixed costs, figure those costs that vary with production, the handling of inventory, and the marketing of the product. These include wages and benefits, materials costs, packaging expenses, advertising charges, transportation expenses, and the like. Always include a figure for earnings and taxes, even if you are the only one doing the work. Self-employment expenses are an important part of the total cost. Add up all variable costs for a month, reduce the total to an hourly rate, and multiply the hourly rate by the number of hours it takes to make and handle an item.

Add the final factor to the equation by determining a percentage for profit. A markup of 100% over costs is common for craftwork. To make the calculation, find the sum of the fixed and variable costs; then multiply this sum by the percentage of profit desired, and add the amount to the other costs. The result should be considered a tentative price.

Adjust a price determined in this way so it remains competitive in the market, as previously explained. Additionally, adjust the price when appropriate to take advantage of some pricing strategy.

PRICING STRATEGIES

Among the general concepts to be taken into account are different pricing strategies that have a market orientation, including those for setting prices initially and for expanding sales thereafter. Accessory, discount, promotional, and psychological pricing are among these.

Accessory Pricing

This form of pricing might be thought of as captive-consumer pricing. A razor company practices accessory pricing if it sells razor blades made to fit only its own holding device. Something similar can be done in many crafts by producing add-ons that go with the basic product. The object is to obtain additional sales.

Discount Pricing

Discounts are offered for several reasons: to encourage prompt payment, to stimulate quantity buying, or to induce post or preseason purchasing. Avoid giving credit on account by offering a discount for immediate payment. Giving a 5% discount for paying by check or cash is preferable because of problems frequently attendant to charge accounts.

Quantity discounting is another inducement worth considering. The idea of the baker's dozen originated as a bonus, a way to induce buyers to purchase in quantity. A variation of this idea might work in your business. Try, for instance, cutting the price of an article in half when an individual's purchases reach a certain dollar level. if you do that, remember always to offer everyone the same deal.

Psychological Pricing

Price seems to communicate something about a product. The public has come to believe this "something" is quality, although such is not always the case. In an actual case several years ago, a local hardware store operator placed a bin full of inexpensive pliers on sale. The pliers were sturdy, though not smoothly finished, but at an advertised price of 50¢, they would make a handy, inexpensive item to have around the house. Few sold. A nearby operator of a variety chain store offered to buy all remaining of the original 500 pliers at 20¢ each. The local operator gladly agreed, even though he would be receiving 5¢ per item less than he paid originally to the wholesaler. He was obviously pleased to be rid of a product that produced little more than a headache. The end to this anecdote took place within several weeks after the new proprietor had placed the pliers on sale. He sold each and every one of the pliers at 98¢ each. As these two stores were located about a city block apart and did similar amounts of business, there was definite evidence of a psychology in pricing at work.

A SCORE instructor suggests this method of pricing crafts: For items to be priced below $5, increase the amount to a 98¢ ending; for those up to $20, have the price end in 95¢, such as $8.95 or $18.95; for items priced between $20 and $50, end each amount in 75¢, such as $27.75; and for items priced above $50, use a 50¢ ending. Somewhat different schemes are also in use, but the general idea is there. Attention to the psychology of pricing, as by asking $29.75 instead of $30.00 for an article, can make a big difference in sales volume.

Promotional Pricing

This type of pricing is helpful in stimulating sales at times other than regular buying periods, such as after the holiday season. "Buy one, get one free" and "25% off all merchandise," are common examples. Shoppers look for bargains. Depending on the type of product you make, you might be able to capitalize on that motivation. By thinking and planning ahead, you can also spread out production schedules via promotions that create sales when desired. You will need to pre-advertise a promotional sale for best results. Your opportunities will be somewhat limited, but the method can be most useful in setting up a demonstration for a select group as opposed to preparing for a public crafts show.

Price Increases

The time to implement a price increase is when demand continually outstrips supply or when costs increase to the point where selling at the same price is no longer desirable. Increase the price of the item just enough to keep supply, sales, and profit in balance. Overpricing could be the prelude to discontinuing a product, so make large increases only when necessary and, hopefully, with no more than a small quantity of the item in inventory.

INVENTORY CONTROL

Except in those home businesses that concentrate on producing and marketing items in unusually large quantities or sizes, the control of raw materials and finished products seldom presents much of a problem for the craftworker. When you handle ordering, storing, and dispensing procedures as previously suggested, the physical arrangements for handling inventory in your home are comparatively easy to manage. Storage is seldom the main problem. The most difficulty arises in supplying the product promptly to consumers.

Ordinarily, keeping a large inventory of finished articles on hand is not feasible in a home business. Samples of quick sellers can be kept on hand along with photographs of others, and multiple pieces can be made in preparation for an upcoming show or demonstration. In that way, large amounts of completed work need not be stored for long periods of time. Keep an updated list of different items and quantities on hand for reference, and, for convenience, keep it near the place of storage, no matter how extensive or limited your inventory might be.

If you build inventory in relation to the space available, keep in mind that such a practice can be costly, especially where year-end inventories are taxed.

Customer Satisfaction

A concern of craftspeople everywhere when deciding how much completed work to stockpile is customer satisfaction. Customers are fully satisfied with delivery only when it is immediate. Waiting becomes less and less satisfying as the time between ordering and delivery increases. The challenge for the operator is to anticipate demand, to produce to meet that demand, and to deliver quickly all items placed on order. Short delays might be tolerated, but extra-long delays could be highly detrimental to your business.

Customers are usually concerned about ordering a handmade article for fear, imagined or real, that the item ordered will not be received as planned for a holiday or some special event. The second concern is that the item placed on order will not be the same as the one demonstrated. In those instances, be sure that the delivery is timely and that the quality of the product eventually delivered is at least equal to the one shown. After all, the reputation of your business will be established by your customers.

THE KEY TO FUTURE SALES

Most of us have heard that customers are a company's best salespeople. We've heard this frequently enough to believe it is true. It follows that to capitalize on this probability, the customer must be satisfied with the product. What happens in the workplace is a crucial factor.

Product Tips

Here is a summarized list of tips to observe in the design and production of your craft:

- Build strength and durability into your product.
- Produce and offer a product-line (variety of items and prices) so as to maximize opportunities for customer satisfaction.
- Build upon, rather than cover up, the qualities of handcrafting.
- Seek customer input and provide opportunities for customizing an article's features.
- Capitalize on methods of streamlining production to make it cost-effective.
- Schedule production so that items on order can be delivered promptly.
- If other businesses compete directly with yours, keep your prices in line with the competition.
- Style your product your way so that its uniqueness is sufficiently obvious to be appreciated by customers.

- Inspect your product for safety and keep off the market every article that doesn't meet rigid standards.
- Gain repeat buyers by offering customers new products, discount prices, and limited repair service.

This list represents some of the most basic considerations in the design, construction, and pricing of your craft. Other factors enter into the complete picture. Among these is the semblance of a life cycle in a product's popularity. In other words, sales will build up and peak, then gradually fall off. To counteract this inevitability, you might change a product's style, reduce its price, build a new line, or undertake a different approach in marketing.

Once you are convinced you have a worthy craft, concentrate on marketing your product so that potential buyers will know it is available. This important step in developing your business is covered in the next chapter.

7
CHAPTER

Market Your Product Effectively

MARKETING IS A WAY of devising effective promotional efforts and directing them where they will do the most good. It proceeds best from the identification of potential customers, their needs, and their desires. Without such knowledge, the selling of the product and the life of the business are left very much to chance.

Selling and marketing are different, although they are related concepts. *Marketing* is the process of creating an awareness of the product; *selling* is the act of exchanging the goods for money. Even the most appealing of products will not sell by themselves, but an effective marketing program will ease the selling process, occasionally reducing it to an effortless exercise.

A complete program of marketing utilizes a number of techniques to promote a product. Publicity, advertising, public relations activities, and contacts initiated through direct selling are the principal categories.

DEFINING THE MARKET

Before making your craftwork available, determine as exactly as you can just who among the general public will buy what you have to offer. A bit of research and analysis can be invaluable in this respect. Although a completely thorough study might be prohibitively costly for your small operation, you must, to the extent feasible, search for and formulate some logical basis for targeting a particular group or groups of people. The observance of both past and current practices could be a helpful beginning.

Market Research

Large, established companies begin a program of marketing by conducting extensive research. They strive to learn everything possible about a product's sales potential before they place it before the public at large. The demographics of market segments, the characteristics of persons likely to be prime buyers, the volume potential of the product, and the extent to which a targeted promotional campaign should be conducted are the kinds of information sought. Some companies employ specialists from outside to do the job. Others involve their own marketing departments. Whatever the practice, the cost is usually substantial.

Market research and analysis are considered essential costs of doing business on a large scale. This is true even when the results of a study indicate the risks of proceeding into production, promotion, and distribution are too great. The price of business failure can far outweigh the cost of the preliminary research. The appropriate attitude for managers of sizable operations is not to question whether the company can afford to do a market study, but whether it can afford not to.

You, like many owners of small businesses, will probably have to do all research and analysis yourself. Chances are you do not have the wherewithal to undertake an exhaustive study. Time, money, personnel, and know-how are the ordinary limitations. Moreover, your product and individual circumstances might warrant little preliminary research. In fact, the requirements for making an in-depth study in your situation might substantially exceed the benefits you can obtain.

These precautions apply to sole proprietorships of different kinds, but especially to those involving the sale of handmade articles. You will have to pick and choose methods that seem most productive. Unfortunately, no statistical data can be found to assist you in marketing your handcrafts. Even the familiar practice of observing the marketing of products similar to yours, such as selling ceramic crafts in a variety store or basketry at a scheduled show, might provide only a scant idea of what to do.

Interviews and Surveys

Personal interviews and surveys by mail are other research methods commonly used in industry, but their applicability to the marketing of crafts has serious drawbacks. For one thing, prospective customers usually want to see a handcrafted item before buying it from a person known only by name. While you could show people samples in a door-to-door survey when trying to get a handle on the work's price and appeal, you would probably accomplish more by actually attempting to sell the pieces than by merely asking questions about them. Also, depending on the time of day you conduct your survey, it might be hard to find people at home.

You can avoid this problem (and the problem of traveling) by mailing out questionnaires. Despite the advantages, the cost involved and an inability to show the actual product must be weighed against the returns likely from this kind of survey. Expenses incurred (easily several dollars per questionnaire) for typing, printing, postage, envelopes, paper, selecting recipients, and compiling results can be exorbitant and reason alone not to use the method. Experience shows that you might have to mail out 2,000 questionnaires in order to receive 100 to 200 returns. Even then, several returns will be unusable due to misinterpretation and failure to answer all questions. Furthermore, you still won't know for sure whether or not a person who indicates on a "check-off" form a preference for buying an item will actually do so after seeing the piece. A response given in relative obscurity that will obviously become part of a mass tally might not be sincere or be based on serious thought.

It is safe to conclude that you would probably be better off investing directly in promoting your product rather than putting money into a survey of questionable value. Since craftwork can be produced in limited quantities and with limited expenses, the potential for gain is much on the side of testing the market through a direct sales effort. Other attempts to define the market should be tried first, in all cases.

Observation and Analysis

The size, financial condition, and product of the average crafts operation will limit its preliminary evaluation of the market to simple observation and logical analysis. Whatever your situation, make an effort to answer these five questions completely when preparing to put your craft on the market:

1. What do you want to sell?
2. Who will buy it?
3. Where is the target area?
4. What means of distribution will you use?
5. How and when will you promote the product?

Chances are that you plied your craft before deciding to place the product on the market. You probably know what you want to sell, and you are prepared to add to the product line. You only hope that buyers will be as enthusiastic about the results as you are.

You are not about to proceed in total darkness, of course, if you have sold some pieces to friends and relatives. Add to your experience the suggestions of other acquaintances whose judgment you trust, and combine them with observations of competitors in your field. Viewed collectively, these facts might provide enough evidence about your market—the age, sex, location, preferences and desires of probable buyers—to go ahead. Your next move would then be to decide how and by what means to promote and distribute the product.

Product Variations and Appeal

In the absence of the kind of information that develops when actually marketing and selling, you would be well advised to give a great deal of attention to any general conclusions applicable to the marketing of crafts. There are several worth noting. One of broad consequence is that crafts oriented in variety, style, purpose, and price to a broad segment of the public will sell in greater quantities than highly artistic, expensive articles of specialized design. Those in this first category will have appeal at all income levels, and they will have uses both in the home and for personal adornment. The other category contains articles sometimes seen in corporate headquarters buildings, museums, and the edifices of wealthy people.

An awareness that women do much of the decorating of homes in America is another important part of the equation. This is not a sexist comment, but an established fact. It is therefore obvious that females of housekeeping age constitute a very large market for crafts. It necessarily follows that product variety and styling can be directed to advantage to that group. This point is worthy of attention whether you are making decorative centerpieces and wall hangings or articles of practical use, including note holders, shelves, cups and saucers, baskets, jewelry boxes, photo albums, bedspreads, or table mats.

The prices asked must vary and be reasonable. Articles priced throughout a range below $20 will generate the most activity.

People of all ages constitute a market for products made for personal use. Purses, wallets, and key cases of leather, ceramic mugs and jugs, cleverly fashioned metal tie clasps and broaches, and wooden toys and jewelry boxes represent product lines that appeal to different groups. Women hold a major spot in this personal-use market, also. They are inclined to fill their own needs in addition to buying gifts for others—the men, other women, and children in their lives. Be sure to keep them in mind when styling items for individual use.

With a bit of judgment on your part, you can define the primary market for your line of crafts. Your next step is to determine where and how you will distribute the line.

PRODUCT DISTRIBUTION DECISIONS

Before promoting your product, decide if you will sell retail or wholesale and nationally, regionally, or locally. Much depends on the size of your business. To sell wholesale or to retailers throughout a large section of the country will require an ability to maintain a constant supply of the product in substantial quantities. Craftworkers are not ordinarily set up to do that, nor do many have the desire to do so. You may be no different. To go large-scale, you will have to employ numerous workers, perhaps purchase volumes of items for resale, and generate and maintain ample outlets for the goods.

The Local Market

Most craftspeople want to market their wares within an area near home. In that way, they can maintain a convenient driving distance while keeping a hand in production. Traveling much beyond the immediate locality, as when attending regional and national shows, could place a strain on a one- or two-person operation.

The possibilities for retailing crafts locally cover a considerable range. Consignment shops, craft or variety stores, bazaars, community and church festivals, sidewalk and arts and crafts shows, a showroom in the home, and neighborhood house parties are the principal places and ways to market such products. Any one of these, or several practices in combination, can produce worthwhile results.

One of the best vehicles for marketing to women is the home party because it takes the product to where they are. The method becomes most effective when combined with promotional displays at local shows and bazaars. This means of marketing can also be scheduled to allow for occasional demonstrations in one's own home and trips to arts and crafts shows in nearby cities.

Store Displays

The retailing of crafts through a store by virtue of outright sales or consignment is also best done locally. Operating through a store can provide, due to close proximity, the advantage of prompt response in supplying products and keeping shelves stocked. On the other hand, proximity does little good in controlling the quality of all items on display, unless you own the store. One potential problem is the need to reduce the quality of your product to remain competitive with articles placed near yours. Doing that could diminish your image and your profit.

Store ownership will give you a reasonable measure of control over what you place on the shelves and the margin of profit, but it will also involve higher operating costs and necessitate employing several additional helpers. Having the necessary capital and keeping an adequate supply of the right merchandise are important matters to take into account when planning to run your own shop.

The money you get to keep could be a significant factor in choosing a method of marketing. Consignment shops, gift shops, and variety stores (whether you sell on consignment or outright) will take as much as 40 to 50% of the selling price. If you're lucky, the charge will be less. You might be better off by marketing your craft directly to the customer. The price you ask should not change much.

Craft Fairs

Selling at bazaars, crafts festivals, flea markets, or other community affairs has other pros and cons to consider. The likely advantage is the publicity resulting from displaying your craft before the public. Since many people who will visit your booth are browsers rather than buyers, you can expect those items in the $1 to $5 price range to sell the best. You can recover the costs of your booth, your merchandise (about one-half the retail price), space rental, transportation, and enough for your time if you have an attractive display and apply above average salesmanship. For many craftspeople, especially those starting out, the benefit of displaying at arts and crafts shows, at shopping malls, and at county fairs will have to be credited more to publicity than profit.

Other Methods

Other, more or less special ways to market well-made crafts are available to the reasonably effective salesperson. Among these are selling crafts to merchants for store-window displays and supplying handcrafted articles to company executives for distribution at retirement parties or as Christmas bonuses. While opportunities of this kind might be few in a given area, they could be an effective supplementary activity even on a very limited basis. What this approach can do for a business's image could be well worth the effort.

Your choice of distribution methods will depend to a considerable extent on how eager and energetic you are. As a rule, the beginning home-crafter will want to concentrate on methods requiring investments in time and effort as opposed to investments in time and money. After you decide on a method, you will need some time to build a positive image.

BUILDING A POSITIVE IMAGE

The factors leaving a lasting impression on customers are both tangible and intangible, but clearly controllable. Both types have an important bearing on how the public perceives the business and the person who represents it. Customers will surely draw conclusions about what they observe and experience, and they will often help establish a reputation by word-of-mouth recommendation. In view of how public impressions can affect a business, an astute owner will do all that is reasonably possible to create an operation that is viewed favorably by customers.

First impressions are especially important. What can you do in your business to control them and create the kinds of reactions that will not detract from your goals? Begin with a quick analysis of your situation. Determine who and what are likely to go before or be presented to your prospective customers, initially. Then do positive things. What you do will reflect directly on the business and the perception of it.

Market Yourself

If you are owner and operator, start by putting things into practice that will make a difference. Here are seven helpful tips on marketing yourself personally:

1. Project an appearance of honesty by being honest.
2. Be positive. Always have good things to say.
3. Be enthusiastic about your craft and your product.
4. Care about your customers and show it.
5. Be courteous, respectful, and prompt.
6. Build a reputation through public relations work.
7. Show that you are successful at what you do.

Although the first three recommendations here should require no further comment, the rest do. Showing that you care about your customers is especially important.

An effective way to show concern for customers is to offer to repair, without charge, any article they buy that might be damaged. To protect yourself, you might stress that repairs will be free for articles accidentally broken while within the purchaser's ownership. The goodwill gained will usually far outweigh the cost involved.

Another way to demonstrate concern is to answer the phone promptly. If possible, answer your business phone after two rings. You will show a quickness to respond without appearing to be overly eager. By the same token, respond personally or by recording machine in a manner that does not detract from the caller's rightful feeling of importance.

The matter of public relations takes on further meaning. The idea is to create personal visibility by participating in noteworthy activities. You can use your work in a civic club, community activity, or other beneficial role to advantage. The idea that you are sufficiently concerned about your community to devote time freely to its betterment can be powerfully positive. If you hold an office, so much the better. The reputation of being a leader in addition to caring about service to others is even more helpful in your business dealings.

As to the matter of success, look the part. How you dress, the accessories you carry, and the car you drive will make a definite impression. You hope it will be positive.

A final point to remember about the personal aspect of marketing is this: No matter how good your product, your business can be tainted by personal behavior. Because of this, you should show concern not just for selling crafts but for supplying people with satisfying products and a beneficial service. Express interest in building quality and safety into your products and for providing such things as biodegradable packaging. You will, by so doing, communicate an awareness of social and environmental concerns. The effect in the marketplace could be very beneficial.

Attractive Printed Matter

Among the first of the tangible things to be noticed by the public, other than the product itself, are business cards, brochures, catalogs, newspaper ads, and, perhaps, outdoor signs. Unlike most personal qualities, many of these things appeal to senses of sight and touch. Professional quality is expected. The look and feel of an amateurish piece will often elicit a profoundly adverse reaction. An easily identified logo, when effectively styled and neatly embossed on printed matter, is an excellent way to promote the business's identification, remembrance, and acceptance.

To be on the safe side, give all of your printed matter a professional look. Typed letters on typeset letterhead and printed brochures, flyers, and catalogs are a must. Use quality paper. Letterhead on 20-pound bond is good. Additionally, have catalogs and business cards printed on substantial stock so they will not fall limp in the hands of consumers.

Names and Slogans

While attractive graphic material will assist in creating a desirable visual image, any slogan or name you use to identify your business will be subject to intellectual evaluation. The impact can be just as significant. Whether rationally or visually inspired, an impression might be long remembered.

The name of a business should be descriptive and easy to remember, and a slogan, if used, should be catchy. Consider these: "The Homecraft Shop" and "Making your house a home." Both the name and the phrase seem to meet the basic requirements, and their brevity makes them suitable for advertising purposes.

On the other hand, too much stylishness or flashiness could obliterate or detract from the message to be conveyed. "Kathy's Korner" might be clever, but it is not as descriptive as "Laura's Leathers." Both are alliterative and personal, but only one really describes what the business is about.

ADVERTISING

Advertising is that form of public communication that businesses buy. It has a place so vital in a planned program of marketing that companies invest about $1\frac{1}{2}$ percent of their annual budget, on the average, in promotional activities and media coverage. While the cost might be considerable, advertising is the only practical way to be certain of reaching the masses targeted.

Mass Media

As with publicity generally, the purposes of advertising are to create and maintain an awareness of the business or its product, to enhance an image, and to support sales. The exact method of achieving each objective will depend on the target group under consideration. Newspaper and radio advertisements, for example, will be most effective when placed with those media to which people in the customer base read and listen. Marketing specialists can tell you which of such media will reach your customers most effectively, but you can make the same determinations without extra charge by talking to the advertising representatives employed by local media.

Media specialists can often provide all you need to know. They will give you information about when to run and how to structure an ad, in addition to specifics on circulation and audience penetration. Seek their advice, and evaluate it. Compare alternatives. To choose to have an ad for radio air at a particular hour merely because it gives you the most time for the dollar could be practically useless if it repeats at 2:00 AM. By asking and listening, you will have the benefit of expert advice on how to avoid such mistakes. You can also learn how to give your newspaper and radio ads a professional tone.

Paying for ads in the yellow pages of the telephone directory and on local TV is a somewhat less certain way to spend money to promote your kind of business. Advertising in yearbooks, sports programs, theater programs, and magazines are other methods of promoting the business and sales that are ordinarily too expensive and are not likely to impact enough of the group interested in crafts. A similar conclusion generally holds for advertising through bus and taxi cards, direct mail, and billboards. An exception occurs when printed advertisements are sent by mail to a select number of regular customers.

Be on guard for any adversity besides excessive costs that might result from advertising. By including your business location in an ad to the public at large, as will often have to be done, you will be giving notice to all types of individuals, including those looking for a profitable burglary. You probably can't afford to stop advertising through the mass media, but you might want to install some kind of security system in your place of business. As suggested in chapter 5, what you decide to do may be controlled by the nature and location of your business.

Catalogs, Brochures, Etc.

In addition to advertising by radio and in newspapers, crafts lend themselves to promotion by distributions of specially printed matter. Some useful and recommended items include: brochures, catalogs, business cards, and posters. The first three can be given directly to customers, while posters should be placed in strategic locations throughout the market area. Simple announcements of sales can be printed on postcards and mailed to selected clientele.

Printed items can be expensive or relatively inexpensive. Generally, costs on a per-item basis increase with the use of color and decrease with the larger quantities. Catalogs and brochures done in four-color printing are more attractive than those printed black on white, but you will have to decide, taking into account the advice of your printer, what you can afford to have done. Whatever you do, make it neat and professional in quality.

One young woman who operates a crafts business uses two sheets of $8^1/_2$-×-11-inch parchment-like paper folded and stapled together on center to form an inexpensive eight-page catalog. The front carries the name of the business, a brief statement of contents, and hand-drawn illustrations. Inside, she identifies the articles for sale in neatly hand-lettered form, with each numbered and priced. All printing is done in black, so the cost of duplicating is minimal.

She includes in her catalog several features worthy of consideration by other marketers of crafts. First, she specifies at the end of the list (on the back page) that she will contribute a certain percentage of sales income to charity. Second, she lists gifts and how people can earn them by hosting sales parties for her. Third, she numbers the items listed for sale beginning at 101, thereby implying the first item listed is not the first she has made. Fourth, and last, she adds a bit more class to the catalog by attaching a small, colorful bow or wooden heart to an upper corner on the front page. Part of her success is undoubtedly due to her ability to make an effective promotional piece from a low-cost informational catalog.

Because catalogs and brochures can be comparatively expensive to produce, consider limiting distributions to people whose interest in crafts is apparent. Handing out literature indiscriminately is a costly and largely unproductive way to promote business. This point is worth considering whether you have people walking by your booth at a show or are contemplating mailing literature to prospective clients.

One promotional item that you should be prepared to give out freely is your business card. Quantities of the cards can be purchased at a reasonable price, and they serve an indispensable purpose. They are evidence to potential customers that you are sincerely in business. Furthermore, they can set the tone and tenor of the type of business you operate. In order to create the desired effect, you will want your cards to be of high quality and to be professionally printed on heavy, durable stock.

Avoid cheapness and a cluttered appearance. Give the name of your business, a small logo (if you have a good one), the address and phone number for business purposes, and either your name as proprietor or a catchy slogan. If your card's finished layout doesn't present much white space to the reader, you've overdone it and made it less readable than desired.

Stick-On Labels

Labels containing your business's name and address, when attached to articles you sell, can be effective in generating repeat sales. They give paying customers and others who admire your finished work a ready reference of where they can obtain more of it. If made with a bit of elegance, such as with black lettering on a gold foil background, the peel-and-stick kinds of labels will provide more than a mere statement of who created the goods.

Fortunately, such labels are not expensive. They can be had for a few cents each when bought in quantities of 250 or 500. Everything considered, they are an excellent way to promote an image and additional sales among satisfied customers and their friends.

Giveaways

Pencils and slim pens embossed or printed with the name of the business are other promotional devices you might want to include among your repertoire of advertising techniques. At a cost of a dime to a quarter apiece, these promos can be used most advantageously as gratuities for established customers or good prospects. They are especially effective at gatherings of customers in house parties.

You might also consider a slightly different twist when displaying your wares at crafts shows, bazaars, and fairs. All you need is a small display area with several feet of frontage, but you must then do something to attract people to it. One useful way to attract passers-by (preferably customers) to your booth is to offer them a chance for a free prize simply for registering their name, address, and telephone number. For the cost of a single item, you will receive numerous leads to contact later by telephone or through mailings.

A Coordinated Plan

A main concern is how much advertising to do and how to pay for it. Drawing up a schedule of activities for the year helps solve problems of coordination. Careful budgeting helps with the financing.

When setting up a plan, think in terms of a campaign rather than a one-shot thrust. Your program should make use of several media, frequent and regular advertising, and stepped-up efforts before holidays. (Refer to the examples in FIG. 7-1.) Several small, provocative ads are better than a large, flashy one. Thus, classified newspaper ads will be more appropriate than display ads. Always use positive wording when writing ads of any kind.

Push for quality responses, not just quantity. When advertising an open-house demonstration before the Christmas season, for instance, you might announce that a door prize of $___ value will be given away to two of the people who attend. Make the rest of the ad the basic inducement. The prize is merely icing on the cake. Hopefully, an ad worded as described will increase the numbers of visitors and, as a consequence, the numbers of people who will actually buy something.

PUBLICITY

If cash flow is a problem, concentrate on generating publicity for your business. There are various ways to make known what you have to offer without spending money out of pocket or extending the advertising budget.

ACTIVITIES PLAN

March		Marketing	Production	Sales Activity
1		Letter to editor	—	Sales party/7:30 Mrs. Jones' home
2		—	Craftwork	—
3	(Sunday)			
4		Design/have printed open-house announcement	—	—
5		—	Craftwork	—
6		Civic club work	″	Telephone leads
7		Prep. poster/display	″	″
8		—	—	City Craft Show
9		—	—	″
10	(Sunday)			
11		Distr. announcements	—	—
12		—	Craftwork	Follow-up leads
13		Prep. radio/news ads	″	—
14		—	″	—
15		Mail invitations to special customers	—	—
16		—	Craftwork	—
17	(Sunday)			
18		News release on crafts/ads out	—	—
19		—	Craftwork	—
20		Sing in com. choir	″	—
21		Call/invite customers	″	—
22		—	—	Open-house sale
23		—	—	″
24	(Sunday)			
25		—	Craftwork	—
26		—	″	Sales party/7:30 Mrs. Bufford's
27		—	″	—
28		—	″	Follow-up leads
29		—	″	—
30		—	—	Bates' party/2.30
31	(Sunday)	Evaluate activities for the month.		

7-1 This one-month schedule of marketing, production, and sales activities points out the need for coordinated planning.

The best publicity is free. Get as much of it as you can. Favorable comments made in public by people who have bought your product can't be beat, and the person who hosts a sales party in her home will be your greatest asset if she speaks praisingly about your work. Although some successful craftspeople rely on word-of-mouth publicity entirely, don't overlook the additional rewards possible from free media coverage.

Media Coverage

Choose the methods of promoting your business through public communications media that work best for you, and build upon them as you gain experience. Be cognizant, in the process, of the benefit of announcing the opening of your business. Contact all media nearby. Those in small communities will publish or air your news release free of charge.

Invite reporters to do a feature on your craft, or write a story yourself and deliver it to the local newspaper editor. Include sharp, 5-x-7-inch black-and-white glossy photographs with anything you present. If the editor sends a photographer, as some editors will for a personal interest story, suggest several shots in your workplace that might be taken. The strong feature about these kinds of articles is they are designed to interest the reader.

Display Techniques

Gather copies of anything printed publicly about your accomplishments. Community work, club membership, election to office, and anything else of a civic or social nature is appropriate. Cut out and make use of the clippings. Display them at shows and attach them to bulletin boards in beauty shops, laundromats, churches, or other community gathering places. Attach your business card to each display. The entire matter will cost you little, but the dissemination of locally published personal information lends prestige and credibility to your work.

The locations noted are good places, as well, for tacking up small posters, printed announcements, or brochures. Displays of photographs showing you standing beside your business sign is another way to promote the operation inexpensively. A neatly assembled group of photographs in clear plastic inserts and fixed in a loose-leaf binder makes an excellent display at shows.

Make an effort to keep your business in the public eye. Additional ways to do this cost free include speaking to local clubs and adult groups about your area of expertise, holding how-to-do-it classes for no more than the cost of materials, and obtaining endorsements from individuals who are popular locally. Of the many things that could be done, your problem will be to limit your involvement to the ones most beneficial to your work.

PUBLIC RELATIONS

Public relations involves activities, intentional or otherwise, that tend to create an impression about your business and different aspects of it. The kinds of public relations activities covered in this section are those that will increase your visibility and acceptance rather than those pertaining to specific operations of the business. In this sense, public relations will be dealt with as it pertains to your personal image. A favorable public perception about you, personally, will do much to foster a positive image of your business and your craftwork.

Public Speaking

There are many things you can and should do to increase your visibility in the community. Begin by giving speeches throughout the area on some subject of interest that might or might not be related to your money-making venture. The club or community action group you have recently joined is a good place to start. If none of the officers asks you to speak, let them know that you can and would like to do so. Experience shows that program chairmen are continually on the lookout for people to address their organizations. By all means, when asked to speak have something worthwhile to say.

When given an opportunity to address a group, prepare thoroughly for the occasion. Outline what you expect to cover by writing down the main points, and rehearse what you will say about each point. Tailor your opening and ending remarks to the group to be addressed. Interject some humor if you can make it relevant, but do not include an off-color joke. (It isn't needed, and some people might be offended if you tell it.) Work out what you will say several days or even as much as a week or two before the time of the presentation. This practice will enable you to sleep on it, adding to and refining the message beforehand. The more thoroughly prepared and knowledgeable you are about the topic, the less likely it is you will be overcome by nervousness when speaking.

Keep your notes handy during the speech, and use them to guide the flow of your message. Pay heed, also, to these final, few suggestions: Relieve tension by taking several rapid, deep breaths of air before going to the podium; look directly at and speak to the audience; and be absolutely sure to end your talk within the time allotted.

Alternatives

If you are too uncomfortable standing before large groups, put your talents to work in other ways. Volunteer your services to serve the elderly or underprivileged youth in your area, become a teacher's assistant in a continuing education class in your community college or nearest vocational school, take an active part in local charity fund drives, or man a booth that one of the benevolent organizations you belong to has set up at the county fair. Exercise good judgment about what you choose to do. The object is to remain visible to the public and in a positive, neutral, or otherwise inoffensive way. To take an active part in a major political party might appear to some people to be a very favorable thing to do, but people of an opposing political conviction might be completely turned off. Your best bet is to keep out of the limelight where controversial issues are involved. The success of your business will be determined, in part, by your personal reputation.

Theodore "Bullmoose" Roosevelt, when President of the United States, once said, "When a man asks if you can do a job, tell him you can; then get busy and find out how." That was the former leader's way of telling people of average cut to be confident about their talents and to make use of them by learning what needs to be known to succeed. The underlying message still applies today. As an entrepreneur of crafts, if you strive for expertise in one or more public relations activities, you will be paving the road to success.

One more suggestion: Do not be afraid to make an error before the public. Ordinarily, the content of an article or speech is soon forgotten, and there are those who will not notice if and when an occasional error is made. The personal exposure is the thing most remembered.

BUILDING A CLIENTELE

Your primary goal in marketing is to locate, acquaint, and interest members of the public concerning your craft. Secondarily, you want to have them continue as your customers once they have bought something. Having buyers who are satisfied with your product, service, and business comprises the basic way to build a continuing association.

Repeat Business

Marketing specialists in the business of promoting magazine sales know how important it is to keep a customer buying year after year. All sorts of gimmicks are used. Discount pricing, offers of free issues, inducements for early payment, special letters that seem to come like clockwork, and returnable, postage-free cards inserted in each copy of the magazine are among the ways they attempt to gain repeaters. The extra, direct effort and expense devoted to retaining a customer or having a previous one begin buying again has evidently become so profitable that the companies make a veritable nuisance of themselves in the process.

You, also, need permanent customers. Unlike an impersonal magazine company (which many are), you cannot afford to have your association with buyers deteriorate into anything resembling a high-pressure confrontation. Actions that seem irritating are often counterproductive and not conducive to repeated buying. Everything from casual conversation to the presentation of a bill has importance in a crafts business, for the relationship you establish will be personal and sometimes close.

Unless buyers are favorably impressed, your prospects of building a clientele you can depend on for future purchases will be greatly diminished.

Express Appreciation

There are a number of workable ideas you can use easily and extensively besides the many promotional techniques already discussed. One of great significance, yet used little, is the habit of sending a personal thank-you for business received. A simple, handwritten note will do just fine (FIG. 7-2). It is a special way of demonstrating courteousness and caring. Although the message might be conveyed by nothing more elaborate than a post card, the cost of the mailing should be a budgeted expense.

As simple as this suggestion seems, the practice is not universal. Think of the companies and professional concerns that have ever expressed appreciation to you in writing for your business. They are probably few and far between. Notes of appreciation are the general exception. In view of this, your business can be made to stand out as being run by one who truly cares enough to extend a special expression of personal gratitude. The effect could be positively memorable.

You can achieve complete effectiveness in using this method only if you always record the names and addresses of buyers. Gather this information at the time of the sale and compile it on a card file. The file is a useful reference for later promotions, as well as for sending notes of thanks.

Don't let your customers forget. Make periodic mailings to them as reminders of upcoming events or occasions for which your crafts just might fill the need. A telephone call once or twice a year could be a preferable alternative to writing, particularly if you are also seeking leads of prospects to call on.

Because customers will not always keep your address on file, every article, whether an initial purchase or not, should have an identifying label attached. The purpose of the label is to provide a ready reference for ordering additional items and to keep your address fixed where it is less likely to be lost or discarded. As previously discussed, commercially made, self-sticking labels that can be attached to an article's back or bottom effectively accomplish this.

Special Services

You might further capitalize on human nature by making available a service doing things that people could do for themselves but prefer not to. Gift wrapping, to suggest an idea, is something many people are not very good at doing and others find to be downright annoying. Why not capitalize on the situation? Offering to mail the purchases for a price can add to your income, in addition to being the kind of thing that will have people coming back again and, hopefully, again.

One Local Drive
Someplace, USA
July 27, 19—

Dear Mrs. Jones,

Thanks so much for your business. You can cherish your purchases for years to come, knowing how carefully each piece was handcrafted.

Appreciatively yours,

Jill
Country Creations

One Local Drive,
Someplace, USA
July 27, 19__

Dear Mrs. Jones,

Thanks again for helping to make my show a success. Please call on me when you are looking for other uniquely handcrafted gifts.

Gratefully yours,

Jill
Country Creations

7-2 Notes of appreciation for new and repeat customers may be handwritten or typed on postcards.

MAKE IT COUNT

Many of the suggestions given in this chapter can, when properly implemented, profoundly affect your business. To ignore them or apply them haphazardly could make a big difference. At the risk of seeming repetitious, there is no good substitute for a well-planned schedule of promotional activities.

Develop your plan of activities by recording those things you can do routinely as part of producing, publicizing, and distributing your product. Set out the things to do in a monthly schedule, tallying and totaling costs in the process. Incorporate the major activities and marketing objectives in the business plan, as shown in chapter 3. It will provide you with a schedule to go by and, at the same time, an assurance that you will be keeping within your budget.

8
CHAPTER

Sell It
Without Hassle

SELLING IS NECESSARY IN BUSINESS. The very essence of business is to produce income by providing a service or by transferring goods to a purchaser for a price. Whether production does or does not have a place in an enterprise's operation makes no difference.

Something similar can be said about the selling of handcrafts. Your mastery of a craft might be evident, but you will be an entrepreneur in the field only when you sell the product. If you have never before sold something, do not despair. Many an untrained person has learned how to sell with a little effort.

Undoubtedly, not all craftspeople who intend to sell their creations take the time to learn how. The practice at public arts and crafts shows illustrates the point. Have you ever observed handcrafters sitting placidly behind their displays, seemingly coming alive only when going to the hot-dog stand or talking to an occasional questioner? Their work is good and occasionally outstanding, you might note, but for some reason not much is being bought. Only at a few booths is there much selling going on. Why aren't more people buying? One reason is that many of the people placing items on display don't have the foggiest notion of what it takes to sell in that environment. They sometimes lack the physical stamina or an appealing product, but most of all they lack salesmanship and marketing skills. The probable result is that some will quit exhibiting their crafts when they might easily have become successful retailers by following a few basic rules.

The significant point to bear in mind is that some handcrafters do sell their crafts successfully at shows, as well as through other ways and means of direct selling. They have learned how to do it, and so can you. Taking heed of the suggestions and procedures given in this chapter could give you the start you need. You might even be pleasantly surprised when proceeding, particularly at how positive the experience can be.

ACCORDING TO TYPE

Salespeople are made, not born. Some become order-takers and some hard sellers. Others develop into more of a consumer-oriented type. What you will become depends very much on what you intend to be.

Order-Takers

To be an order-taker, all you have to do is set up a booth, sit back inactively, and hope that someone will buy something. You might, when the spirit moves you, simply ask the customer if he or she is interested in anything you have to sell. Don't expect much success with either approach, because crafts are basically nonessential items for which no inherent demand exists. They are unlike food and clothing in that regard. People will sometimes buy crafts strictly out of personal motivation, but they have no compulsion to do so to satisfy a necessity of life.

Hard Sellers

At the other end of the spectrum, we have the hard-sell specialists. They are often referred to as "high-pressure," or "one-shot," salesmen. Individuals of this type are frequently encountered pushing sales of encyclopedias, grave plots, or used cars, and they seem to have no reluctance about overstating a product's merits or for running down the competition. They are more concerned with the sale than the customer, a fact that has given selling and salesmen a bad reputation everywhere.

Consumer-Minded Salespeople

The third type of salesperson is more consumer oriented than the other two. These salespeople are concerned about individual needs and desires, and they take their customers' long term interests to heart. They create a feeling of friendship by suggesting solutions to problems, seeking in the process to make the sale and establish a source for subsequent business.

Salespeople of this latter type will never stoop to using underhanded tactics, always remaining cognizant of the legality and ethicality of their intentions. They will observe a 72-hour grace period in which buyers might return merchandise for no particular reason and a full refund of money. They will strictly avoid discriminatory practices relative to age, race, and religion, and never will they intentionally present a product in a misleading light. Neither will they say untruthful things about the competition, nor will they sell anything once used as a new product. In short, they will make a conscientious effort to do what is right.

People who attempt to sell throughout a local territory—as opposed to those who operate in relative obscurity in a large regional or national market area—must be constantly concerned about the kind of personal reputation they are creating. This concern is crucial to the selling of crafts. Crafts are sold through methods of direct selling, which depend on satisfied customers and, to a great extent, on word-of-mouth publicity. A customer's feelings of trust and general liking for the salesperson can then become as important as the product. An astute person will make an effort to cultivate those feelings.

CONFIDENCE AND CHARACTER

Anyone of moral upbringing will want to be guided by principles of honesty and integrity. Those are the kinds of qualities that form the foundation for a business of local orientation. Not only do those qualities come through positively to customers, but they are the stuff upon which one's feelings of self-esteem, inner contentment, and confidence can emerge and flourish.

With confidence, you can accomplish much more than you might have at first imagined. Perhaps, like many handcrafters, you just can't visualize yourself ever asking for money for something you made. Perhaps, also, you have a fear of rejection, knowing full well that some of the people you approach will not buy nor be impressed by anything you have for sale. Neither problem seems to be extraordinary, and neither are the obstacles insurmountable.

Any reluctance or expression of humility along those lines can be overcome by a fundamental change in attitude. The point of change occurs the moment you realize that many people could be benefited by making your handiwork available to the public and that rejection is not fatal. By clearing the air of perceived roadblocks, you can take steps to increase your level of confidence.

The importance of self-confidence in the process of selling can be understated. A defeatist attitude or perceived lack of ability will often elicit a negative reaction. Consider this statement: "I make the stuff, but I'm not a salesman." Or, worse, "All I can hope for is enough sales to cover expenses." Neither will make a favorable impression.

Know the Product

Building confidence takes practice. The first major step is to know what you have to sell and to know it, as they say, "cold." In that regard, you have an advantage. You know all about the construction of the product, because you did it. Add to that a little relevant knowledge of a historical or scientific nature, and you will probably be more of an expert on the subject than any of your customers are likely to be. Develop your presentation into an interesting explanation and you will have most of what is needed to go confidently one-on-one or before a group.

Along with thorough knowledge of the product, you must have an affinity for it. Determine all the truly beneficial ways your product will be of use or service to the customer, and be enthusiastic about the work and its advantages. You will be most successful if you are personally "sold" on the product and show it. The joy of selling something of which you are proud can be absolutely exhilarating, especially at times when paying customers express heartfelt appreciation to you for having brought the work to their attention.

Become a Winner

An experienced sales trainer once told his group of novices that although he had nothing new to tell them, they should remember one thing and put it into practice at every opportunity: "Treat each sales presentation as you would a chess game you sincerely want to win." His advice was sound. Selling, like chess, proceeds from certain rules and a plan, but it also requires an ability to think and modify the plan of procedure as individual circumstances necessitate. How the process proceeds will often determine the success or failure of the outcome.

Unlike winning a game of chess, however, success in selling goes beyond such ingredients as preparation, desire, and ability to think. Mental attitude, personal appearance, courtesy, industriousness, and friendliness are other important qualities in selling. The person who learns to apply them to advantage can reach heights beyond mere ambition.

Rules to Observe

There are, in addition to desirable personal traits, practical procedures of use in making selling successful. Here are several of the most important ones:

- Treat customers as if they are members of your immediate family.
- Set high goals. Keep trying to surpass your previous performance.
- Avoid selling only what sells easiest.
- Recognize that your primary task is to communicate with and to satisfy people.
- Learn from rejection; don't take it as a personal failure.
- Mentally rehearse and review the sales process before each presentation.

A fundamental rule is to view your customers with dignity. How you communicate verbally and through emotional expression will make a difference. Look upon your business as an easy "racket" and your customers will soon get the impression they are being manipulated. At no time do you want them to develop a feeling of being "taken." Make each one feel important and in control, regardless of how little or much is bought at the time.

Customers have a need to be treated respectfully, courteously, and intelligently. A well-placed compliment can do much to build rapport, but the overuse of flattery can undo it altogether. How you handle these human relations aspects of selling can overshadow any expertise you might exhibit relative to the more mechanical aspects of the process.

No matter how much experience you acquire, prepare yourself mentally before each presentation. Cover the basic steps. Give yourself a reminder to remain attentive to both the personal and the business goals.

Memorable Rewards

Selling can be very heady. The rewards are sometimes immediate, and they can reach a level you never expected possible. You probably won't get rich, but you could easily make enough money to continue your craft at a comfortable level of support.

What you will actually accomplish depends on how masterfully you apply procedures of known effectiveness. Although the previous list of suggestions is indicative of how much of an art selling can be, you might find, via diligent application of the step-by-step process below, the selling of crafts can become almost mechanical and a surprisingly easy thing to do.

THE PROCESS

Profit is the bottom line in business, and sales are basic to achieving it. The viability of your business, therefore, is a consequence of how effectively you sell what you make.

Start by ridding your mind of doubts about yourself and your ability. Just as you learned to speak to people, you can learn to speak to them in a particular way. Concentrate on procedures generally accepted in the field of direct selling. Know and apply them and you will sell crafts. You probably will not be extraordinarily successful at first, but you will sell what you make.

The general process consists of six interrelated elements: identifying potential customers, preliminary activities, the presentation, handling objections, closing the sale, and the follow-up. Although details will vary according to individual circumstances, the elements will be discussed essentially in the sequence presented.

1. Identify potential customers The act of seeking potential customers is called *prospecting*. It can be laborious or easy. The techniques vary in practice from blindly canvassing by going door-to-door to greeting prospects who voluntarily come to your place of business. How to avoid much of the drudgery and uncertainty of finding prospects is covered later in this chapter. Be sure to read it, for it will prove helpful to anyone engaged in a crafts business.

2. Preliminary activities The next step preparatory to the presentation entails making plans for and contacting prospective customers. Will the presentation be made by phone, by mail, individually in person, or to a group in a neighbor's home? The answer will be instrumental in making the preparations. Everything that goes into staging for the presentation is prepared at this point, including any props or products that have to be made ready. Exactly what takes place at this juncture will be controlled to an extent by how the prospects have been identified. Prospects taken on referral will naturally not be greeted the same as those casually taking in a display at an arts and crafts sale.

One more thing: Get enough sleep. Being well rested for a presentation should become an established routine. A person who is tired does not have the mental alertness necessary for selling effectively.

3. The presentation   The first point in a sales presentation is to hold the attention of the person or people before you. An effective way to accomplish this on an individual basis is to engage the prospect in small talk. In addition to fostering feelings of relaxation and ease, it provides a few moments for analyzing the individual's mood, attitude, receptivity, and concerns.

Groups must be handled a bit differently. Ask questions in an effort to start everyone thinking, while hoping to have any number of them respond. Even a greeting with casual reference to the beauty of the day is better than saying nothing. An alternate technique is to put some kind of attention-getting gadget into motion.

The main part of the presentation should quickly and smoothly follow. Its purpose is to stimulate interest in the product and develop the customers' desires. During a description and demonstration to a group or an individual, encourage touching, holding, or actually using the product. Direct involvement of this kind helps to maintain attention and create greater interest. Figure 8-1 shows a successful operator at work.

You must not only emphasize the piece's merits and benefits in ownership but also be a good listener so you can adjust your message to satisfy individual questions and comments. Objections are to be expected as a matter of course in the process. You must answer them and, if possible, turn them to your advantage.

4. Handling objections   Resistance to sales in the form of objections is to be expected, for many people will honestly have reasons for not buying while others will pose counter arguments in order to demonstrate their wit or power of control. Two methods are effective in overcoming objections to buying: One is to anticipate and counter them before the prospect raises any, and the other is to invite the prospect to state them, thereby bringing all reasons for rejection into the open so you can address them. If you anticipate objections and think them through beforehand, you can often show them to be irrational, inconsequential, or undefendable (and helpful to the close).

With practice, you will learn to cover the basic elements of a presentation thoroughly and smoothly. Experiment freely and simplify procedures whenever you can. Make a habit of applying the suggestions that work

8-1 The owner of the business shown here derives much of his success from selling by being alert, helpful, friendly, and knowledgeable about his merchandise.

effectively for you. View each presentation as a learning experience, and look at each presentation as a basis for improving the next one.

5. The closing   The part of the process in which the customer is asked to "sign on the dotted line" is the closing. You should attempt trial closes frequently throughout a presentation, such as by asking prospects which color or size they prefer. In the absence of a sale at that point, a questioning technique will often persuade the customer to state his or her objection. Several attempts are commonly made to get the customer to buy.

6. The follow-up   After making a sale, you should contact the buyer to be certain everything is satisfactory and, by showing concern, further promote goodwill. Correct any problem promptly, and remember to use the occasion to obtain additional sales and leads. If the entire process has been effectively handled, the buyer will at the very least remain receptive to possible future sales. A buyer, once identified, is usually worth more than several unknown prospects.

PROSPECTING THE EASY WAY

Because the selling of crafts is a process of intense personal involvement, take initial steps to identify individuals who are potentially interested in the product or who are willing to be approached about it. You can do this through referrals, leads from public announcements, and blind contact. Each approach utilizes techniques worth knowing. The traditional foot-in-the-door approach to prospecting is not one of them.

Avoid the Difficult

A technique of identifying prospects that seems unlikely to be worthwhile for the average craftsperson is *cold calling*. Telemarketing and direct mail efforts use the cold-calling approach. They are commonly directed to men and women by randomly selecting or indiscriminately canvassing households. Because as many as 100 telephone calls or mailings must be made to find a single buyer (and that is when the product can be easily explained by phone), the time and cost of this approach makes it inappropriate for most handcrafters.

The method of canvassing by going house-to-house could be more productive, but the problem there, too, is the limited appeal to be expected for a line of crafts. This method holds out much more promise for someone establishing a regular route for distributing a variety of household necessities. Crafts generally do not fit the mold.

Unrecruited Clients

Fortunately, you can use methods of marketing and selling that have built-in means of identifying potential clients without making preliminary efforts to recruit them. A community sidewalk show is an example. The exhibitors need not have made separate announcements about their plans to attend the show. Prospective customers attend simply on the basis of a general announcement.

People who come to view the exhibits are prized because they already have some interest in the things displayed, or they wouldn't be there. While few of them will have made a prior commitment to buy and some are just lookers, many are there, nevertheless, as viable prospects. Whether the exhibitor does what is necessary to turn the viewers into buyers is another matter. Something similar can be said for merchandising through retail stores, at least in certain instances.

Shows of all kinds—national and regional craft shows, local arts and crafts displays, town-square bazaars, county-fair booths, flea markets, sidewalk markets, and lawn or garage sales—are indicative of a type open to handcrafters to which prospective customers come without much prodding or prior identification. The exhibitor must view practically every person who passes by the booth as a potential buyer. A common difficulty observed is the lack of effort and effectiveness in displaying and selling the crafts. Suggestions on how to make a difference when selling crafts by exhibiting are given in the following list:

Dress
- Neatness and quality count heavily.
- Don't be too casual; no T-shirts or shorts.
- Wear comfortable, non-gaudy attire equal to what the best dressed of the exhibitors present wear.
- Wear comfortable shoes.

Demeanor
- Be friendly and professional.
- Appear eager to help. Keep your hands out of your pockets and your arms unfolded.
- As much as possible, stand up and be ready to greet and aid your customers.
- Do not smoke or eat in view of customers.

Display
- Use a background partition and the dividers to separate your display and to focus attention on it. Your business name can be placed in large letters high at the back, with several shelves of articles attached below.
- Have three or four coordinated groups of articles instead of dozens of small items spread about.
- A device in motion at eye level attracts attention, as does a simple demonstration.
- Use color and lettering for emphasis, but sparingly.

Customer Relations
- Wear a name badge with large, easy-to-read lettering.
- Address strangers with a simple "hello," and quickly engage them in conversation.
- Try to determine the person's interest in a minute or two.
- Suggest reasons for buying different articles, and close the conversation within four or five minutes—with or without a sale.
- Don't hand out literature indiscriminately. Give catalogs and brochures to buyers and others expressing interest.
- Ask each buyer to fill out a slip for a prize drawing, and use these slips for later follow-up.

Special Events

Another type of marketing in which the prospects have an even greater commitment than attendees at ordinary crafts shows is a demonstration at a fund-raising event. A church group or civic organization might have a handcrafter put on a sale for its members and specially invited outsiders, with a percentage of the sales going to the organization. Most assuredly, many of the people who attend will have decided to buy something even before seeing the display. While this practice seems to be somewhat rare, the potential for profits it offers is sufficient to keep a craftsperson alert to such opportunities.

Similarly captive as an audience are those who agree to attend a house party scheduled for the sole purpose of a demonstration and sale. The advantage of this method, like the previous one, is that someone else will identify and invite the prospects to the presentation. Most attendees will be mentally attuned to buying if the person responsible for the invitations has been the slightest bit effective. For the craftsperson who can't devote much time to prospecting, this can be one of the most efficient methods of assembling buyers.

Personal Referrals

The benefit doesn't end there, however. Every prospect, whether buyer or browser, can be a fruitful source for leads. *Leads* are names and addresses of acquaintances who might buy your crafts. How considerate you are in your dealings with each prospect will make a difference in that regard. Remember, always, when following up a sale to ask a buyer for additional referrals that might have come to mind.

Once you have obtained names, addresses, and telephone numbers on referral, you will use them to make arrangements for additional sales presentations, often by telephone. The people you contact who don't decline are good prospects. You should visit them individually in their homes or commit them to attending a demonstration in your showroom. Those who are unreceptive to such ideas initially will sometimes become excellent customers if you make a second attempt at a later time.

Other Sources

Besides personal referrals, you can tap a host of other possibilities. Anyone who fails to keep busy with shows, parties, and open-house displays has little excuse for not finding enough prospects to call on. Among the possibilities for gathering additional leads are: searching the daily newspaper for names of people about to be married or who are identified in an article in some other way, checking courthouse records for new home buyers in the community, obtaining lists of names from a friend in a non-competing business, and telephoning customers you haven't heard from recently. How to turn each lead into a live prospect can challenge the imagination and demand exceptional creativity. As a rule, be prepared to explain how your craft fits each particular situation and concentrate efforts on individuals seeming ready to buy.

You can give newspaper leads a special twist. One effective technique is to contact someone related to the person named, rather than to approach the individual him- or herself. Often, you can approach the prospect's mother most successfully with an explanation of the benefits of purchasing your craftwork as a gift. This approach seems to work best in instances when the mother is contacted shortly after publication of her son's or daughter's wedding announcement. Apply this technique by first sending a letter that contains a clipping of the announcement and accompanying picture, if any, a brochure about your business and the crafts, and a brief handwritten note congratulating her and suggesting she consider your unique work for a gift. If you do this promptly, she might then be very receptive to your suggestion.

Follow up with a telephone call several days after the mailing. Even if the call doesn't result in an immediate appointment or sale, she might give you the name of a grandparent who will also be searching for an appropriate gift. Anyway, if she is left with a favorable impression, she will have a brochure she might want to keep for future reference.

THE SALES PRESENTATION

Personal selling is similar to teaching in that the objective is to have one or more people accept what is said or demonstrated. Success in the undertaking will most likely occur when the presentation has been carefully planned, rehearsed, and refined. Once through the process, or after several practice sessions, applications become easier and virtually automatic. Experience makes a difference. A procedure that might have been recorded in detail in the beginning will not always have to be taped or written out for later use.

Your initial efforts at selling directly to customers should be written out, at least in outline form. Stress the positive. Learn to replace negative words with those having positive meanings. The comparisons in TABLE 8-1 are a representative guide.

A Sample Presentation

The presentation briefly addressed here covers the basics of the presentation. While it makes reference to a particular product and situation, you can readily adapt the outline to fit various crafts in one-on-one or group presentations.

DEMONSTRATION SALE/ETCHED ALUMINUM WARE

Preparation: Display about six trays, dishes, and coasters in different styles and prices—well-lighted. Have additional designs on hand. Spotlight a demonstration area. Provide the brushes, acid, and other tools and materials required for etching. Also, have ready brochures, business cards, order blanks, explanatory poster, cash box, and handcrafted articles complete with packaging.

Introduction: (1) Get the audience's attention. Do something unusual, e.g., popping a balloon with the vibrator, blowing an etched whistle, or

Table 8-1
Watch What You Say

Positives	Negatives
artistic	artificial
attractive	cheap
beautiful	common
complementary	copied
creative	costly
effective	crummy
excellent	crusty
exceptional	displeasing
good	duplicated
great	grotesque
inexpensive	ineffective
likeable	impractical
lovely	mediocre
original	offensive
perfect	ornate
pleasant	peculiar
pretty	poor
remarkable	repulsive
stimulating	revolting
strong	trivial
superior	ugly
unique	weak
unsurpassed	weird
valuable	worthless

striking an etched gong. (2) Put the group at ease with a compliment, simple joke, or brief, relevant story about the item used.

Discussion Demonstration: (1) Go through the construction, step by step. (List them.) Shorten the procedure by having pieces completed to various stages. (2) Pause frequently to explain. (3) Ask questions. Involve the spectators. (4) Emphasize the benefits of owning such pieces. (5) Create further interest by passing a finished piece or two among the audience (designating someone to see that the items are returned). (6) Present and discuss other pieces.

Conclusion: (1) Answer questions and review points as necessary. (2) Stress the advantages of ownership by making the group feel they have an opportunity to get a unique bargain through one-of-a-kind handcrafting, high quality, and affordable price. (3) Thank the spectators and have them register their names and addresses for a prize (and later follow-up). (4) Take orders and compliment buyers for making a sound choice.

Admittedly, this outline does not contain all of the information it could. A beginner will want to list each piece of equipment and material needed, and spell out humorous comments and other points to be presented in a particular way. Some will also want to identify something special, such as the acceptance of payment by credit card, when provided for, while others might also want to highlight points to be covered to offset potential objections.

When you are just starting out, you will benefit by listening to a recording of your delivery. Tape several practice sessions and the first sales presentations, then review the process for any necessary changes in wording or style. Any statements in the playback that have a negative connotation can be avoided in subsequent presentations. This technique helps weed out bad practices before they become habitually ingrained.

Show Enthusiasm

Never overlook or minimize the importance of standing and looking directly at members of the group during a presentation. Always stand in the presence of a prospect, unless you have to sit while demonstrating. (If your feet tire from standing, assume a partial sitting posture on a tall stool. Otherwise, have someone else do the selling.) Your goal is to create a desire for ownership among viewers, but you can't do that very well by sitting passively on your posterior. Enthusiasm is contagious, and you will generate more of it by being on your feet.

Additional Tips

In the process of selling, approach your subject in such a way that the person who buys an article will feel he or she made the purchase by choice, rather than having been sold on it. Have available a variety of items, and suggest different options. Don't forget to mention some of the reasons for making a purchase. The personal uses and opportunities for giving gifts can be extensive.

Occasionally, someone will place an order with you by phone. A much abbreviated presentation is made in such instances, for the individual has already decided to make a purchase. In that case, accept the order first. Then suggest additional items. Read back the order to eliminate mistakes and, thereby, set the customer at ease. Conclude the conversation upon agreeing how delivery and payment shall be made.

USING OBJECTIONS TO ADVANTAGE

A basic rule in selling is not to become rattled by objections. Expect them. Learn to take them in stride, and try to turn them to your advantage. At the very least, don't let them go unanswered.

Product-Related Objections

Price is one the foremost concerns customers have. The matter might not be made an issue, but it must be addressed. Overcome objections to price, whether stated or unstated, by stressing the quality of craftsmanship, uniqueness of design, durability of the product, guarantee of replacement, etc. When the opportunity arises, repeat any favorable comment that has been made by a satisfied buyer for the purpose of minimizing considerations of price. Emphasize exclusivity or other advantages of ownership in the process.

Objections to an item's design, finish, or other features can usually be answered by asking the customer to state personal preferences. Listen closely to each response. If you can meet the description, you've made a sale. If you can't, suggest something similar that you do have. A third option is to offer to make the item exclusively as requested.

Another technique helpful in overcoming an objection is to induce the customer to answer it. First, ask for clarification. In the process of explaining, the customer might actually weaken the argument or give you a clue to diminishing its validity. In instances of multiple objections, work to reduce the number to the lowest level. A single, remaining objection can sometimes be overcome as a result of posing questions about it to the customer.

Personal Factors

Resistance to buying due to some sort of psychological barrier can be very difficult to get a handle on, partly because the customer seldom makes the true reason known. A dislike of the salesperson, an inability to make decisions, resentment at being bothered, and a fear of talking to strangers are representative of this type. The best you can do in such situations is to maintain a positive approach while trying to achieve a breakthrough. Pursue each case with caution, for efforts along this line should not be undertaken to the neglect of the majority of clients normally encountered.

An experienced salesperson will learn to quickly recognize people who are poor prospects by the emphatic nature or manner of their first response. Physical ailments, stressful home conditions, and extremely negative attitudes are not unheard of deterrents to buying. Rather than try to make a buyer out of one who for some reason responds with open hostility, it is better to avoid the risk of verbal confrontation. There are far too many good prospects available to spend time on negative extremists.

THE CLOSE

The closing of a sale occurs at that point when the customer agrees to make a purchase. Efforts to close might occur more than once during a presentation, with successful salespeople sometimes making up to five different attempts. The close occasionally takes place with little effort, but most often the salesperson must make a concerted effort to bring about a successful conclusion.

A successful close will usually develop in one of five ways:

1. Voluntarily—the customer states a desire to make a purchase.
2. Assumptively—the salesperson detects a readiness to buy by virtue of the customer's body language.
3. Directly—the salesperson asks for the sale.
4. Indirectly—the salesperson gets the customer to make a choice of color, size, style, or the like.
5. By inducement—the salesperson offers a financial reward, e.g., a discount, or gives logical reasons for buying.

Inducements

Logical inducements to buy cover a wide range of possibilities. You might mention how much the customer could lose by delaying a purchase, create a list showing a large number of advantages in comparison to the few disadvantages of ownership, explain the favorable things some mutually known and respected person had to say about the product, or reiterate and again "shoot down" the customer's objections. Being persistent without becoming obnoxious is important in closing.

Rewards or bonuses are also useful inducements. Selling at a discount, marked-down pricing, two items for the price of one, and the use of off-price coupons for future purchases are commonly observed techniques in general merchandising. They are not found in use in crafts sales to any great extent, but there is no reason why they can't be used in this work with good results.

FOLLOW-UP AND FRIENDSHIP

The natural tendency in sales is to avoid efforts to close because of the possibility of failure or rejection, yet by getting people to agree to buy your crafts you will be doing them a service. If you think only the seller benefits, you are wrong. Some buyers, in fact, will go out of their way to tell you how pleased they are to be able to purchase what you sell. By keeping those instances in mind, you will always have a powerful incentive to sell quality goods—perhaps even more of an incentive than the money involved.

Reassure the Buyer

Your first duty after collecting money and writing out a receipt is to give the buyer assurance of having made a good purchase. No one wants to feel duped. Buyers will be more inclined to speak with pride to others about their purchase, if you, the expert, tell them what a good deal they have. Verbal reinforcement about the bargain purchased or about how envious others will be when seeing the piece on display can go a long way. That you must be believable goes without saying. The benefits from this practice are twofold: First, it instills a sense of satisfaction about the purchase and, consequently, helps the customer dispel any feeling of uncertainty about keeping or returning the product. The second point, a matter of utmost concern in a locally oriented business, is how much more inclined the customer will be to promote your craft among friends and relatives.

As a next step in the process, discuss the details of delivering anything placed on order. Then ask the buyer for leads on other potential buyers. Be sure to get enough information to find each name in the telephone book, and try to elicit the kind of information that will reflect on the individual's qualifications as a buyer.

After the Sale

Upon returning to your office, record data about the buyers on 3-×-5 cards. You might also rate each one A, B, or C according to their future buying probability as you believe it to be. Leave room on the cards for recording follow-up telephone calls, additional purchases, and when a thank-you note is sent.

The data card is also a place for noting if the person seems to have the personality and attitude needed to host a house party, assuming you use that method of marketing. You will probably be limited to a superficial impression of the person's suitability at this point. A final determination can be more conveniently made after completing a follow-up call.

Direct the telephone call to the buyer not more than several weeks after a purchase has occurred. This is sufficiently important in a crafts business that it not be neglected. In addition to seeking leads and more business, the purpose is to strengthen feelings of satisfaction. Offer to correct any product problems that might be brought to your attention. Ask questions and show concern for the person by seeking advice about the product, your practice, or the presentation. An effectively structured discussion will reinforce personal relations and pave the way for additional sales. Support for your business and its reputation will likely follow.

EVALUATE!

Failing to evaluate sales practices is probably the second biggest blunder among handcrafters who attempt to market their crafts. (The first is a failure to market and sell effectively.) Close observers of activities at public shows will notice, time and again, year in and year out, how certain exhibitors will display their creations in a customary way. Any change is virtually unnoticeable. The exhibitor who previously sat back comfortably and watched viewers walk by will probably be doing the same things this time around. Sales occur almost by accident. One person in charge of a booth might be seen busily knitting and another rocking gently away—both oblivious to happenings around them. A customer interested and courageous enough to ask a question would first have to call the booth attendant forward. Needless to say, not much selling can be seen at booths like those. Neither is there much to evaluate.

Purposes

Evaluations of sales presentations will serve different purposes. They can be used to determine what occurred during certain parts of a show to make it more productive than usual. They can be used to determine which method of marketing is most efficient and most profitable. Evaluations can be used to identify, improve, or eliminate practices that do not pay, and they can be used to determine the times of the year best suited for promoting and selling. Lastly, they can be used as a basis for setting goals.

Over the course of time, evaluation should become second nature and as commonplace as setting out a plan before each sales presentation. You cannot make adjustments intelligently without it.

Periodically, perhaps monthly, review your sales activities and subject them to analysis. Improvement is most probable when you know what to improve. By keeping records of sales events and the results produced, you can compare activities, one with another, and later combine the data to obtain indications of overall trends and effectiveness aggregate.

Procedures

Any of several procedures might be followed. One way suggested is to compare results of presentations of a particular type from one to the next. Another is to summarize and compare presentations monthly, a format for which is presented in FIG. 8-2. The headings suggest topics for evaluating shows individually, as well as in the aggregate.

	No. of Shows	No. of Buyers	Cost of Material	Net Income
Jan.	3	52	$203 00	$735 00
Feb.	6	87	526 00	1908 00
Mar.				
Apr.				

8-2 A simple form for summarizing results is useful in monitoring trends and evaluating performance.

The month-to-month comparison is a basis for evaluating effort in terms of the numbers of shows conducted, expenses in terms of production and inventory costs, and efficiency in terms of income per buyer. You can also readily evaluate differences in profit for the investment in dollars and time. As a further application, you can make yearly evaluations from the data compiled and totaled on this form.

Certainly, an evaluation could go far beyond that presented. The example covers only one method. In actuality, if you are seriously engaged in business, you will want to use more than a single practice. These, then, lend themselves to further inter-comparisons and analyses. The results could show which method or methods to emphasize or discontinue, and they could indicate needs for other major adjustments such as in pricing, timing, and selling.

9
CHAPTER

Have a Party

THE SELLING OF CRAFTS follows patterns of extremes and diversity. A person highly skilled and artistic in wood carving or in metal sculpturing might sell the creations mainly as displays in corporate and professional offices. People who create country-style crafts of wood and fabrics will, by way of contrast, almost certainly market their products in places open to the general public. Although several factors are involved, the choice of to whom and where to sell your handcrafts will depend largely on the type of work produced.

When beginning, the business owner faces an almost perplexing responsibility of choosing among the different ways to sell. A first choice might not be the best and might have to be changed. Businesses seldom continue to operate the way they start out. An operation's type, size, and financing enter into the initial decision. In homecraft businesses, quite often the choice narrows down to what the owner can conveniently accomplish alone or with no more assistance than can be provided by a spouse or child.

PRACTICAL CHOICES

Relatively few individuals who do craftwork have either the interest or the wherewithal to operate elaborate enterprises. Specialty-store retailing and direct-mail marketing are practices that fall outside the realm of ordinary possibility; the demands on capital and human resources are often greater than contemplated. Many craftspeople start out less pretentiously, simply looking for an uncomplicated means of marketing their work.

The possibilities for the usual one- or two-person operation are extensive. Regional and national arts and crafts shows, county fairs, bazaars, sidewalk shows, town-square markets, local fund-raisers, flea markets, consignment shops, and a showroom in the home indicate the variety of places appropriate for selling crafts at a profit. Sales by making house calls to individuals can also be worthwhile, though often with mixed results, but selling in homes by the party plan can be consistently profitable.

Perhaps you have become expert at your craft—at least master enough so that you now feel confident you have something worth selling to the public. How, then, might you begin? Try concentrating some of your energy on the party method. You'll find the techniques given in this chapter to be just what you need to get started in this business, and they'll help you improve as you go along.

THE ADVANTAGE IS YOURS

Ask an experienced salesperson who sells tangible goods directly to households how he would like to have a roomful of customers sitting with pockets lined with cash while he addresses the group, and he might respond by asking whether they are men or women. Give him his choice, then he will probably agree the situation is ideal and worth pursuing. He might even ask, smiling, "When do I begin?"

How Sweet It Is!

All the advantages foreseen by this mythical salesman can be yours by applying the party method. Prospects assembled in one place, prepared to buy, and not having required much effort on your part to get them there are the usual expectations. Moreover, a reasonable amount of prescreening will have been done for you.

Properly done, the house-party method of selling has a number of strong features and advantages. Here are eight of them:

1. It is time-saving. One trip, one setup, and one sales presentation suffices for from 10 to 20 customers.

2. It is a flexible method. Parties can be scheduled to meet your requirements and at your convenience.

3. It places no demand on your facilities. Parties are always held in somebody else's home, and without charge.

4. It requires a minimum of preparation. The hostess recruits guests, acquaints them with the purpose, and prepares the seating and refreshments.

5. It eliminates the salary of a sales assistant. The hostess is selected and given incentives in exchange for supporting your sales effort and assisting you in different ways.

6. It produces a near-captive audience. Guests come with an awareness of the subject and a willingness to listen to the sales presentation.

7. It capitalizes on special motivations to buy. Guests come knowing they will be expected to buy something and that their friend, the hostess, will benefit by their purchasing. Also, when among friends and acquaintances, some people become noticeably competitive in buying.

8. It can be very profitable. A person would have to be extremely inept not to sell at a house party. Given a good product, a person who faithfully follows recommended procedures will discover the house-party method of selling crafts can be most efficient in terms of the time spent for the income produced.

An Adaptable Method

Much of the beauty of the method is its adaptability to almost all crafts. Gifts for friends and relatives, personal wear for the whole family, and decorations or practical items for use about the home will fit the bill. About the only other requirements are quality and variety in the product line.

Extensive application of the method in different fields, in particular by large commercial organizations, attests to the advantages of selling by the party plan. Several nationally recognized firms sell directly to households by this method. Instead of having their sales people call on one person or family at a time, they instruct their representatives to assemble a group of people from different households for each presentation. Although selling to individuals separately remains a viable option, the preference is for the more efficient and, hence, the more profitable arrangement.

Opportunities Galore

Look about your community. You will probably find at least one cosmetics firm or a purveyor of sundry items marketing to homes in the area. By way of contrast, you are not likely to observe a crafts business marketing directly to households, and you are even less likely to locate one that follows the party plan. The advantage is then yours. You have a wide-open territory. Even if you should happen across someone applying the method, your lines of products will probably not conflict. If they do, market yours in another community.

Failure to locate a single crafts business operating in your area by the home-party method is not to be taken as an indictment of the practice. Lack of know-how might be the problem. Crafts people generally are not well-grounded in the method's use. Their first efforts at selling in public usually begin with the obvious and the familiar, displaying in crafts shows and consignment stores.

A LOOK AT ALTERNATIVES

For purposes of comparison, the selling of crafts can be divided into categories by method: exhibiting, through the media, and directly to households. Selling by exhibiting covers all arrangements in which the main emphasis is on displaying the work, such as on shelves in stores or in individualized booths at local, regional, and national shows. Sales using mass communications media are usually directed over a wide territorial range in a decidedly impersonal manner, while selling to households includes the highly personal door-to-door practice in addition to direct marketing to groups assembled in the home. Each method has its pros and cons, but some methods are more appropriate than others for the craftworker.

Craft Shows

The planning, scheduling, designing, constructing, traveling, financing, moving, setting up, tearing down, and evaluating involved in exhibiting at a show can be difficult, tiresome, and time-consuming. If the show is held outside, such as at a town-square or sidewalk show, the weather and protection from it becomes an added frustration. Add to these considerations the fact that many people attending shows are browsers rather than buyers, then you can rightfully question whether there is a more profitable way to sell.

You should not get the impression that selling at shows has problems peculiar to itself alone. Many of the problems encountered there apply to some extent to selling at house parties. The decision, then, centers on comparisons of efficiency and profit. (For more information on the craft-show method, see chapter 10.)

Store Sales

The selling of work through a variety store or consignment shop (fundraisers, also), means giving up some of the income. The person or organization responsible for the selling will always take a share. Expect a substantial cut in wages and profits, since the sales price listed must be kept reasonably the same as when selling locally by another method. A further problem occurs by virtue of having your products displayed in competition with others—sometimes with many others. You would have to exercise extraordinary influence in order to gain the most favorable placement in those places.

Despite the shortcomings of having another do the selling, there are several advantages to be recognized. First of all, you do not have to invest much time in selling, leaving yourself free to concentrate on other things. Additionally, you gain from the exposure and promotion of your product in public. These two factors combine to make the practice a good supplementary approach to selling crafts directly to households.

Media Sales

As explained in the previous chapter, selling through the media can be extremely costly. The investment in a direct-mail, telephone, or magazine campaign can be not only considerable but exorbitant, particularly as the breadth of coverage and repetitiveness of solicitations increase. Not to be confused with advertising by television, radio, or newspaper insertion—all of which can enhance personal selling efforts—mass-media methods of selling attempt to obtain immediate sales and orders for the product. They are not likely to be profitable when shipping costs are close to the price of the product. The margin of return could be a substantial problem.

By way of further concern, people want to see handcrafted articles before they buy them. To try to get them to choose an item sight unseen has very serious drawbacks.

House to House

People peddling a variety of low-cost, perishable items that fill personal or household needs can expect to profit by traveling from house to house. Their wares are appropriate for marketing through an established route—an advantage you do not have. You must create a desire for your crafts without the benefit of being able to return on a biweekly or monthly frequency.

An improved way to sell crafts in the consumer's home is to begin with leads of prospects (see chapter 8). This practice can be successful, even though rejections might outnumber appointments. For convenience, set up a number of presentations within proximity of each other. Any difficulty in that regard might be offset, at least in a way, by inviting the prospects to a showroom in your home.

Weighty Evidence

As you can see, the evidence weighs heavily in favor of the party plan. Unlike the potential for gaining viable customers by the other methods described, most of the people attending a crafts party are committed to buying something. This is a rare feature. The receptive attitude and inclination of people who go to house parties is a result of knowing what to expect and expecting to purchase something. About the only situation producing an equally strong motivation to buy is a fund-raiser for a church or civic organization in which the members are assembled for the purpose of purchasing the merchandise presented. The problems for the craftworker are the limited opportunities for supplying such events and the need to donate part of the earnings to the charity. Furthermore, some organized fund-raising shows sell only donated goods of the kind ordinarily displayed at garage sales.

One more factor tipping the scale in favor of the house party is the freedom to schedule the meetings when you want them. Space for a booth at public shows must be reserved well in advance and according to the dates set by others.

All things considered, the party approach to selling crafts appears to be a better way to proceed. Both beginners and experienced marketers can use it to advantage.

THE HOSTESS HOLDS THE KEY

How successful you are in recruiting a good hostess will make a big difference at party time. The right person will perform all of the duties you expect, and she will have the kind of outgoing personality that has a positive influence on selecting guests, preparing them for the presentation, and making the sale a success.

~ A WORD ABOUT GENDER ~

If experience acquired over the past 40 years holds true, women still comprise the primary group of buyers at home parties. Men are not usually inclined to attend craft parties in the home, even when asked merely to accompany someone. Anyone who thinks this somehow disparages women or their role is free to invite all males or only mixed groups in an effort to change conditions. The probable result, however, would be a short-lived business. Some success might be realized, but time and effort might be spent much more wisely by focusing on the group for which the house party has been a proven success.

It is equally logical that the person selected to host a house party and invite the guests should also be a woman. Sexism, in the disparaging sense the word is used, has nothing to do with it. Past successes and intelligent recognition of personal relationships and preferences cannot be ignored. Even today, some women, perhaps many women, would not accept a man's invitation to a crafts party he intends to host in his home. Besides, women are more likely than men to be proficient at arranging all the essentials for a successful gathering in the home.

The gist of all this is merely to advise beginners and other uninitiated individuals to follow practices that have been extremely successful in the past. For this reason, recommendations given hereafter regarding the plan will target women as best for setting up and attending crafts parties. Nothing said should be taken either as belittling men through their exclusion or as portraying women in anything but an exclusively favorable and enviable light.

The Selection

When selecting a hostess, choose someone from among those who have already purchased your craftwork, preferably one who does not hide her enthusiasm for it. If you're lucky, you'll find a person who has been somewhat lavish in buying your work in the past and who continues to express warm feelings about it in public. Additionally, she will reveal qualities of friendliness and leadership. Both are necessary.

The next step is to evaluate her appearance. She must be neatly dressed and tidy. (You can only assume therefrom how her home will be kept.)

The final point in selecting a hostess is to obtain her agreement to do all of the work. First, you want her to provide the setup in her home, supplying enough chairs and table space for the gathering. Second, you want her to invite and prescreen the guests. Third, you want her to serve refreshments, lead the small talk, and later support the sales effort. Aside from cleaning up afterward, she doesn't have much else to do—all for the inducement of a gift or two. It can be done, and you save in the process.

Duties

The person you select should own a home, rent a place of living, or share a place with husband and family. Having a residence for which she has major responsibility, her immediate thoughts will turn to accommodating and making the place ready for a large group. The mixture of chairs resulting from the need to borrow is expected and matters little. The need for a clean place matters a lot. This latter concern usually can be dismissed without comment; most people naturally want to put a good foot forward for a gathering of friends and acquaintances.

Other responsibilities of both major and minor consequences fall on the hostess's shoulders. She must instruct guests where to park for the meeting, greet them at the door, prepare and serve a light snack (usually coffee, tea, soft drinks, and cookies), lead the casual conversation prior to the presentation, and assist you or your salesperson in presenting and selling the handcrafts. She will have the further duty of straightening up the place and returning chairs after the meeting.

One of her main responsibilities is identifying, screening, and gaining the commitment of a sufficient number of guests. What qualifications should the group of guests possess, and how many should there be? Fourteen is a good number. You can deal with that size of group effectively, but don't fail to suggest recruiting one or two more to allow for last minute withdrawals. The hostess will decide whom to invite. Friends, relatives, neighbors, other acquaintances, and friends of friends (about in that order) are the logical ones. Should she fall short of the desired number, you might invite several of the prospects identified on your list of leads— providing, of course, that the hostess doesn't mind.

As to the guest's qualifications, instruct your hostess at the outset to select people who like crafts and who have the wherewithal to buy something. Adult working women and homemakers alike are good prospects. Have the hostess explain the purpose of the meeting to them, and assist her by providing brochures to distribute to the invitees. If you have had any newspaper coverage of your business, make copies of it and place those in her hands, as well. The guests who accept the invitation will then know what is planned, why they are being invited, and that you have roots and some credibility in the community.

Be sure your hostess thoroughly understands the purpose of the meeting and the benefit to her of inviting a sizable group of qualified customers. She has a commitment to fulfill. You can only be confident about the outcome to the extent of her willingness to carry through her part thoroughly, intelligently, and conscientiously.

The Incentive

The hostess should be given an award (one of your creations, of course) for arranging the party. Offer her additional awards, or items of greater value, according to several levels of purchasing attained by the buyers (for example, for $100 in guest sales, offer her a craft worth $5, for $200, one worth $15, and so on). It is distinctly to her advantage to invite people who are likely to participate in the buying. An alert, positively motivated hostess will need little prodding on that score.

Fortunately for both hostess and salesperson, those who accept an invitation to a sales party are inclined to buy. They know, or suspect, their hostess can benefit by their actions, and they will try to please her. The closer in friendship they are to her, the stronger will be this psychological inducement to please. You can make the most of the situation by presenting awards in the presence of the group at the appropriate time.

The handling of awards in the special way suggested here is a useful technique. Everybody involved in the sales party benefits. The hostess increases her awards, you gain in sales, and the customers satisfy many of their future shopping needs with purchases of unique merchandise. If your articles are truly unique and of good quality, as they are expected to be, there should be no reluctance to sell as much of the work as you can and to reward the hostess for her part in the process.

GETTING READY

A house party begins with an idea, a plan, and a schedule. You must know what you want to do and how to go about it. Only in that way can you explain everything involved and expected of the hostess. You must also know when you want to hold the meeting so you can find a time that is mutually agreeable. Occasionally, you will have to approach several people to find one available and willing to serve as hostess when needed.

Scheduling

Set the date for a house party according to your schedule. The holiday seasons are especially good, but sales presentations of this kind can be held effectively throughout the year. About the only exceptions are the holidays themselves. Be sure when arranging your schedule to allow enough time for producing the articles to be sold, bearing in mind the different sales presentations you want to accommodate.

As to the day and time, choose a weekday evening or a weekend afternoon. Avoid mealtime and the period immediately before. Also, try to avoid times when many people in the area are busy with other activities, if such are apparent. Base your selection on sound reasoning. Schedule a meeting for an evening to begin at 7:30 PM and end by 9:00 PM. A meeting on a weekend might begin at 2:00 PM. The hour-and-a-half proposed maximum length for a meeting will usually be viewed by the hostess's guests as a reasonable limit.

Try to secure a commitment to host a party at least three weeks in advance of the time set. Your hostess will need some flexibility in arranging details and selecting guests. Guests, in turn, will expect to be given a minimum of about two weeks' notice.

The Goodies

Refreshments for the party should be light. Instruct your hostess in this matter. You don't want her to lay out such an extensive spread that there is no time for anything else or it overshadows your presentation.

As to the choice of refreshments, base the decision on your budget and the particular needs of your hostesses. Most hostesses will welcome a chance to "show off" their culinary skill or a favorite caterer to their friends and relatives. This way, too, any comments regarding food or its serving can be directed to the hostess, leaving you free to present, discuss, and sell your crafts.

The Product

Variety in the product line is one essential; variety in pricing is another. As much as possible, make items large and small, expensive and inexpensive, and for decorative and practical uses. If a holiday or occasion of known importance will occur in the near future, develop some of the pieces about that theme. Articles specially fashioned in that way will favorably impress customers and give them another reason for buying. The following are days of the year that suggest different motifs:

April Fool's Day	Hanukkah
Arbor Day	Independence Day
Armed Forces Day	Labor Day
Boss's Day	Mother's Day
Columbus Day	New Year's Day
Christmas	Presidents' Day
Easter	Secretary's Day
Father's Day	St. Patrick's Day
Flag Day	Thanksgiving
Grandparents' Day	Valentine's Day
Graduation	Veteran's Day
Halloween	

Place on the back or bottom of each finished piece a sticker with your business's name and address on it. A design in black lettering on a gold background will remain as a special reminder and reference for the future.

Provide a second attachment, either a sticker or tie-tag, on which to record the article's price. Write in the amount in ink. Leave room on the label for additional entries, as for writing in a new price in the event the original is to be deleted.

The articles might vary in value from several dollars to hundreds of dollars, but plan to take along a sizable quantity of items in the $5 to $20 range. If you go to a house party prepared to sell only high-priced artwork, you will in all probability have little if anything to show for your effort. An occasional sale of a very expensive piece is about all the average craftsperson can expect.

Packing

Pack damageable crafts carefully. Use bubble-plastic sheets for padding (the loose kernel-type of packing material can be very messy), and place the small items in cartons of no more than two or three different sizes. If you maintain some similarity in size, you can use the cartons later for shelving the display. Wrap large items separately, using sheets and spreads made for covering the craftwork before the demonstration.

For very large items and those too numerous to transport, provide a photograph album. It should contain close-ups of projects that either are on hand or could be made on order. Several shots, also in color, showing work being done in your shop might be included to lend a bit more credibility to the presentation.

After packing each carton, label its contents on the outside in a visible spot. List each and every item. You'll be glad you did.

Display Accessories

In addition to providing covers for the display area, you must make, or have made, several devices by which articles can be conveniently shown. Three sections of peg-board framed in wood, painted light gray, hinged together, and fixed with fasteners that will allow for easy removal and reattachment of small pieces during the presentation is one way to do it. Make the assembly tall enough to be visible to a group in sitting position. For demonstrations, equip an easel with backboard and ledge, and carry along a shielded floodlight for casting light of high intensity on the demonstration area. A useful, supplementary device for this setup is a board showing a handmade article in different stages of completion.

Because some rooms are poorly illuminated, it is a good idea to pack an extension cord and a small electric lamp and extra bulbs. A dull, dingy room is not conducive to your purpose. Furthermore, you might want to highlight a part of the display during the meeting.

Thumb tacks, a roll of masking tape, a flashlight, pliers, screwdriver, and hammer are other accessories that could come in handy. They aren't always needed, but they're worth taking along—just in case.

Miscellaneous

In addition to crafts and all the ancillary pieces needed for displaying them, you must prepare for the sales presentation by making ready the various things useful in selling. Pads of order slips with carbon duplicates, a small battery-actuated calculator, a cash box, copies of your brochure (for any who didn't receive one before), copies of your catalog, a stack of business cards, separately packed gifts for the hostess, a ball-point pen or two, paper clips, small tablets for the guests to write on, and sharp wooden pencils for everyone should be considered essential. For promotional purposes, you might have the pencils imprinted with the name and telephone number of your business.

Because you will be meeting a group of strangers, you will need some means of keeping their names in view. Use nameplates of folded poster board or the commercial stick-on type.

Also, take along an instrument for recording credit-card transactions, if that is the way you normally operate. At other times a stapler is useful, while a briefcase for carrying the entire lot is a solution to a constant problem.

One point remains to be addressed before the day of the party. Call the hostess to find out how her preparations are going. A contact a week ahead of the meeting time could be all that is needed, but lend assistance and follow up later if she is encountering any difficulty.

GOING TO THE PARTY

The meeting has been scheduled, the craftwork done, the display prepared, the packing completed, and the hostess made aware of her responsibilities. What else must you do? Decisions about who should go, what to wear, and the vehicle to use remain to be settled.

People who are sole proprietors and operators of craft businesses seldom have a problem deciding who will prepare the sales presentation and deliver it. They make the articles and expect to do the selling. Occasionally, someone whose business situation permits will hire a salesperson on a commission basis to help out.

To keep costs to a minimum and to maintain closer control than is possible by paying an outsider, train a member of your family to do some of the selling. A spouse or responsible child can be taken to several house parties as an observer and assistant, being given increasingly more responsibility with each meeting. Eventually, the assistant can assume the duties of salesperson. This system of development results in relief for the proprietor virtually whenever desired, and it makes representation possible at two house parties at once—a matter of some consequence during seasons of high volume buying.

The question of what to wear at a house party can be settled in part by recognizing that the meeting is being held for the purpose of transacting business. To be in keeping with this purpose, you must dress in business attire. An exception to this rule occurs when one's garb is selected to be compatible with the merchandise, e.g., Scandinavian folk crafts.

As with dress, so it is with the vehicle you drive. It is likely to be seen by your customers, and that can have an irreversible psychological effect on attitudes toward you and your craft, so keep it clean and polished.

It is to your advantage to be seen driving a vehicle of good quality. If you feel uncomfortable with yours, consider borrowing one for the occasion. A vehicle large enough for packing and transporting your merchandise and equipment is essential in any case.

AFTER ARRIVING

Parking the vehicle, unpacking cartons, setting up the display, and greeting guests are matters requiring attention after you pull into the hostess's driveway. In time, these duties will become routine, but they should never be carried out without giving thought to the consequences of what you do. As salesperson and owner, you are the one with the most to gain or lose. You do not want even the most trivial of actions to detract in any way from your ultimate objective.

Give yourself enough time to accomplish what you have to do so as to be free to greet guests as they arrive. Ordinarily, plan to arrive about three-quarters of an hour before the scheduled time for the meeting. This should provide enough time for unloading your vehicle, parking it out of the way before guests begin to arrive, and setting up your display.

Parking

Are there other special rules to follow when parking at a house party? The answer is definitely, "yes." A major one is to be aware that customers expect you to leave the convenient parking spaces for them. By parking your conveyance where they have to walk past it (worse yet, around it), you run the risk of inviting the kind of criticism that will be shared in later conversation. The best practice is to park across the street or to a side of the lawn, if lawn parking is intended. Always leave the driveway and spots adjacent to it for use by the guests, and never disrupt neighborhood traffic patterns.

The Setup

In the meeting room, your first duty will be to position the tables and chairs to your convenience. You will need a side table or two on which to arrange some of your products and, perhaps, sales literature. You might also stack a few of the cartons in tiers on the tables. These will serve as shelves. Move the guests' tables and chairs about as necessary to provide an unobstructed line of sight to the speaker's area.

Make your display area as neat as possible under the circumstances. Oftentimes the result will be less than ideal. You might have to leave some items in their boxes. One suggestion for making the area reasonably neat is to cover the display table and cartons with a pressed cloth. Then, with the display set in place, lay a cover over the assembly. (Preferably, use something more elegant than bed sheets or tablecloths.)

The reason for covering the display is to keep it out of view as the group assembles. This helps assure the different pieces will not prematurely become a topic of conversation nor effectively eliminate the potential for surprise. Expressions of approval are far more valuable to you if audible to the entire group than when lost in the din of private conversations.

Creating Friendships

Put your display in order as quickly as you can, for you have other things to do before the sales talk. You must review with the hostess procedures for greeting the guests, serving the refreshments, and assisting in the sale. Your next step is to help greet those guests who have yet to arrive. Since the hostess will soon be busy preparing for serving, she will likely ask a friend who arrives early to greet the guests for her.

Everyone arriving should sign a guest book, which you provide if the hostess doesn't have one. The greeter should also point out to each where the lavatory is located. You can help by showing guests where to place foul weather gear, if any, and by showing them where to be seated in the party room.

As each is seated, fill in the person's name in large letters on a name card using a felt-tip pen. Do the writing yourself. Double check that all spelling is correct. This will help avoid an unwanted error, while further imprinting the names and faces in your memory.

The hostess should serve the beverages and cookies when most of the guests have arrived, and both you and she should enter into the small talk. The idea is to keep it going and everyone involved. You, personally, want to get to know the guests, including those reluctant to enter into the conversation.

During this preliminary period, your hostess must remain in obvious control. First of all she should not make ash trays available in the room, and early on, she should announce that smokers are entirely free to use another (designated) room for smoking. (You must refrain from smoking altogether, as well as from chewing gum, regardless of what others do.)

Secondly, she must limit the conversational period to about 25 minutes, counting from the time the guests were told to be present. This she does by announcing after a period of about 20 minutes has gone by that your presentation will start in about five minutes, suggesting in the process enough time remains for a refill on beverages for any who want more. She should then follow up by saying that you, the presenter, are also providing another special treat, whereupon she passes about a box of high quality mints or chocolates. Whether or not everyone partakes of the extras offered is not important. The impression created is the thing of importance.

At this point, the hostess should have the tables cleared of cups, glasses, and all paper products no longer being used. She should also announce she will return in a few minutes to introduce the program. Upon returning, she should face the group from a point near the spot where you will be standing.

ADDRESSING THE GROUP

Now is the time when a hostess will show her true worth. Most women will be gracious in serving and handling compliments, but not all are skilled at making introductions. What you would like to have said and what she actually says might not be the same. Be prepared for whatever occurs. She might blandly restate your name and what you do, leaving it up to you to request open questioning, informality in speaking, and the use of your nickname or given name, as you prefer. Never show disappointment. Be gracious.

A live-wire hostess, by way of contrast, might express appreciation to the group for attending, mention the rules by which you like to work and be addressed, and finish with a restatement of the purpose of the meeting and a word of praise for your craft. Any complimentary statement she makes about things she has bought from you before will be a strong plus. You have reason to be especially grateful when that happens.

The Opening

How you start makes a difference. Look directly into the faces in the audience, wait until all guests turn their attention your way, and speak slowly. If any nervousness persists, be prepared to direct the group's attention to something besides yourself. You should not delve into a lengthy introduction, regardless.

Any number of openings can be used, but whatever you decide to do should be entirely positive. One acceptable way to begin your presentation is to thank the hostess and ask the group to applaud her for all she has done. When expressing your appreciation to her, use that moment of opportunity to praise her for being an outstanding customer and supporter of your work. As always, be truthful and accurate in what you say. What you say honestly can be said with conviction and without the fluff and puff of excessive flattery.

Early on, compliment the group. You will find something good to say if you've studied the people present. Suppose, as sometimes happens, a husband who came along for the show is the only male present among the group. That fact can be addressed with a slightly humorous twist. You might make reference, if you're a man, to something about only one thorn being among all the lovely roses present. Then courteously welcome him and the others. A female presenter might use the same situation to comment how nice it is to have a splash of shaving lotion among the fragrant perfume, adding something to the effect of how lovely everyone looks. The attitude of the group, the humor or intelligence expressed in earlier conversation, and the friendly relationship with the hostess are several areas to explore for ideas to develop into a favorable opening.

Humor can be a very effective ice-breaker. Some salespeople, in fact, will make a habit of cataloging stories for introducing and livening up their presentations. That practice is recommended, generally. Humor is not essential, but it can be advantageous when intelligently used. One rule is to keep it relevant to the subject. Others are to avoid its overuse and never to tell an off-color or lewd joke. Be careful about puns, as well, for some people are inclined to view them derisively.

Creating Interest

Promptly after delivering your opening comments, turn the group's attention to your craftwork. You might say, "I'm here to show you some things in which I take great pride." Remove the cover from the display at this moment, and switch on the auxiliary lighting for emphasis. Explain briefly the benefits of owning or buying the items for gifts and how you will be giving everyone a chance to study them closely. Pay heed to any comment made. A softly spoken exclamation of a positive nature can be followed by an enthusiastic agreement on your part, such as: "They are attractive, aren't they?"

A slightly different, but effective, attention-getter is to begin with a single, unique item. Cast the floodlight on the item while holding it up for everyone to see. An antique, an artifact of more recent vintage, or an unusually expensive piece made of the same material as your products is one way to impress your audience. Such an item is more meaningful if you make comparisons with the methods of construction you use. If you are truly prepared, your knowledge of the craft from a historical standpoint will begin to show. Factual statements of that kind will add to your credentials as an expert or authority in the field.

Be judicious in making the opening remarks. Build upon any interest generated by moving on before that interest wanes, and never dwell on a topic to the point of boredom. Condition your listeners to ask questions if you move too fast.

Focus the group's attention on the articles you brought for sale. Start with the most expensive item you have. Talk about its construction, its finish, its quality, and where such an exceptional piece can be used. Then turn the piece over and read its price from the label attached. Say no more. Certainly don't try to sell the piece, but turn quietly to a second article.

There are good reasons for starting with your best and most expensive work. To begin with, you will show evidence of having attained a high level of craftsmanship (or artisanship). The customer is inclined to remember the first piece shown and to keep in mind the standard to which it was made. It serves, potentially, as a model for work to be made to order.

The second, and sometimes overlooked, reason has to do with price. The initial price given might seem out of reach to many of the observers, but everything following thereafter will seem more affordable. The effect is largely psychological. Only on rare occasions will someone purchase the very expensive lead item. It's a great day when that happens.

Follow the first article with items more moderately priced. Present and discuss mid-range articles primarily, occasionally filling in with those having higher and lower price tags. End each presentation by visibly referring to and matter-of-factly reading the price as labelled. By following this practice consistently, you will firmly establish evidence of having thought through pricing beforehand. Customers can become noticeably concerned when the salesperson quotes prices not previously recorded—thinking, perhaps, there might be an error in recall or the price is being adjusted on the spot according to some notion of ability to pay.

After presenting several articles, instruct everyone to write down all items they would like to review later or want to buy when the presentation is over. Take a few moments to distribute packets containing paper and pencil. Include in each packet an order blank and catalog, that you explain will be referred to later. (Although these materials could have been distributed before the presentation, you would still have to take time out to discuss their purpose and use.)

Benefits of Ownership

The purpose of telling about and showing the different articles you have handcrafted is to create a desire among the customers to buy them. Present a piece to the group assembled as shown in FIG. 9-1. Point out the qualities of the product, and bring the customer's sense of touch into play. Do this by passing about several durable items. The feel of genuine leather, polished metal, woven fabric, smooth wood, glazed ceramics, or another material used in your craft can have greater appeal when handed from individual to individual than anything you might say.

Suggest items that might be given as gifts, but also mention that many customers want to keep some pieces for themselves. Make a point about the personal item the hostess owns (hopefully, is wearing or has at hand) that she once bought from you.

Insofar as possible, do some name dropping. Reference to a person well-known in the community who buys some of your work every so often is the kind of unspoken testimonial you need to bring out. Perhaps you have had a different repeatable experience, such as the lavish, almost embarrassing, praise by a neighbor about an article she bought similar to the one you are holding at the time. Or you might be able to report how one person kept telling another about how lovely an item is so that it has now become the most

9-1 Pride in workmanship and obvious enthusiasm go a long way toward selling crafts at a house party.

popular of all you have to offer. The kinds of useful references suggested here naturally increase with your experience in selling.

An individual's desire to own a piece intensifies as increasingly more people demonstrate their desire for it. When several people are observed buying a particular piece, you can expect multiple purchases of it to follow. A buying frenzy might even occur among some groups. Capitalize on this emotion. Encourage such buying by stating how popular a good seller has become, and tell a story, if true, about how the exquisitely designed piece was first placed in a customer's home where it captured the enviable eye of visitors.

If you've won a ribbon in a show, don't pass up the opportunity to make that fact known either. Be proud of what you do, and show it. Many customers will be as impressed with your accomplishments as they are with the quality of the craft.

In addition to promoting individual pieces, have several baskets containing various pieces of your work on hand. These baskets should vary in size, content, and price. Emphasize how popular the gift-basket idea has become, and suggest how the customer can select the contents as best suited for the person for whom the basket is intended. You will probably find that the selling of crafts by the basket, with an opportunity for the customer to choose what goes inside, can be very profitable.

Holidays and personal events are occasions for which gifts are normally given to friends, family, and relatives. Be cognizant of the days and events, and don't let them go unmentioned. A number of useful ideas follow:

Anniversary	Friendly prank
Awards banquet	Going-away present
Baby shower	Holiday gifts
Birthday	Home renovation
Bon voyage gift	Hostess gift
Bridal shower	House warming
Career change	Job promotion
College entrance	Mortgage burning
Commencement	Personal needs
Ethnic celebration	Retirement gift
Family reunion	Wedding

Add to the list any unusual ideas or humorous applications you know about, such as the item a lady once bought as a gift for her pet after its operation.

A CHANGE OF PACE

Do something to break up the routine of showing and talking about item after item after item. Don't let monotony take hold. Monotony leads to boredom, boredom to disinterest, and disinterest to complacency about sales. Frequent questioning and an interesting demonstration, coupled with a constant display of enthusiasm, will do much to help your efforts.

Questioning

During the course of the presentation, involve as many of the group in the conversation as you can by encouraging them to raise questions. Ask questions yourself, if necessary. Direct some to probable buyers and some to reticent onlookers. Phrase your questions so as to receive more than a simple yes or no. "What do you think of this piece, Julie?" is a query appropriate for someone who obviously likes the piece and your work. For others, a less specific phrasing is sometimes better, such as, "Lorraine, what do you like best, so far?" How the answers come forth will give you an idea of how well you are getting across, and occasional exchanges of the kind suggested here will help maintain alertness throughout the assembly.

Questioning sometimes brings out objections to buying, although most people who are reluctant buyers will often keep their opposition to themselves. Those are the difficult ones to deal with, because you have no idea what's holding them back.

You're better off having a person blurt out some negative comment than having him or her say nothing at all. Don't be flustered when it happens. Above all, don't show anger, and don't disparage or belittle that person—ever! Try to reason about the comment, or prove its fallibility. The lady who tells you your craft won't fit in with the decor in her home, for example, leaves the way open for several possibilities. First, ask her why not. Her description might actually identify a style you have yet to show. If that line of pursuit doesn't pay off, use a second approach by asking her about the different individuals and events for whom and for which she normally buys gifts. Go over them with her, if need be. Remember that person. You might have to continue the question-and-answer routine later when dealing with her alone.

Learn to question objectors so that they will arrive at their own conclusions, rather than having you tell them what to think. The idea is to maneuver them into removing their own barriers. In an example of this, suppose you are being told a particular item would be acceptable if only some feature were different. Don't respond by offering to make it to order. Instead, ask the customer to explain exactly what should be changed. Then ask the person if he or she would buy one made that way. If the answer is "yes," make known it's a deal. You'll make one exactly as desired.

Don't try to bring out all objections at once. Raise questions and offer explanations throughout the presentation. Do this just enough to keep the presentation from settling into an unexciting monologue.

A Demonstration

A short, snappy demonstration is a good change of pace. Interrupt the showing of merchandise when you have gone through about two-thirds of the number of things you have to sell. Place the demonstration board on the easel, and direct the floodlight onto it. Give a relatively brief explanation of how your material is handcrafted into a finished piece. Show the steps (which you had prepared before) and the tools used, if convenient. Do no actual handwork, unless it can be easily and quickly carried out. A few comments about how your work contrasts with mass produced pieces will add to the diversion and, very possibly, buyers' interest. The exclusiveness of owning a one-of-a-kind handcrafted piece in contrast to multiple produced ware is a legitimate and proper point to emphasize at this time.

This pause is also a time to make a few passing comments about another person's craft. Mention the work of some well-known artist or expert, if such has not already been brought up by a customer. Compare that person's work with yours, but never in a negative way. You gain the most by implying you're in the same league with a big hitter. By belittling another's accomplishments, you might effectively diminish the outlook for your own work and open the door for its criticism.

WRAP IT UP

The steps to take after showing the items for sale include presenting the hostess's award, giving the group extra incentives to buy, and closing with individual sales. From your opening remarks to the time you begin to write orders, the entire presentation should take no more than 40 minutes. Observance of this time limit will leave about 25 minutes for writing orders and collecting payments, with the program finishing close to the time scheduled. For an evening program, this will be about 9:00 o'clock.

Presenting the Gift

Bring your presentation of products to a close on time or as soon as you feel the audience is ready, whether or not everything has been shown. Cut it short, too, when time is about to run out. Simply mention the existence of any remaining articles and assure the guests that these will be made available for viewing.

The next step is to turn the flood lamp toward the ceiling, set the easel aside, and ask the hostess to come forward. With the hostess standing before the group, present the award she has earned for hosting the party. Have her unwrap the piece at that time. Make a mild fuss about it, and praise both the hostess and her work. Call for applause and join in vigorously. Finish the brief ceremony by stating that she might earn additional gifts, which depends on how much everybody buys.

Capitalize further on this inspirational moment by directing attention to future parties. Seeing the rewards for being hostess, some of the customers present might be interested in booking a party. Mention how this might be done by expressing that desire to you at the end of the show, and perhaps include a small reward for those who give you a definite date for a show.

Add on the Extras

Having created a measure of excitement and interest, you are now to the place where you want to clinch your prospects' desire to buy your craftwork. To do this, be prepared to offer them an incentive or two. People look for bargains, and there are many you can choose among. Consider these: 3-for-2 types of purchases, buy-one-get-one-free offers, cash discounts graduated according to level or purchases (e.g., 2% over $20 and 5% over $50), free gifts for the top two buyers, and 20% off the list price of any item bought after an individual's purchases reach a certain amount. Decide on something not likely to cut too deeply into your profits, and announce your offer so everyone will hear it.

Then make another point. Explain how you will repair free of charge any piece accidentally broken. Protect yourself by restricting the deal to the period of the buyer's possession. Couple this guarantee with an offer to make any item in a customer's choice of colors, and you will create a still more powerful incentive.

To stimulate interest even further, announce you will donate a certain percentage of your income to the United Way or some other worthy organization. While you might not be able to determine the exact benefit, the effect is much like icing on the cake.

Write the Orders

You have finally come to the point of closing. You are about to take orders—many, you hope. Explain to everyone how to list the items they want on the sales forms, how all customers should feel free to inspect any of the items on display, how to use the catalog for comparing items and prices, where to consult brochures and the photo album for other ideas, that you and the hostess are there to help, and how you will review each order form as the customers are ready to make payment. Make clear, also, that the order forms should contain all items desired; you will sort out later which articles can be taken along and which must be placed on order for later delivery. Having covered those routines, give the group another opportunity to ask questions.

The sales slips used in the closing process require further explanation. A $5\frac{1}{2}$-×-8-inch size is adequate if it contains about 15 or more lines for entries. A shorter form, say, with room for only five entries, might create the undesirable impression that you obtain very few purchases per order. A type that has a place for the customer's name and address and columns for quantities, descriptions, single prices, and total amounts is best. Preferably, use two-part forms, with a carbonless duplicate as the second sheet.

While the customers are writing down selections, circulate among them and offer suggestions to whomever seems hesitant. The hostess, when she finishes her own order list, can also lend suggestions to her friends. Try to get a picture of the dollar amount of the purchases proposed, and give outspoken acknowledgement to any who are writing big orders.

At a point when the writing of orders seems to be ending, stand before the group and ask for their attention one final time. Explain that you have made a quick calculation of the orders, and are pleased to announce that the hostess will qualify for another gift with a bit more ordering. Suggest, if the truth of the situation so warrants, one purchase more per person will do it. Remind them to think well ahead to occasions when they will again have to shop for gifts. They will probably be doing both themselves and you a favor by buying one of your exclusive articles while the opportunity is at hand.

Also, ask the customers to bring their lists to you when they are finished ordering, and ask them to list the names and addresses of people you might call on later. Have them write the leads on the tablet paper while waiting to check out.

Go over each sales slip as presented, check the prices, and add the amounts with your calculator. Don't forget to figure in the sales tax, but before accepting payment, inquire of each person if they are considering anything else for later procurement. Review the advantages of buying now for those who hesitate. Occasionally, one will express pleasure at being reminded.

Since payment will sometimes be made in cash, you should be prepared by having stocked your cash box with small bills and coins in various denominations. Trying to scrape together enough currency among the customers can be a difficult, if not frustrating, alternative.

Review the lists of leads, and make an effort to add names as the customers check out. Assure each person that you will keep the source of leads confidential if so desired. You will probably gain a few more leads by doing that.

Be thorough and considerate when closing. Go over the list of purchases to be sure the buyer has the items paid for, is aware of when items on order will be ready, and knows that you will be calling soon. Next, reinforce the customers' decisions by extending compliments in one way or another by referring to the intelligence of their choices or how friends will be noticeably envious. Finally, express your sincere appreciation. Send each customer on his or her way with the purchases, a copy of the sales slip, a catalog, your name card, the pencil, and a request to call you if anything else comes to mind.

After the guests have gone, settle with the hostess. First take care of her order; then give her any gift she has coming. Leave her feeling good about the party or, at the very least, about her role as hostess. She might, if asked, be of further help by giving you some advice about which of those present would make good hostesses.

Bring the party to a close by packing your belongings and heading home. Use the time while driving to reflect on everything accomplished and to review procedures for the follow-up. A number of things remain to be done. You must finish and deliver articles placed on order, sign up hostesses for new parties, send notes of appreciation to customers, and contact people on your lists of leads. The most immediate concern could be the results obtained at the party.

REVIEW THE RESULTS

There are three ways to review and analyze a house party: (1) Give it a quick overview and internal analysis, (2) compare it with other house parties, and (3) compare it with other sales methods. Each has its purpose, and each should be applied routinely.

The Once-Over

Begin reviewing results on the drive home from a party while everything is fresh in your mind. Identify high and low points, evaluating each to determine which are worth repeating and which need to be changed. You should have more good than bad to recall, but no matter how successful the occasion was from the standpoint of sales, you will find something to change. No party will ever be perfect in all respects.

The basic concern is improvement. Conscientiously think through things you might have done or said differently. Then devise strategies to accomplish them. The kind of mental exercise suggested here is the key to making each subsequent party a little better than the one before.

Recording the Facts

Unlike the purely cerebral review just mentioned, this second method begins with a recording of facts. Those facts include the kind of data routinely noted about the location, the hostess, driving distance, date and time, and numbers of people who attended the party. Additionally, matters of income, profit, sales tax, and various expenses are to be put into the record. These data serve not only for comparative purposes but also for reference in filing tax reports. The form presented in FIG. 9-2 is an example of a form for the kind of information you need.

Most items on the form are self-explanatory. However, several items in the expense category must be clarified so as to assure constant usage from one calculation and comparison to the next. The cost of articles sold, the cost of the gifts, transportation expenses, and personal expenses are particularly in need of clarification. The first of these, the cost of articles sold, is the total of all expenses for producing and packing the pieces. The gifts for the hostess and any promotional purpose are similarly based on cost. Profit is excluded in both calculations.

Transportation, by way of contrast, may be based on either of two calculations: the actual expenses or an estimated cost per mile driven. The latter is easier to apply (simply use the figure allowed by the IRS). Actual costs require keeping expenditures for gasoline, oil, repairs, etc., over a long period and reducing them to a mileage basis.

Reusable accessories are ordinarily figured as deductible expenses in the year when purchased. The procedure for this exercise is to divide the cost of new purchases by the estimated number of uses for the year. No amount would be deducted for such items in subsequent years.

The last of the items to be mentioned in the context of expense deductions are the personal expenses. They are likely to be a flat zero. Legitimate expenses occur in this category only in instances such as renting a room overnight on a long trip to a house party. Another rare possibility is

PARTY PLAN SUMMARY

Date:_____   House Party #_____

Hostess:_____   Address_____

_____

Miles one way:_____   Time arrived:_____ Time left _____

No. customers invited:_____   No. attending_____

No. leads obtained:_____ No.items sold:_____ On order:_____

INCOME

    Gross sales.....................................$_____

    Sales tax collected........................ _____

EXPENSES

    Cost of articles sold......................$_____

    Cost of hostess gifts.................... _____

    Cost of selling (commission or wage)....... _____

    Refreshments: coffee, tea, etc............ _____

    Promotional items: catalogs, brochures,etc. _____

    Expendable accessories: order forms, etc... _____

    Reusable accessories: easel, tools, etc.... _____

    Transportation............................ _____

    Personal expenses......................... _____

                          Total Expenses....$_____

BALANCE

    Net income (profit).........................$_____

9-2 Data of use in evaluating and comparing results of party sales can be recorded on a form such as this.

the prorated cost of an item of clothing bought and worn exclusively when selling.

Analysis and Comparison

The data entered on the form provide the basis for a wide range of calculations. These can relate to costs, profits, price, and efficiency. Examples are:

Cost basis
  Cost per customer in attendance
  Cost per hour involved
Profit basis
  Profit per order written
  Profit per lead obtained
Price basis
  Price per item sold
  Price per item sold in top one-third
Efficiency basis
  Ratio of items backordered to items sold
  Percent of items sold with a price under $20

A quick analysis of the foregoing calculations indicates many are averages. Although you can easily develop others, the most beneficial practice is to settle on several calculations useful in making comparative analyses to decide which practices in the sales plan to delete or modify.

You can make comparisons from one house party to the next, as long as you record the data consistently. These comparisons might indicate something you can do or say more effectively at the next party, which level of products are the most profitable over the long run, or when a change in pricing is appropriate.

Comparisons among different methods of selling are equally beneficial. In fact, by comparing results obtained through house parties with those in crafts shows, you might have the hard evidence you need to decide if you should be concentrating energies on one or the other. Quite likely, you will find some difference. Whether that means avoiding one altogether or using it as a supplementary practice will depend on how effective you are in conducting business by each method.

Regardless of the method you use, you must have a desire to succeed. You must set goals for yourself and strive enthusiastically to achieve them. Unless you make an honest effort in this regard, you could easily become complacent about results. Worse yet, you could fall into the trap of creating and justifying reasons for failing.

Success in selling does not occur automatically, nor is it a consequence of innate talent. Hard work is essential. Whether you are following a party plan or practicing one of the methods described in the next chapter, if you conscientiously and diligently apply yourself, you can expect to be successful. A book can only point out how; the doing is up to you.

10 CHAPTER

Expand Your Horizons

THE TASTE OF SUCCESS whets the appetite. Experience the joy and reward of selling crafts profitably at your first house party or crafts show, and you will probably look eagerly for opportunities to do more of the same. This is a natural reaction. It normally leads to further sales activity.

Perhaps, in time, you will think about expanding your business if it has gotten off to a good start and seems to have the potential for greater profits. You might consider a supplementary practice of one kind or another, or you might even think about taking an entirely different approach to marketing and selling your work. Whatever the preference think about it carefully. Any radical change can be risky. The person of average means would be wise to avoid a sort of knee-jerk reaction to any urge to plunge ahead. A gradual, well-planned procedure for increasing business is better.

BUILD ON YOUR SUCCESS

Let's assume you have established a successful business selling by the party plan. Further, you want to increase your income. The logical beginning is to make the most of what you are doing. Before striking out in different directions, learn to conduct a thorough and complete follow-up. It is the easiest way to capitalize on any successes already realized. Although any profit obtained from a sale made on first contact is most of what you can expect to gain, you will overlook an opportunity to increase your sales by doing a poor job of following through.

Follow Up the Sales

Within a week or two of making a sale, contact your buyer by telephone. Your note of thanks will have arrived on postcard by that time, and the recipient will have had time to thoroughly contemplate the purchase. Start the conversation by inquiring whether everything about the purchase is still all right. Your expression of interest will demonstrate your personal concern (a gesture seldom occurring in business today) while helping to give your customer feelings of post-purchase satisfaction.

Modify this procedure in instances when you are delivering a product that has been placed on order. Face-to-face discussion at the time of delivery will take the place of much of the conversation when following up entirely by telephone.

The procedure and timing of the contact are not as important as your attitude. By showing respect and valuing your customer, you will create an atmosphere conducive to future sales. Sincere concern, courtesy, and the pleasantness that goes with friendship are fundamental to full acceptance of your message.

If some problem is brought to your attention, correct it cheerfully or offer to do whatever the situation dictates. It is better to replace an item with another of equal value than to run the risk of having a disgruntled customer spreading an unwanted message about the community. Don't expect repeat business from the one who remains unhappy, but at least leave the subject knowing you have made a positive effort to be helpful. Negative reactions will be rare, unless your methods or product are bad.

Another use of the follow-up call is to see if the customer would like to make further purchases. Exercise your creative wit; think of your customer's reasons for buying initially to see if these will suggest applications for other items, such as add-on accessories or articles to complete a full series.

Use the follow-up also as an occasion to obtain more leads, and gather enough information about the individuals recommended to consider them among your future prospects. Additionally, encourage your customer to host a house party. End the conversation with a further expression of appreciation and a request to be contacted as needs develop in the days and months ahead.

Plan for Expansion

The underlying purpose of business expansion is greater income and profits, which depend on increasing the sales volume. More sales, in turn, necessitate increased production and bookkeeping capabilities. A disregard of these facts can lead to trouble. It is safer to strive for a doubling of sales by bringing production and supply along as needed than to double production and hope that sales will catch up to the supply. This is an important difference for most craftspeople. A large variety store might eliminate an unprofitable display of craft supplies without much consequence, but a small-time operator in a similar situation could be left holding an expensive bag of crafts. You must be flexible and able to adjust to demands in the marketplace. An oversupply or overproduction of crafts of a given kind can run completely counter to that logic.

Develop a plan for expansion reflective of your desires and capabilities. This might include one or more methods of creating new business without abandoning the house-party plan. You can solicit new business by finding new localities for marketing, by scheduling additional house parties, and by increasing the use of mailing lists, publicity, and advertising.

To proceed impulsively and without careful analysis could be disastrous. An error costing several hundred dollars in one context could cost thousands in another. You must thoroughly think through your plan for expansion, and even then it's not a given that there will be no errors (although thinking ahead will help reduce the chances of expanding too rapidly). Carried out in detail, a plan spanning a year or so will indicate how boldly expansion shall occur in light of the limitations that exist in the particular business.

A plan for expansion will, in short, help minimize the risk. It should follow the general procedure recommended for creating the original business plan. (See chapter 2.)

SUPPLEMENTARY PRACTICES

In-home open-house displays, craft shows of various kinds, sales through retailers, and a diverse range of miscellaneous methods of selling comprise the recommended ways of filling in between scheduled house parties. Most of these involve selling through variations of exhibiting. Their purpose is immediate profit and long-range promotion.

Business and Professional Clients

Look about your community and the cities nearby for opportunities to supplement your regular sales practices. Begin by making lists of professional businesses, corporate industries, and the specialty stores throughout the area. Concentrate on those seemingly most suited to your talents.

Corporate organizations and professional personnel, especially those catering consistently to the public, usually design their buildings to impart an appearance of success. The waiting rooms for visitors are almost always finished in exclusive decor. Your craftwork might be just the thing for the purpose. With a little effort, you might find doctors, lawyers, and business executives who will pay a handsome price for your creations and the opportunity to display them in their offices or in a building's lobby where the public will see them.

The thought of importance when marketing in this arena is that established executives and professionals generally seek things a bit out of the ordinary. They prefer to display items not readily observed elsewhere, and they are usually willing to pay a premium for rare works of high quality. Knowing this, you hold an important opening card. Unless you are well acquainted with the person—the doctor, lawyer, company president, or whomever you intend to see—you must be prepared to discuss with the receptionist how your craft can be important to the one in charge.

Because your first move will be to create a favorable impression on the receptionists or secretaries responsible for making appointments, you do not want to seem cavalier or attempt to brush those people aside. They will sometimes screen out or divert unimportant calls, whether made in person or by telephone, or they might subtly cast a negative light on your request. Whether you have an appointment or drop in unannounced, you want to see a boss who still has an open mind about your work. Have with you a sample handcrafted in appropriate style and quality when visiting, show it and your portfolio of photographed work to the person who greets you, and strike up a friendly conversation while gaining that individual's opinion of how your craft can add to the decor.

As much as you can, present necessary and sufficient reasons for the top person to see you. Observe these additional tips:

- Be well-dressed for the occasion, and be confident you can do commission work of high quality. Otherwise, forget it.

- Don't tremble at the thought of talking to important people. Most of them are considerate individuals who will give you a fair hearing if you have something worthy of their consideration.

- Your prospects are usually busy people, so promise that several minutes is all you will need to explain your unique work. Schedule an additional meeting if commissioned or asked to present a proposal.

- Think through the different applications a prospect might consider, including a handcrafted logo for the corporate board room and a custom-made gift for the boss's home.

- If asked to leave a catalog rather than talk to the boss, explain your reason for wanting to show a real sample of the individualized work you do in this area. Then resolutely request a mutually convenient appointment. Leave a brochure or photographs of previous work if you must, but only as a last resort.

- Don't let a neatly decorated lobby and reception area dissuade you. A change might be in the offing, or there might be several out-of-view possibilities that are not immediately apparent to you.

- Strive for a written contract (a commission to do the job at your price) or, in lieu thereof, an opportunity to present a proposal to the decision-making group or person in charge.

- Don't give up when first rejected. Try to keep the door open for a future possibility. Leave your business card, and offer to call back in a year or so.

Window Displays

Retail stores offer a slightly different opportunity. Instead of limiting your offer to outright sales, you might propose to create a window display of your wares free of charge. That approach could be all that a balky store owner will need to be convinced to go along. You gain exposure and publicity without making a huge investment. As a way of overcoming resistance to your idea, offer to set up your display with the aid of the store's professional decorator. Acceptance of your proposal by an owner or manager whose business is in a position to employ a decorator could depend entirely on the desirability of your work as well as your willingness and ability to produce sufficient quantities of the product for sale on the premises. Be prepared, also, to have your proposal rejected as being inappropriate for the situation.

The proprietor whose business is not in direct competition with yours might be most receptive to placing your craftwork on display. Specialty-store owners are often good prospects. For example, one exclusively in the business of selling carpet might be convinced that having some of the pieces arranged to a side of the show window will be the kind of eye-catcher needed to make passers-by stop and peruse everything on display. Paint stores, bookstores, and picture-frame shops are among the variety of operations worthy of investigating for such possibilities.

Select a store doing a good business, and avoid any that markets cheap merchandise. You want your name and craft associated with the best. By the same reasoning, put on display only things of high quality and uniqueness. Follow this advice even if you produce an inexpensive line.

Given the opportunity, make sure your display looks professional. Use an attractive style of lettering to identify yourself or your business and either a phone number or an address where orders or inquiries can be handled. Limit the display to several attractive pieces, at the most, rather than a conglomeration of items that seem to lack coordination and harmony.

Obtaining permission and arranging a store-front display to the proprietor's satisfaction is only the beginning. The next thing you will want to do is monitor results. Undoubtedly, as time permits you will watch how people moving along the sidewalk react to the display. That information, coupled with any successes observed by the proprietor and the number of sales inquiries occurring, will eventually come in handy when seeking a new location for the display.

As a final word about this method, be aware that it will be more of a promotional technique than a means of creating immediate sales. Image and awareness are the main concerns; therefore, keep the display fresh. Change articles every several weeks. Furthermore, do not keep a display in the same location month after month or until it no longer is an attraction to the people who frequent the area. Seek a new location when the display no longer seems to be a point of interest to most observers or when some other negative factor enters in, such as dust being allowed to collect visibly but without apparent effect on an unobservant storekeeper.

Exhibiting

When in need of a quick way to supplement selling by the party plan, the normal inclination is to turn to one of the purposely organized opportunities close at hand. These include the craft shop that will take work for a percentage on consignment, a local bazaar that can be entered for a small fee, and a regional craft show or two. Each will help expose your work to the public, but the amount of profit likely from exhibiting by these methods will vary widely. With experience and by applying cost comparisons as explained in chapter 8, you will be able to tell which method holds the greatest opportunity for you.

Be aware, though, that the amount of money you will earn from each item sold will be less when sold in a store or at a show than if you do the selling yourself at a house party. Store owners will take up to 50 percent of the selling price, and costs for such things as booth construction and space rental at shows will sometimes eat away much of the profit. These methods of exhibiting can be useful, nevertheless. Tips on making them profitable are given later in this chapter.

The Showroom at Home

Before stepping into the organized show circuit to supplement your income, consider setting up a showroom in your home on a year-round basis. Convenience and low cost are among the desirable features. Unlike attendance at public craft shows, you need not be bothered with transporting goods and equipment or with other problems associated with a non-permanent display. Showing the crafts in the home can be an inexpensive adjunct to selling by the party plan, while still allowing for participation at public shows of one kind or another.

A place to show your products to customers in the home is a natural extension of the home-based business. You can show visiting customers where and how the crafts are made, and you need keep only a simple display ready for their observation. An important requirement is to keep all areas tidy, whether a makeshift office, workshop, or display section in the living room.

A showroom in the home offers advantages not readily duplicated in some of the other settings. Several are:

- Its location is permanent, thereby lending itself to consistent promotion and identification.

- It can be kept open year-round or be closed virtually whenever desired.

- It is suitable for specially promoted open-house sales campaigns, mainly around the holiday season.

- It is a ready alternative for customers who cannot attend shows scheduled at special times or in far-away locations.

- It can usually be operated by oneself or one's family, eliminating the need for outside help.

- Its location in the home provides for a certain convenience in performing chores, constructing crafts, and attending to the showroom as needed.

- Its presence eliminates traveling for the purpose of consummating a sale.

- It avoids or holds to a minimum rental costs and certain operating expenses.

- It can actually reduce tax on the home through depreciation on the qualified portion of the residence.

Considering the various advantages, you would be wise to publicize the opportunity to make purchases at the home. This advice is worth following whatever your regular method of selling, and it is particularly pertinent when you are planning to hold an open-house sale. A well-publicized special event of this kind can be one of the most profitable methods of supplementing scheduled party sales or craft-show activities.

OPEN-HOUSE SALES

Initiate an open-house retailing venture only after making sure it is legal at the location chosen. Check the local zoning ordinance and licensing requirements. Such restrictions do not ordinarily apply to garage sales, but the merchandising of crafts from your home would likely be considered by the authorities to be an entirely different matter. The making and marketing of homecrafts should always proceed within the law, regardless of where the selling might take place or how easily the legal requirements might be circumvented.

If you are not permitted to sell from your home, check out the possibility of open-house selling at a friend's or relative's residence. This alternative loses some of the advantages of your home location, but it just might do in a pinch. A better alternative, though not always possible, is to obtain a variance from the restrictive ordinance.

After taking care of the legal matters, direct your attention to how best to operate the sale. Decisions about timing, that is when to hold the open-house, are a basic concern. Additional concerns pertain to promoting and handling the event.

Timing

What is the best time of the year for selling crafts from the home? The answer is simple: When a customer comes to the door. That could occur almost any time. The alert entrepreneur will try to remain prepared for those eventualities.

There are, or course, days of the year when the public does most of its shopping. Nationally, the day after Thanksgiving produces a higher level of sales than any other day of the year. That particular day, traditionally, is the beginning of the shopping season for the Christmas holiday.

The evidence seems clear. You will want to prepare enough crafts to schedule a major open-house event to occur soon after Thanksgiving. A two- or three-day sale is appropriate, preferably on a weekend. Time the event to begin about Friday noon and to carry throughout the day on Saturday. Allow the sales period to extend well into the evening on both days, and if you live in a locality where retailing on Sundays is common, you might also schedule the open house for the afternoon of that day.

Work other events into your schedule. Don't hesitate to hold more than one open-house event during the Christmas season. Properly promoted, the extra sales effort might prove to be more profitable than several presentations at crafts shows and house parties during that period. Open-house presentations can be held at other times of the year, too. The spring and fall months are good for an occasional special of that kind.

Promoting

Several weeks before a scheduled open house, begin the promotional campaign. There are two target groups: the general public and customers who have previously bought from you. For the former, select among and use newspaper advertisements, radio announcements, posters, and single-page flyers as previously suggested for publicizing the business. Adapt each item of publicity to the specific event, and watch your budget as you finalize details.

Treat previous customers specially. After all, they have bought before and might do so again. One way is to mail to each person whose name is on file a copy of the flyer announcing the sale. Include on the sheet clearly drawn directions to the house. Offset the impersonal effect of the piece by attaching a small, handwritten note to an upper corner. The stick-on variety of note paper is excellent. It should contain the person's name, a brief "Hope you can attend," and your name. If you know the invitees well enough to use nicknames (theirs and yours), so much the better.

You can also hand out flyers at crafts shows, community events, and the house parties you attend. You might have them delivered with the daily or weekly newspaper, if the expense is not too great, or you might have youngsters deliver the flyers door-to-door in selected communities. Instruct all young people employed for hand delivering the flyers to place the sheets in coiled fashion between the door knob and door jamb of the front door but never, for legal reasons, in a resident's mail box.

Publicity for an open house during the Christmas season requires adaptation to the specific situation. Distribute flyers and direct other announcements about an event to the public at least several days before shoppers go on their celebrated annual shopping spree. Do this even if you plan to hold your sale a week or two after Thanksgiving. The advance notice will help many potential buyers plan their purchases with your crafts in mind. A second reminder, preferably through the local media, can be made a few days before the opening of your sale.

The success of any open-house sale is contingent upon creating enough interest so that a sufficient number of buyers will attend the event. While a simple announcement will be adequate for some people, an added incentive will capture the desire of others. Publicize a bargain, a discount on purchases, or a valuable door prize. Any of these suggestions can be used to build attendance during the time set out.

Always be truthful in what you say and do, and by all means avoid a reputation of deceit or cunning. "Everything must go" sales are the kinds of come-ons that cautious buyers will look upon with skepticism. An illustrative example of this occurred when a certain proprietor advertised a going-out-of-business sale with all the finality he could muster. He was taken at his word when he first published the notice, but his reputation diminished when he remained in business and tried the same ploy a year later. It was further noticed that he had increased prices on all merchandise considerably and immediately before advertising a 30% discount. Unfortunately, this deceitful practice has been used in more than one city. The moral is: A shyster might profit for a time in some areas, but he can't expect to remain in business for long in a close community. The person who runs a homecraft business should be especially cognizant of this warning.

Recruiting by Phone

The moment has arrived. You've thoroughly advertised the event, you've distributed directions widely, you've made your telephone number known for any who need further directions to your home, you've offered expensive incentives, and you've stockpiled a large quantity of articles that have been your best sellers. Everything is ready, you think. But nothing happens. Chances are you've started too early in the day for some customers, others are planning to come tomorrow, and many aren't planning to come at all.

Don't stand by idly if activity doesn't explode as hoped. Make the most of the lull. Begin calling that list of leads you've kept for this occasion. Be cheerful, enthusiastic, and as convincing as you can be in the minute or two of phone-time available with a prospect. Briefly introduce your business, emphasizing the kind of crafts you produce and the neighborly nature of the operation, and promptly compliment the person for having been recommended to you. Let her know how much her willingness to listen is valued and appreciated. Then talk about your sale, the bargains and discounts, other reasons for attending now, and how convenient it is to drive to your place.

Next (and this is very important in establishing need), ask the prospect whether she has completed her shopping for the holidays, and follow through to the extent needed by suggesting how your crafts make unique gifts, whether for family or friends and regardless of the season or gift-giving occasion.

Keep cool and persistent to the end. Your object is to have the prospect tell you that she will be coming to your show. Emphasize that attendance is not an obligation to buy. Terminate the conversation by thanking the prospect, and if everything goes as planned, say you're looking forward to meeting her at about the time she said she'll arrive. This last comment is a way of verifying and further elevating the prospect's acceptance to the level of a commitment to be fulfilled. It is the kind of clincher needed to assure attendance.

Surely not everyone who agrees to attend will be a buyer, but you could gain, even then. People who actually see a product, including people who don't buy something, often tell others about skillfully and uniquely fashioned craftwork.

The Sale

Upon their arrival at the house, give customers the kind of special treatment not often experienced in the ordinary retail shop. Offer them coffee and cookies along with a warm personal greeting. In order to do this promptly with each new arrival, you might need the assistance of a capable friend. You will then be better able to allocate time among shoppers, buyers, and new arrivals.

A friendly, relaxed atmosphere is conducive to selling in this setting. For that reason, have a table and chairs placed off to the side where customers might sit while sipping coffee and leisurely passing time with others. Keep the table supplied with copies of your catalog and order forms.

A point of immediate concern is the attitude of prospects when they first arrive at your home. You can't control everything that might affect people negatively, but you can take steps to alleviate irritations that have developed as a result of your situation. Get to the point by showing enough concern to ask visitors if they had any difficulty finding either your home or a parking spot. Apologize if need be, but the mere asking will often put the subject directly out of a customer's mind. Sympathize with people who tell about troubles beyond your purview, and thank others for bringing to your attention a difficulty that you might be able to do something about.

Make your place easy to identify, and assist with the parking of automobiles. Place an attractively lettered sign identifying your business in front of your home. If permitted, set the sign on posts at a spot on the lawn where it can be easily seen from the road or street, and plant a bed of neatly arranged flowers or bushes around its base. Illuminate the sign with a floodlight for the benefit of nighttime visitors. Use such a light, also, when the local ordinance restricts the sign's location to the surface of the building.

Much of the selling at an open house will involve observation and explanation. This process is not unlike that between a salesperson and a customer in a retail store. The main difference is that you must talk to each and every customer—explaining techniques used in making items on display, suggesting items for different occasions and deserving people, and reminding them that some customizing of merchandise will be done if requested.

In instances when demand exceeds expectations, you will run short of one or more items. A practical solution is to sell the last piece on hand while gaining the buyer's permission to leave it on display until the show is over. The piece will then serve as a model for others to place an order.

Complete each sale much as you would when selling at a house party in another person's home. Remind buyers of other possibilities, collect payment for all goods bought, express appreciation for their business, and ask them to recommend the place to others. About the only thing you should do differently is to forego asking customers for a list of leads, especially if other people are waiting in line. Besides, you will have the buyer's name and address on the duplicate sales slip for following up at another time.

CRAFT SHOW SALES

The opportunities to display and sell crafts at shows are extensive. You can choose among and make reservations to attend shows sponsored and widely publicized throughout the year, or you can hold your own show as sole exhibitor when and as you see fit. The first of these, the sponsored shows, are commonly held in cities and towns throughout the country, while the latter method of presentation is best arranged by renting space in a neighborhood shopping mall. The make-up of the display is essentially the same in either case.

Sponsored Shows

Craft shows organized by sponsors vary according to location, participation, and cost. Those promoted on a regional, statewide, or national basis are usually attended by exhibitors in great numbers and from a wide geographic area. They are often held in exhibition halls in large cities, are attended by both amateurs and accomplished professionals, and will always attract a fair share of exhibitors who seem to enjoy traveling by van or mobile home from one show to the next. The costs of renting space, transportation, and living away from home are evidently no deterrent to many who travel afar to display their craftwork.

Locally sponsored shows, by way of contrast, are held in such diverse locations as town squares, school buildings, and civic centers. These shows draw exhibitors primarily from the immediate area, with many of the participants involved in craftwork as a part-time hobby. For some, it is a first attempt at merchandising crafts.

The community show is generally a profitable way for charitable or civic-minded sponsors to raise money and a convenient way for exhibitors to place their crafts before the public, with the cost of renting booth space frequently viewed by exhibitors as going to a worthy cause. Whether or not the effort turns out to be profitable seems to make little difference. Exhibitors come back again and again in increasing numbers, and agencies continue to sponsor the shows on a regular basis. Agencies often take turns several times a year in the typical small city or town. Crafts festivals, bazaars, sidewalk sales, community fairs, handicraft exhibits, charity raffles, block parties, and hobby shows are indicative of the various titles and popular themes.

Much of the popularity of local shows among exhibitors is due to proximity and cost. Traveling is minimal, and advertising expenses can be avoided altogether. About the only special outlay, other than for a license and booth materials, is for the space. At a cost of about $10 or $20 a day, a purveyor of handcrafts can rent a space with a 10-foot frontage. Areas of the exact size and location desired must often be reserved well ahead of time.

Anyone contemplating showing crafts in a locally sponsored setting must remain alert to the announcement and make reservations promptly. Look for announcements in your daily newspaper, and check with your chamber of commerce. Also, direct inquiries to any club or organization you know to have sponsored a show in the past. If, however, you intend to participate in a regional or national show, begin your search by reviewing magazines that regularly list such events.

Is selling at crafts shows really profitable? That all depends. The result is contingent not so much on when a show is held as on what and how one's craftwork is presented.

Through careful observation, you can profit from the results experienced by exhibitors of different crafts. Spend an hour or so at a show in your area. What you can learn about selling in that environment could make the difference between success and failure in your next show.

A Case to Consider

Consider the following: A charitable group operating in a city of about 20,000 population annually sponsors, in their words, "The Grand Crafts

Fair." They publicize each fair via word of mouth, radio announcements, and newspaper releases. They also contact craftspeople who have exhibited in previous years. No other publicity is specially targeted for the event, except for posting on a movable bulletin board the date, time of day, and the event's full name. The board, with this one announcement, is placed for one week on the lawn of the high school where the fair is to be held.

Only one day, a Saturday, is scheduled for the fair, with the public invited to attend between the hours of 9:00 and 4:30. Exhibitors are allowed to set up tables and booths before 9:00 PM of the previous evening. All displays are arranged along the hallways and throughout the cafeteria. Further instructions call for all exhibits, tables, booths, and trash to be removed after the show by 7:00 PM.

Visitors arriving for the show have no difficulty finding a place to park in the large school lot next to the side entrance. Upon entering the building, each person is greeted by a member of the sponsoring group and given an inexpensively made brochure. Those two things set matters off on a positive note. They are helpful, for inside the building's alcove the hallways soon become jam-packed, almost to the point of chaos.

The brochure is most useful for sorting things out. Made of two sheets of ordinary 8½-×-11-inch paper, photocopied on both sides before folding and stapling on center, the assembly contains a neatly illustrated front cover, a local firm's advertisement outside back, and a layout of all 110 booths with numbers corresponding to an identifying list of exhibitors. A page of the brochure is devoted to names of companies making special contributions to the sponsoring group's benevolent project, and another section invites visitors to attend the sponsor's raffle booth where 80 or more prizes donated by exhibitors will be given away. Also identified is the place to purchase lunch.

In view of how effectively organized these shows usually are, one might expect sales to be extraordinary. The numbers of citizens normally attending would seem to substantiate that expectation. In actuality, however, the results vary considerably.

Points to Remember

The experience at a recent show, which was organized as just explained, illustrates this point. Handmade merchandise of many kinds—quilts, wooden cutouts, stuffed animals, laser-engraved boxes, wax ornaments, country carvings, floral arrangements, pet poles, ceramic ware, needlepoint pictures, tooled leather goods, pine-cone decorations, gingerbread house gifts, woven baskets, decorative bows, and unpainted toys—were among the items displayed. Some things sold well and others seemed not to sell at all. One group of exhibitors, a number of ladies from a local church who made and sold different flavors of hard candy, took in over $800 for the day. It is worth noting that their product was packaged in 1½-pound quantities in clear plastic sacks and sold at $3 to $3.75 each, depending on the flavor.

Of the people attending the show, roughly 85 of every 100 were women. Men and a few young boys and girls comprised the balance. A similar distribution was found among the exhibitors.

Buying patterns had a definite relationship to gender. Those things that sold best, as might be expected, appealed to women. Men didn't buy much, but when they did it was often at the direction of a spouse.

Gender seemed to have little to do with sales effectiveness, however. What did make a difference was whether the salespeople were on their feet, eagerly and enthusiastically helping customers. Both capable men and women were observed. Unfortunately, there were fewer of those than the other kind. Many sat placidly back, hoping a customer would ask about something displayed. Other problems along this line occurred, too. One of those involved a lady who left her 12-year-old son in charge of the booth, but without leaving information on prices for him and the customers. That she lost sales of her beautiful ragule ceramic ware was an evident fact.

The exhibitors who seemed to be the busiest and most successful had something in common. They displayed only a few different products or a single line. Like the candy makers, they did not have a huge conglomeration or seemingly endless variety of articles on display. Of all the comments heard by shoppers, the one standing out most clearly was the concern (much in the order of expressing defeat) about having too much to choose among. Booths with a few coordinated groupings of articles were a welcome sight among the many displaying dozens, even hundreds, of different items. The women shoppers were heard to comment most often and favorably about the articles seen in one or two uncluttered displays (FIG. 10-1).

Successful booths had still another feature in common: a clearly identifiable and orderly arrangement. The business's name and hometown were displayed along with neatly arranged products on a back wall or supporting arrangement, and the area was separated when possible from other booths or tables by a space of several feet. Some used decorative dividers, as well. There was never any doubt about where the successful displays began and ended. The visual separateness achieved seemed to create a psychological distinctiveness among the general run of the show.

This particular show brought out several other points to bear in mind, besides how sales can be affected by the attractiveness of the product and the display. One was cost. Very expensive items did not sell well. Twenty dollars was about the top limit, with items of less than $5 moving most quickly and often.

Location, a difficult matter to decide upon in advance, was another problem for the exhibitor. Booths situated a short distance from the main entrance did well, especially those that were attractively decorated and professional in appearance. Among the worst places, at least at this fair, were the stations on the second floor. No matter what time of day, the traffic by customers was always less there than it was along the first floor booths. Other poor locations included those with inadequate lighting.

10-1 Pegboard makes a functional backdrop for displaying small articles. Keeping the product lines limited and the display uncluttered aids the customer's decision-making at a show.

It is evident from this description how beneficial observation can be. You can pay for a space and do nothing special, or you can go to the show prepared to make the most of it. You can, for example, take along a lengthy extension cord and flood lamps for lighting your display in the event you get stuck in a dark spot. This one act alone might make a world of difference.

The General Procedure

Anyone planning to sell at a show, whether as a fill-in or on a regular basis, will soon become aware of the numerous things to be done. In fact, preparing for a show will ordinarily take longer than manning a booth and following through afterward. An idea of the division of effort needed might be apparent in a list of activities to be observed by exhibitors. The procedure from preparation to completion is as follows:

Preparation
1. Consult your schedule of activities and select an open date.
2. Estimate the costs and determine your cash flow.
3. Make reservations early for booth space, being prepared to pay a

flat fee or from 10% to 20% of intake, and find out what regulations and restrictions apply.

4. Make personal arrangements, such as for transportation and a motel room if traveling a distance from home.

5. Determine the licensing requirements and update or upgrade yours if need be.

6. Design and construct the booth, display decorations, and accessories.

7. Prepare the crafts to be sold and displayed, observing price and quantity variations.

8. Employ help or enlist assistance for setting up, operating, and dismantling the display.

9. Promote attendance to your exhibit by informing regular customers when and where you will be selling.

Showtime

10. Transport and set up the display and sales necessities.

11. Man the booth and provide for substitution at lunchtime and occasionally during other open hours.

12. Show your product by means that make it seem not only desirable but necessary.

13. Practice methods for safekeeping your display and cash box.

Post-Show Activities

14. Remove any garbage and trash.

15. Dismantle the booth and pack all accessories and display items.

16. Transport everything to your home or to the next show.

17. Evaluate the experience.

18. Do the paperwork: thank-you notes, data files, and bookkeeping records.

19. Complete and deliver articles placed on order at the show.

20. Follow up new customers and leads as time permits.

DISPLAY TECHNIQUES

Aside from the personal aspect of selling, much of the success of selling crafts at a show relates to the exhibit itself. The arrangement of the display, the use of an attention-grabbing device, the use of posters or similar "silent salesperson," application of a special promotional activity, and demonstration of a related process are five of the techniques to be elaborated upon in this section. They are applicable wherever one's work is placed on display, although not all will be used everywhere or every time.

The Arrangement

A flat table or two of about five-foot length each is the minimum needed for a display, but a better arrangement can be had by adding a backdrop of about seven- or eight-foot height. Customers need to know whose work is being sold and, secondarily, where the business is located. They want to take this in at a glance and get an idea of what is being sold. This information can be quickly transmitted by having a professionally arranged, uncluttered group of products attached next to the lettered business identifier, with the name plate placed slightly above eye level and the representative product or small group of items fastened directly in the line of sight. A floodlight directed to that area will help make the entire booth stand out.

Be imaginative. Arrange the display to capture attention rather than overwhelm viewers with a seemingly endless number of items. Use color grouping, bright streamers, banners, a poster or two, a treasure chest filled with a coordinated array of items, or something cleverly designed to relate to your craft. Country crafts, for example, can be given a homespun effect if a corner is designed in a barnyard decor with straw, corn shock, pumpkin, burlap, and several crafted animals set among them. Here, again, your creative talent will pay off.

Another rule to observe is to avoid clutter in the placement of cartons, supplies, and extras. A good cover draped over the front table and extending clear to the floor will form a useful hiding place. People are much more likely to stop at your booth when it is evident what you are selling than if they can't readily sort out what is intended to be seen.

Look at your competitors' displays, noting which seem to draw the most shoppers. Borrow useful ideas and apply them in your own way. Experiment freely. Strive for something a little different each time. If you settle for a humdrum display, you might be pitifully outdone by an adjacent exhibitor, but you will probably hold your own at any spot in an exhibition if yours is one of the outstanding arrangements in the show.

Be fully aware, no matter what kind of show you enter, your first object is to capture the attention of viewers. Do something to cause the audience to slow down and stop. Results thereafter depend on the effectiveness of the arrangement at the booth and your personal actions.

Attention-Getters

An effective technique for gaining the immediate attention of people walking by your booth is to create action in the display. An inexpensive, handmade action-toy will do, but you might choose to purchase a device for the purpose. Battery-operated gadgets of all sorts are now available at a reasonable price. Barking dogs, mooing cows, tumbling clowns, rotating rabbits, marching soldiers, and musical carousels represent some of the things adaptable to different needs. Applications utilizing push-button music boxes, pulsating or blinking bulbs, and small musical harps offer other possibilities.

Whatever you do, do sparingly. You want to create attention, not boredom. Try to make an application fit the scheme of things instead of looking like a commercial gimmick. Examples of appropriate applications are the placement of a chirping bird or two in a display of birdhouses and feeders, attaching to a stuffed reindeer a plastic nose that blinks in red when selling at Christmas time, and displaying a small article (of virtually any kind) on a musical box having a rotating platform. For optimum results, place the item both where it is immediately apparent and where it serves as a transitional piece in the display.

In a rustic setting, as when selling creations done in the country style, a stuffed rabbit tumbling on a horizontal bar or a small, grunting mechanical pig corralled in a barnyard are possible applications. Due to their nature, whimsical devices can become the center of humorous reference. Generally, they need be given no more than off-hand and quickly passing attention.

On-the-Spot Promotions

You can also draw people's attention by focusing on the merchandise. This section suggests ways to do that and more. These additional techniques are designed to create attention and to reward those who take some specified action. The reward is the inducement. An offer of a special price on a product is a common example of this. A variation is to post notice of a 25% discount on all purchases after buying the first item at regular price.

Very lucrative specials and extra-large discounts are sometimes geared to needs as they develop. A line of merchandise that is not selling well will often be discounted heavily to move it before the show ends, or an entire display will be reduced radically in price near the end of a show in an attempt to eliminate much packing and further handling. Selling above cost is preferred, but selling at a price that has no profit margin at all can be desirable on occasion. The craftsperson who ignores the realities basic to these illustrations might soon be saddled with a lot of merchandise that has little buyer appeal.

Along with discounting, another popular promotional technique is the offering of a prize. "Register to win" or "Guess the weight" enticements are frequently posted at show booths as a way of obtaining leads and, ultimately, new customers. Often, those registering are not the least bit interested in your craft. Despite this, the technique is a useful door-opening device. It pays off most handsomely for exhibitors who are effective in following up by telephone.

A good countertop promotion will create traffic and a measure of excitement. Inexpensive balloons and samples of candy are examples of give-aways used effectively with certain displays. As one person stops and shows interest, others will naturally follow. It is your job then to capitalize on the opportunity.

Posters

Posters are an item that, although not essential in all situations, can be helpful in holding the customers' attention. There are basically two kinds of posters: the informational and the inspirational. The former tell something you want the customer to know, such as "credit cards accepted," and the latter are geared more toward stimulating the customer's imagination.

The informational poster will engage the audience's attention primarily because of the practical content. A message so intended should be brief, simple in design, easy to read, and unambiguous in meaning. The functional layout in FIG. 10-2 is illustrative of this kind of poster.

Inspirational posters, by way of contrast, are used more for effect than information. They add flair and a touch of class to an exhibit while conveying a unifying thought. In many instances, they appeal to a viewer's sense of humor and creative inclinations.

You will often find such posters are most appropriately positioned when placed next to a group of items that have something in common. A

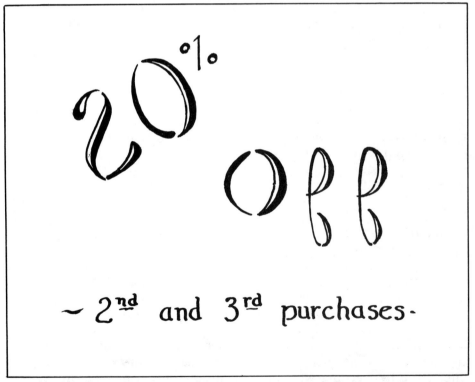

10-2 A well-made poster for promoting sales can be very effective at a booth if the deal is a good one.

sign reading "Bunny Bazaar" beside an array of cuddly rabbits exemplifies this point.

Make use of posters in your display only if they are not amateurishly done and if they do not detract from your crafts in any way. Use no more than one or two posters at a time, and have them attractively and sparsely lettered.

As a final suggestion, attach all your posters to something solid so they will remain securely in place. You don't want to be constantly picking up and re-setting one that tips over at the slightest breeze or an accidental brush with a hand.

The Demonstration

An action-packed method of getting people to stop at your booth is to perform some of the steps involved in making your product. The method is much as explained for demonstrating procedures at a house party, but with important differences. At a house party the audience is seated and quiet; at a public show they are on their feet: Some are standing, some walking about, and some talking. To compensate for this difference, use a table or stand of 48-inch height placed to one side of the display, perform the kinds of operations that can be readily seen by people positioned to the front, and speak louder and slower than you normally would. Supplement the lighting to obtain maximum visibility at that point. Additionally, work with an assistant. You don't need one at a house party, but you do need someone to help you at a show. A well-trained person can tend to sales activities while you are engaged in the demonstration.

A demonstration at a show must be further tailored to the audience, due to the transient nature of those in attendance. Since every person present is free to move on to another booth at almost any moment, learn to judge when most observers have seen enough to get the gist of how you do it and cut the activity short. Intersperse your commentary with references to products on display, and call attention to any bargains available. Conclude each segment by asking the group to register for the prize and to look over the merchandise. A reiteration of suggestions and reasons for buying the handcrafts is an appropriate way to finish.

During the final moments of each session, identify one or more people in the audience who seem especially interested in your work. Pick up a piece of the merchandise and have them hold it and pass it about. This act alone might be the prelude to making buyers of observers.

Whether you choose to demonstrate your craft or use another method of capturing people's attention, remember that show visitors are bombarded. They see an assortment of displays, some with effective eye-catchers and some just so-so. You can make yours among the most impressive by learning what the regulations for displaying are in each instance and by observing and analyzing how competitors conducted their affairs at previous shows. Further develop your display in light of the suggestions given in this text. You are not obligated to spend a great deal of money, but what you do must stand out by being different.

OPEN A SMALL STORE

Perhaps you've reached the point where you want a change in your approach to selling. A store might have suddenly become vacant, and you've become confident about your ability to risk a potentially more profitable venture. Possibly, too, you've simply grown tired of attending parties and shows. Anyway, you want to set up an operation where customers come to you. A store is what you need, you believe.

Think twice before proceeding. Analyze what you propose to do in terms of the money needed, the workload, employment, paperwork, legal assistance, and the like. Chances are your life will change dramatically. Even if nothing else changes you can be sure you will become more involved in the business of selling other people's crafts than your own. You will become less of a craftsperson and more of an entrepreneur; otherwise, you can't expect to handle the quantity of merchandise necessary to make the venture profitable.

If you decide to go ahead, consider beginning with a small operation. You, like most people, will probably be better off by keeping the financial risk to a minimum. Overhead expenses alone will seem huge compared to those previously experienced when working out of your home, and those costs, regardless of the size of the new operation and its physical structure, are just the beginning of what you will encounter.

Carts and Kiosks

Look to a shopping center or mall for an opportunity to open a small operation. A center near you might have a kiosk (a newsstand type of store) or a cart available to be leased. The kiosk offers permanence. A cart can be rented for shorter periods of time and, generally, can be moved about to find the best spot for doing business.

The costs and amount of business expected will vary considerably, primarily in relation to the popularity of the center. The cost of renting a cart, for example, can vary from several hundred to several thousand dollars monthly in busy shopping locations and seasons, while gross income can exceed rental costs by as much as 20 times. Not all locations are highly lucrative, so it behooves the prospect to investigate widely and compare the findings.

Some centers are very restrictive about the time and place for selling from carts and other temporary setups, and some do not allow non-permanent kinds of displays at all. Neither are kiosks extensively provided or readily available in many shopping malls. When a desirable opportunity does emerge, by all means fully consider the ramifications of entering into an agreement before plunging ahead.

What are some of the considerations? In addition to securing a lease agreement that meets your terms, you will need a license to do business where intended, an adequate supply of the crafts you intend to sell, and sufficient help to do the selling. A license is obtained through normal procedures and previously explained channels, but you will probably have to increase the quantity of merchandise beyond that which you produced for your home-based operation. You must be able to keep a steady supply on hand, because you will now be selling much more continuously than before.

There are several courses available to you. You can increase the supply of your own product by hiring helpers and farming out construction under contract, or you can take on merchandise in consignment and through purchasing. Either way, you will be introducing costs not part of a small, one- or two-person business. The resulting negative effect on markup, you hope, will be adequately compensated for by an increase in sales volume.

The selling phase, too, is likely to cost more. The need to remain open for business from about 10 o'clock in the morning to as late as 9:00 at night, six days of the week and on Sunday afternoons, is not a schedule that an ordinary family can keep. You will probably have to hire employees.

Storefront Operations

A fixed location with a show window facing the foot traffic, whether in a shopping center or downtown location, is a slightly different way to step out. One concern is how to keep the show windows interesting and exciting. The merchandise, itself, will make a difference. Variety is one essential. Whereas a single item can be effectively displayed in a cart, a larger choice will have to be displayed and offered to customers in a store. Thus, hand-cut sheepskin seat pads might be all that is needed to make a profit in one situation, while a selection of handcrafted leather goods would attract the larger number of customers needed in the other.

A mall or shopping center location can be quite attractive to the entrepreneur. Parking is usually adequate, snow removal is another's responsibility, and such things as heating are no problem or extra cost. The conveniences are purchased with the lease.

While the rent for a downtown location might be low, be prepared when opening a store along a city street to cover the other costs encountered. All utilities, advertising, starting inventory, insurance, remodeling, sidewalk care, window washing, and a lengthy lease represent some areas of cost not of much consequence, if any, in other kinds of situations. Fees for attorneys and accountants are also likely to be considerable. The need to borrow operating capital to enter into and manage the store successfully could be the most stressful aspect of all, particularly if you've been unlucky enough to choose a spot where business is dying.

BORROWING CAPITAL

You must have some money of your own to start a homecrafts business, but you will need more of it to switch to a store operation. The need for a facility separate from your residence will result in significantly higher costs, and operating expenses will surge dramatically. Due to the need to keep the store open full time, employing and training helpers and finding and dealing with suppliers become constant concerns. Knowing how to obtain enough money to cover all of these additional expenses (and your living costs) during the first eight months or more of operation could be a major hurdle. Qualifying for and obtaining the money in time to land that special location you have identified could be the second problem.

The Proposal

Your initial obligation is to prepare a complete proposal that states what you plan to do, gives sound projections for the venture's profitability, and clearly sets out the request for capital. You will also have to include, whether as part of the proposal or in a separate presentation, a description of your experience and any other evidence that you can conduct the business successfully. Most lenders will also require evidence of personal worth and ownership as a basis for putting up collateral for a loan.

A proposal must impress the lender. Therefore, it should be complete and neat. Ten to twenty typed pages should be adequate, with a brief summary placed immediately after the title page. Make yours similar to a business plan that places most emphasis on financial information. List personal data and identify references on the last page.

Although you might be personally known to the lender, give references who can speak about your character and your ability in business ownership. Evidence of your ability to succeed financially in the private sector will be most valued. With the recent failure of many lending institutions resulting from poor loans, you can expect all money lenders to be extra cautious and to check out a borrower's background much more thoroughly than in years past. The kind of reputation you have established in your homecraft business will undoubtedly be investigated, so you might as well include among your references the names of people who can speak with firsthand knowledge about your managerial skills.

The financial part of your proposal must include both short- and long-range projections. Present detailed lists with dollar amounts of start-up costs, including fixtures and equipment, beginning inventory, office supplies, decorating and remodeling expenses, legal and professional fees, licenses and permits, market research, advertising, and operating cash. Include with these all other capital and operating expenses needed during the first year.

Every probable cost must be accounted for. Utilities, insurance, taxes, interest on the loan, wages, rent, travel, and maintenance are representative items. If you expect your business to grow, expense statements for later years, say, the third and fifth years will show the lender how carefully you are looking ahead.

As part of the projected operating statement, include income and balance statements. Show the projected gross sales, the cost of sales, profit, and your salary. Don't overstate your case. Unusually large profits and overly optimistic projections for growth are common errors to avoid. Your credibility could be brought into question if you do not do a realistic job in this respect.

Include in your proposal evidence that you are conscious about the need for adequate cash flow. You pay bills with cash, not with projected profits. A neat balance statement with assets exceeding liabilities will look good, but it won't pay the bills. Unless you can set aside enough funds to tide you over the rough times and can be reasonably assured your earnings will replenish and provide the money needed, you will surely be starting on the road to disaster. In other words, you're about to go broke.

Sources

If you are uncertain about what to include in a proposal, seek the advice of knowledgeable people in your community. You could consult a local banker, but since that person might later be asked for a loan, you probably will be better off going to someone else.

You need not consult someone who will charge for the advice, either. Doing that could result in an unnecessary expense. Try, instead, someone you know in the business sector, such as members of your local chamber of commerce. The SBA is another source for free information and advice on preparing a proposal.

In addition to helping to prepare your proposal, a retired executive in the SBA will instruct you concerning the procedure for borrowing funds and the SBA's role in providing backing. The procedure, briefly, is to seek a loan from at least two federally insured lending institutions, and if turned down, to apply to the administration for a loan guarantee before again seeking a loan. Guarantees of up to $50,000 are available to people who qualify.

The traditional approach to borrowing capital is to go to a relative or friend. If you do that, do not be lavish in your request and do so only if you are truly convinced you can repay the loan. To default on your obligation might not only lead to financial disaster but also to the complete deterioration of personal relations. It is for this latter reason alone that some financial consultants advise strongly against borrowing from individuals with whom there exists a close relationship. Relatives are prone to be swayed more by emotion and personal feelings than to raise sound, businesslike precautions about making the loan.

A final, but significant, word of caution is in order in concluding this topic. Avoid borrowing from venture capitalists. People who advertise the availability of money for initiating or expanding a business are on the lookout for financial gain, very often exceptionally huge gain. Generally, their rates are high, and they take a firm hold on the business's conduct and operational practices. As one might expect, the venture capitalist is shrewd enough to have a loan agreement written so as to avoid financial loss in the event of a default in payment of the interest due. The kinds of conditions encountered in such an agreement could easily lead to the most calculating, unforgiving, and ruthlessly cold business association imaginable.

11
CHAPTER

Keep Track & Measure Your Success

A GOOD, COMPREHENSIVE SYSTEM of record keeping is vital in business. It need not be elaborate, but it must provide adequately for financial accounting and internal management. It must enable the business owner to prepare and substantiate tax claims, to convince money lenders of the need for any loan requested, and to recover data (financial and non-financial) for the analysis and planning of business activities.

Small business operators generally do not have the time or the inclination to do complex record keeping. Besides, many have not progressed to the point of employing an accountant or other assistant to help them. For these reasons, the average craftsperson needs a system that is easy to use. Components of a system appropriate for a small crafts business are explained in this final chapter.

RECORDS AND BOOKS

The business owner must separate business activities from non-business activities and taxable income from non-taxable income. Aside from the fact that tax-collecting agencies require written documentation, no one can direct affairs effectively by relying entirely on memory. Recalling details from day-to-day operations that have long ago transpired can tax the best of us. Memory fades with time. Clearly, tangible evidence as kept in a systematic arrangement of records is needed for purposes of management and operation. A bookkeeping system meets only part of the requirement.

Knowing the Difference

Record keeping and bookkeeping, though integrally related, bear differentiation. *Bookkeeping* is the process of keeping account of the financial affairs of the business. The completed books are records, as are the back-up papers which document the financial transactions.

Record keeping is a more inclusive term. It is the practice of committing all kinds of business activities to writing or print and of maintaining documents for the purpose of later retrieval, analysis, and reporting or planning. A complete system of records makes possible the timely retrieval and substantiation of financial data for filing federal, state, and local tax forms. It has the additional, important purpose of providing data for determining such things as which methods of selling used are best, when the slow days and the busy periods occur, when to advertise, and when to take vacation. Having information about customers readily at hand is another reason for keeping records of the non-financial kind.

Keep It Simple

You might devise your own complete system of record keeping, or you can purchase books containing forms and descriptions for the financial part of the process. Whatever you do, try to keep the paperwork to a minimum for the kind of business you run. For a small home business operated by yourself and organized as a sole proprietorship, you can probably get by using the cash method of accounting, a single-entry system of bookkeeping, and a few forms for maintaining operational data. With a little effort, you can learn to do all you need to do without paying an accountant. Hire professional help if your business grows in size and complexity to the extent that you don't have the time or the knowledge needed to do the bookkeeping part yourself.

Large, complicated businesses place special demands on bookkeepers. Accrual accounting, double-entry bookkeeping (which for many would mean a semester in college), and numerous extra records are necessary. Hiring one or more employees and allowing customers to purchase merchandise on account will increase record keeping to an even greater extent. Payroll accounts and tax records are needed for the former, and accounts receivable records for the latter. The accrual method of accounting will also become necessary, just as it is for merchandise and materials in inventory. Large-ticket capital and vehicle purchases are other expected occurrences in a large organization, with each such purchase necessitating year-by-year accounting and depreciation records.

Because the law does not require any one system for entering data and organizing financial records, the owner retains some freedom in the matter of record keeping. Clarity and completeness are the basic requirements. Along with wording to this effect, tax-collecting agencies are emphatic in stating the need for filing reports accurately, on time, and with documentable support. Discipline yourself to keep records of all transactions and compile the information in a way you understand it.

Record Files

Ideally, all of your business records will be kept in a fireproof location, but the extent of such protection is most likely to be limited to storing the bookkeeping journals in a fireproof safe or filing cabinet. A two- or four-drawer filing cabinet of the fire resistant variety is especially recommended. It could be a small investment for the added protection it offers, even though there might be room for only current and the most important records.

Keep all receipts, bills, canceled checks, bank statements, etc. that relate to your business. Accordion folders and ordinary manila file folders, all of the same legal or letter size, are excellent for keeping the papers separated according to income and expenses by the month. It is also advisable to staple canceled checks to the bills for permanent filing.

A set of books, called *journals,* is also needed. Entries are made as explained later. The type of book or columnar pad to purchase for this purpose will depend on the method of bookkeeping adopted. Office supply stores customarily carry a variety of styles to meet different needs.

Records that relate to operations other than directly in a financial way are preferably kept on 3-×-5-inch cards. Customer files are of this kind. They can be easily alphabetized and separated chronologically, and their smallness limits the amount of information each card can contain to important notations only.

The maintenance and filing of special records, such as concern insurance, equipment, and inventories, require different treatment. Set up file folders for each as a first step. Keep the insurance policy, premium notices, and canceled checks together in one folder, and mark on your annual schedule the date premiums are again due. As with all important papers, file records of personal and business affairs separately.

Equipment and Supplies

Records of equipment and inventories of supplies can be kept on sheets in sizes convenient for filing in folders. Capital equipment, that is, items of permanence with a normal life of a year or more, should be identified, the date and cost of the purchase listed, and the method and amount of annual depreciation shown. If, however, the cost is small and is taken as an expense of operating, no depreciation schedule need be kept. In that case the piece of equipment is treated as an operating expense, with the record limited to data at the point of the purchase.

To be complete, a record of an asset used both for personal and business purposes must show the date and cost at the time of acquisition, the percentage of business use, and any changes in the basis (e.g., improvements) of the item. The record is used to compute and report the gain or loss when selling or otherwise disposing of the asset.

Supplies and saleable items placed in inventory are treated differently. They are subject to depletion and, therefore, should be identifiable on records as to purchasing information and year-end carry over. A convenient method for a small business is to post a sheet in the area where materials are stored, Each time an item is removed that fact is noted on the sheet. Periodic and end-of-the-year reviews of the posted sheets will identify items needing replenishing, as well as provide data for determining the cost of goods on hand for tax purposes. Both the craftsman who makes items for sale and the one who purchases completed items for resale need this kind of record.

Other Records

The types of records you will keep in addition to those already mentioned depends on the specifics of your operation. If, for example, you use your car for business, you must keep day-to-day expense (or mileage) records, and you will need various daily, weekly, monthly, quarterly, and yearly payroll and tax withholding records if you employ someone. Banking transactions, sales-tax collections and receipts, and petty-cash accounts, by way of contrast, are among the records which almost every owner-operator must maintain.

An owner-operator must also keep self-employment records. Business earnings, whether in the form of wages paid to oneself or profits as sole owner, are the basis for computing and filing self-employment tax. It is part of the system for providing social security coverage for people who work for themselves.

SCHEDULING, POSTING, AND RETENTION

While the previous section contains suggestions on what to file and how to do it, in this section emphasis is placed on when to file and post information and how long to retain it. As a general recommendation, develop a workable system. Routinely sort and separately file bills and receipts. Be timely in the process. An excellent way to invite trouble is to toss the papers into a drawer or carton, leaving them there until the end of the year when the sorting and posting operations become considerably more involved. About the only practice worse is to discard the papers too soon.

Retention

As to length of time to keep records, use your judgment but be careful to comply with requirements of the IRS. Retain information on file as long as it remains useful in analyzing trends and making comparisons relative to the management of the business, and hold onto original copies of financial data and journals for the length of time needed for tax purposes. The IRS stipulates a minimum of three years for ordinary expenses, four years for employment taxes, and longer for ongoing accounts.

To be on the safe side, retain all journals and tax returns for at least three years beyond the time of leaving or terminating the business. Keep all back-up bills, receipts, and check stubs for five or six years, and maintain records of capital acquisitions, equipment depreciation calculations, and loan payments for several years beyond the full life of each claim as it pertains to the business. Prematurely discarding financial records could be an extremely costly mistake, particularly if you are ever investigated by a federal revenue agent.

The amount of storage needed to retain a craft business's records should present no major problem. A single drawer in a filing cabinet is large enough to keep an ordinary accumulation for a number of years. After the initial five-or-six-year build-up, many of the oldest papers can be removed and discarded as new ones are added to the file. From that time on, the files tend to stabilize in size.

A General Schedule

A good habit to get into is to perform activities according to some logical scheme or order. You will save time in the long run by doing this. Not always can you comply with a schedule for handling financial matters exactly as written, but you will soon realize the advantage of making an effort to perform duties routinely in the manner presented below.

Daily
- File mail and receipts received.
- Update inventory records for inflow and outflow.
- Record time, mileage, and petty cash expenditures.
- Pay bills (by check) to meet discount deadlines.

Weekly
- Make bank deposits of income.
- Enter deposits in checkbook and record books.
- File sales slips and update customer files.
- Enter week's cash and check purchases in books.
- Mail invoices (if you permit buying on time).

Monthly
- Reconcile checkbook with bank statement.
- Pay fixed charges, e.g., rent and utilities.
- Tally receipts and expenses and compute balance.
- Compute cash flow and adjust next month's plan.

- Order supplies as needed.
- Tally logs for traveling, transportation, etc.

Quarterly
- Make and record required sales, business income, and self-employment tax payments.
- Submit and record taxes withheld for employees.

Yearly
- Make all end-of-year payments qualifying for tax deduction.
- Bring books to a close and compute end-of-year net worth statement.
- Prepare and submit income tax returns.
- Prepare next year's budget and update the business plan.

Whether or not you need a professional to assist you in carrying out your fiscal responsibilities will depend largely on how confident you feel about performing the activities explained hereafter. You might want to hire a tax accountant, as many businesspeople do, but you might profit by following through on your own. Even a partial effort at maintaining your own system can be a cost-saver.

Materials Needed

To keep books, you need a sharp pencil and specially sectioned paper. Always do the posting of figures in pencil (a fine-line mechanical pencil is good), and keep a good eraser at hand. The lined paper on which data are to be entered for permanent keeping might be loose leaf or bound, have headings either entered or unstated, and contain rows and columns divided in quantities large or small. The choice will depend to an extent on the system of bookkeeping chosen.

Unless you have reason to do otherwise, use the single-entry system of bookkeeping. One of its overriding advantages is that you don't have to keep a set of ledgers and journals. One-time entries as they occur will suffice. Simply maintain a daily record of receipts, disbursements, and related activities in a consistent and usable form.

You are at liberty to set up books by purchasing columnar pads which contain sheets lined in the numbers of rows and headings suitable for your purpose. A well-stocked office supply store will have a large variety to choose among. Select columnar paper adequate for making entries daily and for tallying monthly. You will also need to make the selection according to the number of accounts you keep. A three-ring notebook cover with insert dividers is suggested for storing completed columnar sheets.

As an alternative, you might wish to use a commercially prepared bookkeeping record. Books of this kind, also available in office supply stores, eliminate the need for writing in headings of your own. They might give you a few more accounts than needed, but they often include other helpful information about record keeping and tax reporting.

Another item of considerable value in bookkeeping is the calculator. Although any type at all will simplify the adding of columns of figures, a variety which can be set to provide a printed read-out in addition to a digital display is to be preferred. This type will make an easy task of checking arithmetic computations for accuracy. Ease in verification is important; accuracy is essential.

A small, transportable electronic calculator of the type suggested can be an extremely useful instrument. For a purchase price under $50, you can acquire the capability of performing any calculation you will ever need in bookkeeping and records analysis. In addition, you will have a device to use in place of a cash register at crafts shows or house parties, not to mention the many other practical applications for the calculator about the home. All things considered, you might discover it to be an indispensable tool for operating your business.

SIMPLIFIED BOOKKEEPING

The system of bookkeeping recommended for a small crafts business should make possible the recording of data in categories much as required for income tax reporting. Secondly, it should make possible the recording of transactions conveniently and as they occur in common, everyday activity. The system and its components as described here meet these requirements. Anyone who can make accurate arithmetic computations should have no difficulty following the recommendations given. Simplicity is maintained by first selecting an uncomplicated accounting method.

Cash and Accrual Accounting

Choose an accounting method that fits your needs, and apply it consistently from year to year. Some small businesses regularly use the cash method, others accrual accounting, and still others a hybrid of the two. The methods determine when and how to report income and expenses. The differences in results are basically inconsequential, except, perhaps, at the end of one tax period and the beginning of another. Placing every financial activity in a reporting period according to a consistent rule is of concern to the IRS, especially.

For most crafts businesses, a hybrid method of accounting will suffice. By this method you use accrual accounting for purchases and sales involving delayed payments or inventories of goods and the cash method for all other income and expenses in the business. If you do not maintain an inventory (an unlikely occurrence in a handcrafts business) or do not need to maintain receivable and payable accounts (which you can readily avoid doing), you might use either the cash method or the accrual method exclusively.

The cash method is easily understood and widely used. It permits the recording of income when actually received and expenses when actually paid. The method works this way for receipts: A payment in cash is recorded on the day received, no matter when the merchandise was or will be delivered. This is true as well for income payments by check, money order, or credit card charge slip. It doesn't matter, for example, if you receive a check in payment on December 31 but do not actually deposit the check until after the new year has begun. The cash record would show payment constructively made in December. By this method, if a sale occurs sometime before payment is made, it is the date of receipt of the cash or instrument of payment that is recorded.

Purchases work similarly. The day a check is written for the goods delivered or to be delivered is the day of a cash payment. The date on which the sale was made is not the determining factor. An exception occurs when paying in advance so that such expenses (e.g., insurance premiums) can be deducted only in the year to which they apply.

Suppose, however, you make a practice of selling on time, as when taking orders for goods on account. You must then use the accrual method. You record the income when you earn it, that is, when you make the sale, even though you may be paid a month later or in another tax year. Under this method, expenses are deducted when you incur them, regardless of whether or not you pay them in the same year. You will also have to keep accounts receivable and accounts payable records to be in full compliance in this respect.

The method by which books are kept for goods placed in and sold from inventory is similarly dictated by the IRS. Inventories include all finished or partly finished goods and materials that will become a part of the merchandise you intend to sell. Since some of these things carry over from one year to the next, you will have to use the accrual method of accounting for sales and acquisitions. The value of the closing inventory is subtracted from the cost of goods in inventory to determine the cost of goods sold during the tax year.

Decide on the method you want to follow, and implement requirements of the IRS as they apply. Then be consistent in application. With a little experience, you will find that even a hybrid method is not a difficult method of accounting to use.

Single-Entry System

As suggested previously, use a single-entry system of bookkeeping if your business is not large or complex financially. The single-entry system is easy to maintain, but it does not have the built-in checks and balances of a double-entry system. By the same token, neither does the single-entry approach require knowledge and use of debits, credits, ledgers, and journals.

Single-entry bookkeeping allows you to keep track of income and expenses by simply recording cash receipts and disbursements on a daily basis and following through monthly with a summary of those financial activities. Periodic and year-end net worth statements and balance sheets can be readily drawn therefrom. Whether you perform these operations on paper or with an automatic data processing system makes no difference as long you can maintain adequate permanent records. For many people, a paper-and-pencil record will prove to be entirely adequate and comparatively inexpensive.

Financial Records

The recording of financial transactions in a clear and accurate way is essential for the effective operation of your business and for reporting taxes. Forms in extensive variety (some indispensable in any business and some needed only for special operations) can be purchased or developed for keeping track of progress. Those from which a selection can be made for a handcrafts business include the following:

> *Basic Business Records*
> >Checkbook
> >Daily register of receipts
> >Daily register of disbursements
> >Monthly summary of receipts and disbursements
> >Annual balance statement
>
> *Special Purpose Records*
> >Employee compensation records
> >Logs of car expenses, traveling, and business gifts
> >Depreciation records
> >Accounts receivable and payable records
> >Inventory account

A form for computing cash flow is also commonly recommended by authorities, for the viability of a business generally depends on the availability of cash when needed. Forms for this purpose are most useful for making projections, that is, for budgeting. Projections of monthly and accumulative profits show how much money is expected to be on hand throughout the year. An after-the-fact computation of cash flow occurs automatically in this system.

SAMPLE BOOKKEEPING SYSTEM

The system illustrated on the following pages covers the basic forms needed for a sole proprietorship. It is a single-entry system, and it is appropriate for the cash method of accounting for everything but matters related to inventory. While the system is designed for use in preparing income tax returns, you might have to add special forms to it to accommodate your particular operation.

The Bank Account

One of the first things you need to do when setting up a financial system for your business is to open a checking account. Open it in the name of your business, and make all payments related to the business through it. By paying all bills for the business from this purposely designed account, you will have a written record of each transaction and you will be keeping all your business finances separate from your personal ones.

Basic to the effective use of a business checking account is the understanding that every purchase and every payment chargeable to the business be made by check. Bills for crafts supplies should obviously be paid that way, but so also should personal draws (payments to yourself) and funds for placement in petty cash. Write checks for these latter purposes to yourself, never to "cash," and write the purpose on the check and check stub.

Similarly, payments for expenses that are only partly chargeable to the business must be paid from the business's checking account to the extent necessary. Building rent, for example, in situations where the cost would be properly divided according to the facility's use for personal and business purposes, might be paid by two checks written in the proportionate amounts. If that practice seems like a cumbersome way to obtain a record and keep the business account in balance, develop an alternative to making partial monthly payments. Work out some procedure for paying less frequently but in larger amounts from the business's checking account. Paying the applicable portion of the rent for the business on a quarterly or semiannual basis might be a convenient and easily followed practice, but if the amount does not exactly match the total amount of rent due, you might find it easier to write the business check to yourself and pay the total rent by personal check. Be certain when delaying transfers in this way that all payments are duly recorded and made in full by the end of the tax year.

Another point of concern in using a bank account for purposes of transaction and record is reconciliation with the monthly bank statement. Deposits, withdrawals, and interest earnings (or charges) as reported by the bank must balance with your record. As a minimum, this will mean you must add to your record the amount of interest earned for the period (or deduct the service charge) and adjust for outstanding checks and unlisted deposits when making the comparison. A well-kept checkbook will help substantiate entries in your income and expense records.

Petty Cash

Although every business payment will have a canceled check for back-up, there are some things for which you will pay cash. Incidentals, such as a pencil for bookkeeping, gasoline for the car, typewriter tape, and so forth, are often most conveniently paid for without taking time to write a check. For that reason, transfer $50 or $100 to a petty cash box, and carry a small part of it with you. Remember to mark on a sheet kept in the cash box the exact amount of money you take out each time. At the end of the day when a purchase has been made in cash for the business, make sure the purpose of the purchase is shown on the cash register slip and place it in the box for later reference and permanent storing.

When the petty cash fund is nearly exhausted, summarize the items and draw a check from the business's checking account to cover the exact amount expended. The check is then cashed and the fund replenished. At all times, the cash on hand plus the expenditures listed must equal the original amount placed in the fund.

Daily Expenditures Register

An easily managed, adequate way to keep details of expenditures is to record them chronologically as they occur. Figure 11-1 illustrates one of the acceptable formats. This arrangement makes possible the separation of expenditures into three major groups: one for deductible expenditures,

DAILY EXPENDITURES

Month _____ 19__

Day	Check No	Payee	Acc't.	(A) Deductible		(B) Mfg/Inv'try		(C) Non-Deduc.	
1	153	Somer's Office Serv.	12	59	97				
3	154	Crafts Supply Co.	27			132	28		
3	155	Owner's Draw	32					200	—
4	156	Daily News (Ad)	2	35	30				
8	157	County Auditor (license)	10	20	—				
10	158	Bud's Painting (shop Area)	29			85	—		
30	173	Dave's Home Rentals 15/29		15	—	35	—		
30	174	Public Power & Light 23/29		5	78	13	49		
				293	27	221	80	625	—

11-1 A single-entry form for daily expenditures may be made up like this one on lined sheets from a columnar pad.

another for expenses related to production and inventory, and the third for nondeductible business costs. Entries are made as they occur throughout the entire month.

Check numbers, names of recipients, dates of payments, and amounts of the payments are recorded routinely on the form. Also, account numbers are entered so as to define to which account on the monthly summary sheet the various entries shall be transferred. Whether or not all three columns will be needed for recording expenditures depends specifically on how the business is conducted.

A description of the columns will help clarify where to enter the different categories of expenditures.

Column A   This column includes deductible expenses—that is, those costs directly deductible on the federal income tax return, including operating expenses which are not made part of the cost of goods sold. Every business has deductible expenses. The costs of marketing, selling, advertising, distribution, and direct repairs to an office and showroom are among them. Indirect costs are other allowable deductions, such as for partial use of the home, but only to the extent insurance, utilities, rent, real estate taxes, and so forth are proportionately allocated according to personal and business uses. The business portion might have to be further divided to reflect costs incurred through manufacturing and inventory (placed in column B) and other aspects of the operation, including office and display room activities (placed in column A).

Column B   This column provides for the costs of manufacturing and of holding materials and completed crafts in inventory, while providing a ready reference for later reporting the costs of the goods sold. Many businesses involved in making handcrafts can benefit by using this category, for production and selling activities are likely to carry from one year into the next. As a consequence, the business falls under IRS uniform capitalization rules, and the accrual method of accounting must be used to separate and report the costs of handcrafting and storing.

Briefly, a handcrafts operation in the business of producing articles for sale must compute the costs of raw materials, storing, production labor, depreciation of equipment, and indirect expenses (part of the rent, utilities, etc.) as they apply in preparation for computing the cost of goods sold when filing the year-end tax return. Those costs relate to the inventory and are figured separately from directly deductible office and merchandising expenses. In some instances, costs for a particular item might have to be split and entries made in both columns A and B. For example, interest payments on a business loan would be divided 60/40 between the two columns if the loan were for the total business operation which has a 40% involvement in manufacturing and inventory operations and the balance in other business operations.

As previously explained, some businesses are exempt from certain requirements. Resale businesses are among them. The law currently permits an exemption from the uniform capitalization rules if articles (including handcrafts) are purchased for resale and annual income is not beyond limits. Moreover, certain small-business operators can produce and sell a product and remain exempt from the uniform capitalization requirement. Artists and photographers are specifically included in this special class. Because of this and the fact that some crafts have reached a high level of artistry, some handcrafters could have a good legal argument for exemption on those grounds. It is strongly suggested, therefore, that you consider asking the IRS for an opinion as to the status of your craft. You have nothing to lose by requesting an opinion regarding your need to separate the cost of goods sold from ordinary operating expenses. If you do call an IRS office, record the respondent's name and ask for the opinion in writing for future reference.

You should also obtain copies of IRS publications and tax forms which apply. Study them. They will help you understand the reasons for maintaining books in a particular way. How the records are kept might vary; how the tax returns are prepared is a legal matter.

Your objective is to make record keeping no more involved than it has to be. You might find the tax-filing requirements of the IRS to be replete with complex rules for your small craft. If they make your record keeping procedures involved, don't despair. After the initial decisions have been made, the recording of data on expenditure forms will tend toward the routine.

Column C The third column in the form is for setting apart expenses incurred as they relate to items not deductible on the federal business income tax form. Part of a loan for the business is an example. The portion of the monthly charge which is for interest is to be taken as a business expense and should be subtracted from the total payment before entering the non-deductible amount for the principal in part C. Additionally, payments on your salary and the federal tax on the business's income are not deductible expenses and must be kept separate. The purpose of placing these expenditures in a category by themselves becomes apparent when computing monthly cash balances and when filing the annual income tax return.

Monthly Expenditures Summary

The form to which entries from the Daily Expenditures Register are transferred is shown in FIG. 11-2. At the end of the month, figures in each account are summed for transferring, previous totals are written in, and year-to-date totals are drawn. The final figures are useful in computing cash-flow balances.

PART A. DEDUCTIBLE BUSINESS EXPENSES

1. *Accounting:* Bookkeeping expenses and costs for an accountant.
2. *Advertising:* Printing circulars, radio and newspaper ads, etc., and costs of pencils, business cards, and similar giveaways.

EXPENDITURES SUMMARY

Month _____ 19 __

Acct. No.	Account	This Month		Prior Total		Total to Date	
(A) 1	Accounting			125	—	125	—
2	Advertising	35	30	57	25	92	55
3	Attorney						
4	Car/Truck						
5	Commissions						
6	Depreciation						
7	Freight						
8	Insurance						
9	Interest						
10	License						
11	Maintenance Supplies						
12	Office Supplies						
13	Pension/Profit Share.						
14	Postage						
15	Rent/Lease						
16	Repairs						
17	Tax, Sales						
18	Tax, Self-Emp.						
19	Tax, State Unemp.						
20	Tax, Local						
21	Telephone						
22	Travel/Meals/Lodging						
23	Utilities						
24	Wages						
25							
	Total – Deductible Exp.	293	27				
(B) 26	Labor						
27	Material/Supplies						
28	Merchandise						
29	Other						
	Total Mfg./Inventory Exp.	221	50				
(C) 30	Fed. Income Tax						
31	Loan Principal						
32	Personal Draw						
33							
	Total Non-Deductible Exp.	625	—				

ENTER HERE ALL ACCOUNT

TOTALS FOR THE MONTH FROM

THE **DAILY EXPENDITURES REGISTER**

11-2 Expenditures on the daily form are summed by account and entered on a summary sheet for the month. Year-to-date calculations are included.

3. *Attorney*: Legal expenses incurred in the business.

4. *Car/truck*: Operating costs for the business. Mileage log required. Depreciation, if applicable, might be listed in account No. 6.

5. *Commissions*: Payments to consultants and contractors.

6. *Depreciation*: Annual, deductible depreciation taken on capital expenses.

7. *Freight:* Freight charges on delivery of purchases.

8. *Insurance*: Business insurance premiums.

9. *Interest*: Interest on business loans and applicable mortgage charges.

10. *Licenses*: Legal fees for operating your business.

11. *Maintenance supplies*: Cleaning supplies such as brooms, soaps, etc.

12. *Meals/entertainment*: Meals away from home on business and expenses of entertaining customers. Keep an expense record.

13. *Merchandise/materials*: Articles bought for resale and raw materials to be used in the craftwork. (Enter amounts if not required under Part B).

14. *Office expenses*: Costs of operating and maintaining a business office.

15. *Pension/profit sharing*: Cost to you for plans benefiting employees.

16. *Postage*: Costs of using U.S. Mail service for business purposes.

17. *Rent/lease*: Rent applicable to the business.

18. *Repairs*: Repairs to equipment, machinery, and facilities used in the business.

19. *Tax, sales*: Amount of sales tax collected on goods sold.

20. *Tax, Social Security*: Enter the employer's share of this tax and any self-employment tax paid.

21. *Tax, state unemployment insurance*: If subject to this tax, enter the tax you pay as employer.

22. *Tax, local*: If so charged, enter the amount of business tax paid to local governments.

23. *Telephone:* Charges for a separate business phone or the long distance business charges for a personal phone.

24. *Travel:* Expenses incurred for such things as lodging, transportation, and incidentals on out-of-town business trips. A detailed expense record is required.

25. *Utilities*: Those costs for electricity and heating chargeable to the business. Also, water if used in production.

26. *Wages:* Salaries and wages paid to employees, if any, including deductions for income and social security taxes when paid.

PART B. COST OF GOODS SOLD

27. *Labor*: Salaries, wages, and benefits paid to persons involved in the production and storage of merchandise. Exclude pay to yourself.

28. *Materials and supplies*: Merchandise and raw materials purchased for production and inventory.
29. *Other expenses*: overhead (rent, heat, etc.), packaging, and freight-in costs.

PART C. NON-DEDUCTIBLE EXPENSES

30. *Federal income tax*: Income tax for a sole proprietorship is considered to be the same as personal income tax and is not deductible.
31. *Loans*: Payments on the principal of business loans fit this category. The interest payments are deductible in account.
32. *Personal draw*: The salary you pay yourself is not a deductible business expense.

One important point needs to be emphasized about the Monthly Expenditures Summary. If you find your business is required to report only deductible expenses on the federal business income tax form, you will not need to fill in Part C, cost of goods sold. Accounts in Part A, deductible business expenses, will then accept all expenses incurred. As it is, the most likely need for a handcrafts business is to separate and record expenses incurred for manufacturing and inventory-related activities, on the one hand, and for all additional business expenses, on the other.

Receipts Register

The recording of income is a relatively easy task. The main reason is the IRS requires only that you report it all, not its specific source. A form suitable for maintaining a complete account is presented in FIG. 11-3.

Total sales receipts, net receipts, and sales tax collected are basic dollars-and-cents entries. The days of the month on which the various collections occur and on which funds are deposited are also written into the form. The final deposit of receipts must occur after all income for the month has been received. By so doing, the total deposits for the month will be equal to the total receipts for that period.

Monthly Balance

Figure 11-4 illustrates how to make a comparison of income and expenditures. Balances for the month and for the year to the present time are obtainable. At 12 times during the year, you will have an indication of how well the business is doing financially. Of course, factors besides those shown could enter into determining if the balance is adequate for individual purposes. The magnitude of personal expenses and whether there is an additional source of income are real considerations for any entrepreneur.

RECEIPTS REGISTER

Month _____ 19 __

Day	Net Sales		Sales Tax		Total Receipts		Deposits	
2	121	55	7	29	128	84		
5	417	50	24	05	442	55	571	39
6	29	95	1	80	31	75		
9	92	33	5	54	97	87		
10	4	25		26	4	51		
25	210	25	12	62	222	87		
30	3	25		20	3	45	17	86
	1207	07	72	42	1279	49	1279	49
	4008	58	240	51	4249	09	4249	09
	5215	65	312	93	5528	58	5528	58

11-3 A form for recording income by the day can be kept very easily in a single-entry system.

Tax Year

You must maintain records for an annual accounting period equal to your tax year. If you operate as a sole proprietor, the tax year for your business must be the same as the year you use to report federal income taxes as an individual. For most people in a handcrafts business, this means the calendar year, beginning January 1 and ending December 31 will be the tax year and the period on which to base record keeping. Fiscal years, which end in any month except December, are more appropriate for large organizations and corporations.

SOME HELPFUL HINTS

Numerous suggestions have been given throughout this text for simplifying your work. Apply them whenever you can. Otherwise, the paperwork can become overbearing and relatively unproductive. Several of the sug-

BALANCE SHEET

Month _____ 19 __

	This Month	Year to Date
RECEIPTS (Gross)	$1,279⁴⁹	$5,528⁵⁸
EXPENDITURES		
(A) Deductible	293³²	678⁷¹
(B) Mfg. & Inventory	221⁸⁰	992¹¹
(C) Non-Deductible	625⁰⁰	3,150⁰⁰
	$1,140¹²	$5,020⁸²
BALANCE (Profit)	$139⁴²	$507⁷⁶
– portion of rcp'ts.	10.9%	9.2%

11-4 A monthly balance shows cash flow for the business and how it is progressing.

gestions you might consider for your business as they apply to financial records are repeated here.

About Capital Assets

The law allows you to treat all or part of the cost of qualifying business property (purchases of equipment and machinery) as an expense rather than a capital expenditure. The cost of such property might be either deducted, subject to limits, in the year purchased or be capitalized and depreciated over a number of years. It is generally to your advantage to take the deduction. You can reduce taxes immediately and avoid keeping depreciation records year after year.

Currently, the total cost you may elect to deduct might not exceed $10,000 for the tax year, nor may it exceed your taxable business income. In other words, the deductible limit will be the lesser of $10,000, your taxable income, or the cost of the property. Fortunately, you are accorded the privilege of carrying forward and later recovering any part of the cost not deductible in the year when the property was placed in service.

There are other limitations. Those to be mentioned here pertain to the partial use of property in the business and to the purchase and use of a passenger automobile. When you use property for both business and non-business, you are eligible for this section 179 deduction only if more than 50% of the property's use is for business purposes. For an automobile, the current first-year deduction under this rule is limited to about $2,660. The actual amount is determined by multiplying this figure by the percentage of business use. Be sure to check with IRS publications regarding the several limits, as such restrictions might change yearly.

Time Payments

By avoiding time payments, that is, selling and purchasing on credit, you can avoid some record keeping and frequent headaches. Records of accounts receivable and accounts payable are a basic requirement when selling and buying on time, as is accounting by the accrual method. Moreover, billing expenses and losses due to uncollectables are common when selling on credit, and a loss of discounts is probable when much of your own buying is done on delayed payment. If most of your crafts sell for under $50, you will ask for more trouble than you need by accepting credit rather than demanding payment in cash, by check, or with a credit card.

As experience painfully shows, the acceptance of payment by check isn't always a sure-fire thing. The "bounced" check is an occasional problem. You, not the bank, will be stuck ultimately with collecting payment in restitution. Your first step is to contact the customer. If that doesn't bring a positive response, you have available the final option of filing a suit in small claims court, though the need for action of that nature would seem to be extremely rare in a handcrafts business.

An unpaid bill or uncollectable debt of any kind is a bad debt, and the amount should be listed in the section on deductible expenditures. Enter it as a bad debt in the form.

When buying materials for your business, avoid the extra record keeping and any interest charged for late payment. You'll be much ahead by taking advantage of discounts offered for paying promptly in cash.

Employment

The hiring of a single employee can increase the paper load tremendously. You can save by using members of your family. Or, you might hire outside contractors. Both methods have their advantages, but be prepared to keep payroll and various tax records if you do hire hourly or salaried employees.

When becoming an employer, you will be subject to additional regulations at the federal and state levels of government and, perhaps, the local level as well. Records must then be kept regarding income tax withholding, unemployment insurance, workers' compensation insurance, payroll, quarterly tax submissions, social security tax, and in some cases accident, safety, and employment data and reports. This is not to say that employment isn't profitable. It certainly can be. The only purpose is to call to the attention of handcrafters of modest beginnings that expansion of the business along these lines will require more knowledge and record keeping.

Publications

Booklets published by the SBA are good for helping an entrepreneur get started in record keeping, and the guides put out by the IRS are indispensable at all levels of advancement in business. The SBA charges a small fee for some publications. Those prepared by the IRS are entirely free. Find out what is available from these agencies, and obtain what you need for your library. One that every person in a handcrafts business should have is IRS Publication 334, Tax Guide for Small Business. It will be invaluable when preparing financial records.

Professional Help

The final suggestion to be given here might seem to be overstating the obvious: Employ an accountant if you find you need one. Select a professional who has had experience advising small business owners; otherwise, you might be paying for a learner. Remember, too, the more you have learned and done relative to keeping financial records, the less costly the employment of a professional will be.

How much work you hire an accountant to do will depend on the extent of your own knowledge and how much of the work you want to do yourself. In many businesses, the larger, more complex the operation becomes, the more likely much of the bookkeeping will be turned over to an accountant. In small operations, as a rule, professional assistance is called upon primarily for help in filing taxes.

NET WORTH STATEMENT

Don't strive for frugality in record keeping at the expense of significant information. Whether you like it or not, you must perform some paper-and-pencil operations. An important one that hasn't been mentioned before is the computation of the business's worth. At a minimum, you will want to make this determination yearly.

A complete financial analysis will tell you how your business is faring. A cash flow calculation gives only part of the answer. Its shortcoming is a lack of accounting for some of your business assets.

A net worth statement has several purposes. First of all, it can indicate if some change is needed, whether that be increasing sales, reducing costs, or both. It can also be used as the basis for presenting a case to a lender when attempting to borrow money. Whatever else might result, a number of such statements taken over a period of time will show trends and, possibly, the staying power of your business.

NET WORTH STATEMENT
December 31, 19__

ASSETS (What you own)
    Current Assets
        Cash in Bank $_____
        Petty Cash   _____
        Merchandise/mat'ls
          in inventory   _____
        Accounts receivable
          (if any)   _____
          Total $_____
    Fixed Assets
        Tools/Equipment (cost) $_____
        Bus. Vehicles (cost)   _____
        Buildings (cost)   _____
        Less Depreciation
          Reserve   (_____)
          Total $_____
    Total Fixed Assets $_____

LIABILITIES (What you owe)
    Current Liabilities
        Accounts Payable $_____
        Note/Loans Payable   _____
        Fed. Income Tax   _____
        Total $_____
    Fixed Liabilities
        Mortgage Payable $_____
        Debt (Long Term)   _____
        Total $_____
    Total Liabilities   ($_____)

RESIDUAL $_____

11-5 An annual statement of net worth is important for knowing how the business, with all its assets in-cluded, is doing.

Figure 11-5 contains the factors to be taken into consideration in a net worth statement. A quick review of the statement will indicate how relatively uncomplicated its preparation is, especially in a small business that has a minimum of capital assets.

Internal planning, rather than tax reporting, is the reason for computing your business's net worth. The IRS wants part of the income, regardless of whether your business is flourishing or struggling. Your concern is to direct the business on the basis of sound evidence so that you will have enough income left for personal needs after paying a share to the government.

THE PLUSES AND MINUSES

The accurate recording and reporting of financial data as required by agencies of government constitutes an important part and reason for record keeping. The other major purpose is to provide information of value for steering the business in a positive direction. Thus, there are calculations worthy of recording besides those previously shown. One of these shows expenditures as a percentage of income.

Percentage-of-Sales Analysis

Using the annual profit and loss statement as the basis, you can create a more complete picture of how your business is functioning by computing percentage distributions of costs. We are naturally inclined to think in terms of the whole, the 100%, and divisions within as fractional or percentage parts of that whole. Raw figures in dollars and cents are meaningful in the sense of showing magnitude, but computations showing the expenditures as a percentage of sales income adds another dimension in meaning. Suppose your car expenses for business purposes one year came to $3,700. Would it also be worth knowing this cost was 6.7% of sales income for the year? The answer becomes apparent with experience.

Percentages are useful not only for comparing cost distributions within a year but also for evaluating proportionate distributions from year to year. The trends so revealed become the basis for making adjustments in expenditures among accounts and in planning future budgets. In short, the percentage-of-sales method of analysis is an excellent planning tool.

The idea of the percentage record can be used in another way. Advertising costs, for example, can be further subdivided. In place of just determining the total cost and percentage amount for the year, the expenditures for advertising can be separated and ranked according to how the dollars were spent. In this method, the media used—newspapers, radio, direct mail, posters, etc.—are listed along with their component percentage parts of the total cost of advertising. The result obtained is an extension of the basic analytical technique.

Make the Most of It

The underlying objective in business is to make a profit. While profit is money, it is only partly a measure of success. Success also relates to the achievement of goals such as service and customer satisfaction. Profit might be most essential, for nobody would consider themselves to be very successful in business without it. One can joyously relish the knowledge that the business makes every effort to please customers, but such feelings are likely to be short-lived in a business hampered by negative cash flow and a year-end loss.

Whatever goals you might set for yourself, it is imperative that you strive to achieve the level of performance planned for your business. Analyze the record; then maximize sales and net income accordingly. The kind of calculations indicated in FIGS. 11-4 and 11-5 will be useful in that regard.

Make a systematic appraisal of activities in relation to the outcomes desired. In addition to the comparisons already described, you might make use of performance data based on cost/profit ratios. These are especially meaningful for comparing expenses within a year and from year to year. On the basis of what you learn, devise strategies and adjust procedures to make the most from the effort invested. Practices of the kind suggested here can have a significant effect on the progress of your business.

Income tax form: Schedule C

SCHEDULE C
(Form 1040)

Department of the Treasury
Internal Revenue Service   (0)

Profit or Loss From Business
(Sole Proprietorship)
▶ Partnerships, joint ventures, etc., must file Form 1065.
▶ Attach to Form 1040 or Form 1041.   ▶ See Instructions for Schedule C (Form 1040).

OMB No. 1545-0074

1991

Attachment
Sequence No. **09**

Name of proprietor	Social security number (SSN)

A Principal business or profession, including product or service (see instructions)

B Enter principal business code (from page 2) ▶

C Business name

D Employer ID number (Not SSN)

E Business address (including suite or room no.) ▶ ....
City, town or post office, state, and ZIP code

F Accounting method: **(1)** ☐ Cash   **(2)** ☐ Accrual   **(3)** ☐ Other (specify) ▶ ....

G Method(s) used to value closing inventory: **(1)** ☐ Cost   **(2)** ☐ Lower of cost or market   **(3)** ☐ Other (attach explanation)   **(4)** ☐ Does not apply (if checked, skip line H) | Yes | No |

H Was there any change in determining quantities, costs, or valuations between opening and closing inventory? (If "Yes," attach explanation.)

I Did you "materially participate" in the operation of this business during 1991? (If "No," see instructions for limitations on losses.)

J If this is the first Schedule C filed for this business, check here .... ▶ ☐

Part I   Income

1	Gross receipts or sales. **Caution:** If this income was reported to you on Form W-2 and the "Statutory employee" box on that form was checked, see the instructions and check here ▶ ☐	**1**
2	Returns and allowances	**2**
3	Subtract line 2 from line 1	**3**
4	Cost of goods sold (from line 40 on page 2)	**4**
5	Subtract line 4 from line 3 and enter the **gross profit** here	**5**
6	Other income, including Federal and state gasoline or fuel tax credit or refund (see instructions)	**6**
7	Add lines 5 and 6. This is your **gross income** ▶	**7**

Part II   Expenses (Caution: Enter expenses for business use of your home on line 30.)

8	Advertising	**8**	**21** Repairs and maintenance	**21**	
9	Bad debts from sales or services (see instructions)	**9**	**22** Supplies (not included in Part III)	**22**	
10	Car and truck expenses (see instructions—also attach **Form 4562**)	**10**	**23** Taxes and licenses	**23**	
11	Commissions and fees	**11**	**24** Travel, meals, and entertainment:		
12	Depletion	**12**	**a** Travel	**24a**	
13	Depreciation and section 179 expense deduction (not included in Part III) (see instructions)	**13**	**b** Meals and entertainment		
14	Employee benefit programs (other than on line 19)	**14**	**c** Enter 20% of line 24b subject to limitations (see instructions)		
15	Insurance (other than health)	**15**	**d** Subtract line 24c from line 24b	**24d**	
16	Interest:		**25** Utilities	**25**	
a	Mortgage (paid to banks, etc.)	**16a**	**26** Wages (less jobs credit)	**26**	
b	Other	**16b**	**27a** Other expenses (**list type and amount**):		
17	Legal and professional services	**17**	....		
18	Office expense	**18**	....		
19	Pension and profit-sharing plans	**19**	....		
20	Rent or lease (see instructions):		....		
a	Vehicles, machinery, and equipment	**20a**	....		
b	Other business property	**20b**	**27b** Total other expenses	**27b**	

28	Add amounts in columns for lines 8 through 27b. These are your **total expenses** before expenses for business use of your home ▶	**28**
29	Tentative profit (loss). Subtract line 28 from line 7	**29**
30	Expenses for business use of your home (attach **Form 8829**)	**30**
31	**Net profit or (loss).** Subtract line 30 from line 29. If a profit, enter here and on Form 1040, line 12. Also enter the net profit on Schedule SE, line 2 (statutory employees, see instructions). If a loss, you MUST go on to line 32 (fiduciaries, see instructions)	**31**

32 If you have a loss, you MUST check the box that describes your investment in this activity (see instructions)   **32a** ☐ All investment is at risk.
32b ☐ Some investment is not at risk.

If you checked 32a, enter the loss on Form 1040, line 12, and Schedule SE, line 2 (statutory employees, see instructions). If you checked 32b, you MUST attach **Form 6198**.

For Paperwork Reduction Act Notice, see Form 1040 instructions.   Cat. No. 11334P   **Schedule C (Form 1040) 1991**

Part III Cost of Goods Sold *(See instructions.)*

33	Inventory at beginning of year. (If different from last year's closing inventory, attach explanation.) . .	33
34	Purchases less cost of items withdrawn for personal use	34
35	Cost of labor. (Do not include salary paid to yourself.)	35
36	Materials and supplies	36
37	Other costs	37
38	Add lines 33 through 37.	38
39	Inventory at end of year.	39
40	**Cost of goods sold.** Subtract line 39 from line 38. Enter the result here and on page 1, line 4 . .	40

Part IV Principal Business or Professional Activity Codes

Locate the major category that best describes your activity. Within the major category, select the activity code that most closely identifies the business or profession that is the principal source of your sales or receipts. **Enter this 4-digit code on page 1, line B.** *For example, real estate agent is under the major category of **"Real Estate,"** and the code is "5520."* **(Note:** *If your principal source of income is from farming activities, you should file **Schedule F** (Form 1040), Profit or Loss From Farming.)*

Agricultural Services, Forestry, Fishing
Code
- 1990 Animal services, other than breeding
- 1933 Crop services
- 2113 Farm labor & management services
- 2246 Fishing, commercial
- 2238 Forestry, except logging
- 2212 Horticulture & landscaping
- 2469 Hunting & trapping
- 1974 Livestock breeding
- 0836 Logging
- 1958 Veterinary services, including pets

Construction
- 0018 Operative builders (for own account)

Building Trade Contractors, Including Repairs
- 0414 Carpentering & flooring
- 0455 Concrete work
- 0273 Electrical work
- 0299 Masonry, dry wall, stone, & tile
- 0257 Painting & paper hanging
- 0232 Plumbing, heating, & air conditioning
- 0430 Roofing, siding & sheet metal
- 0885 Other building trade contractors (excavation, glazing, etc.)

General Contractors
- 0075 Highway & street construction
- 0059 Nonresidential building
- 0034 Residential building
- 3889 Other heavy construction (pipe laying, bridge construction, etc.)

Finance, Insurance, & Related Services
- 6064 Brokers & dealers of securities
- 6080 Commodity contracts brokers & dealers; security & commodity exchanges
- 6148 Credit institutions & mortgage bankers
- 5702 Insurance agents or brokers
- 5744 Insurance services (appraisal, consulting, inspection, etc.)
- 6130 Investment advisors & services
- 5777 Other financial services

Manufacturing, Including Printing & Publishing
- 0679 Apparel & other textile products
- 1115 Electric & electronic equipment
- 1073 Fabricated metal products
- 0638 Food products & beverages
- 0810 Furniture & fixtures
- 0695 Leather footwear, handbags, etc.
- 0836 Lumber & other wood products
- 1099 Machinery & machine shops
- 0877 Paper & allied products
- 1057 Primary metal industries
- 0851 Printing & publishing
- 1032 Stone, clay, & glass products
- 0653 Textile mill products
- 1883 Other manufacturing industries

Mining & Mineral Extraction
- 1537 Coal mining
- 1511 Metal mining

- 1552 Oil & gas
- 1719 Quarrying & nonmetallic mining

Real Estate
- 5538 Operators & lessors of buildings, including residential
- 5553 Operators & lessors of other real property
- 5520 Real estate agents & brokers
- 5579 Real estate property managers
- 5710 Subdividers & developers, except cemeteries
- 6155 Title abstract offices

Services: Personal, Professional, & Business Services
Amusement & Recreational Services
- 9670 Bowling centers
- 9688 Motion picture & tape distribution & allied services
- 9597 Motion picture & video production
- 9639 Motion picture theaters
- 8557 Physical fitness facilities
- 9696 Professional sports & racing, including promoters & managers
- 9811 Theatrical performers, musicians, agents, producers & related services
- 9613 Video tape rental
- 9837 Other amusement & recreational services

Automotive Services
- 8813 Automotive rental or leasing, without driver
- 8953 Automotive repairs, general & specialized
- 8839 Parking, except valet
- 8896 Other automotive services (wash, towing, etc.)

Business & Personal Services
- 7658 Accounting & bookkeeping
- 7716 Advertising, except direct mail
- 7682 Architectural services
- 8318 Barber shop (or barber)
- 8110 Beauty shop (or beautician)
- 8714 Child day care
- 6676 Communication services
- 7872 Computer programming, processing, data preparation & related services
- 7922 Computer repair, maintenance, & leasing
- 7286 Consulting services
- 7799 Consumer credit reporting & collection services
- 8755 Counseling (except health practitioners)
- 6395 Courier or package delivery
- 7732 Employment agencies & personnel supply
- 7518 Engineering services
- 7773 Equipment rental & leasing (except computer or automotive)
- 8532 Funeral services & crematories
- 7633 Income tax preparation
- 7914 Investigative & protective services
- 7617 Legal services (or lawyer)
- 7856 Mailing, reproduction, commercial art, photography, & stenographic services
- 7245 Management services
- 8771 Ministers & chaplains
- 8334 Photographic studios

- 7260 Public relations
- 6536 Public warehousing
- 7708 Surveying services
- 8730 Teaching or tutoring
- 6510 Trash collection without own dump
- 6692 Utilities (dumps, snowplowing, road cleaning, etc.)
- 7880 Other business services
- 6882 Other personal services

Hotels & Other Lodging Places
- 7237 Camps & camping parks
- 7096 Hotels, motels, & tourist homes
- 7211 Rooming & boarding houses

Laundry & Cleaning Services
- 7450 Carpet & upholstery cleaning
- 7419 Coin-operated laundries & dry cleaning
- 7435 Full-service laundry, dry cleaning, & garment service
- 7476 Janitorial & related services (building, house, & window cleaning)

Medical & Health Services
- 9274 Chiropractors
- 9233 Dentist's office or clinic
- 9217 Doctor's (M.D.) office or clinic
- 9456 Medical & dental laboratories
- 9472 Nursing & personal care facilities
- 9290 Optometrists
- 9258 Osteopathic physicians & surgeons
- 9241 Podiatrists
- 9415 Registered & practical nurses
- 9431 Offices & clinics of other health practitioners (dieticians, midwives, speech pathologists, etc.)
- 9886 Other health services

Miscellaneous Repair, Except Computers
- 9019 Audio equipment & TV repair
- 9035 Electrical & electronic equipment repair, except audio & TV
- 9050 Furniture repair & reupholstery
- 2881 Other equipment repair

Trade, Retail—Selling Goods to Individuals & Households
- 3038 Catalog or mail order
- 3012 Selling door to door, by telephone or party plan, or from mobile unit
- 3053 Vending machine selling

Selling From Showroom, Store, or Other Fixed Location

Apparel & Accessories
- 3921 Accessory & specialty stores & furriers for women
- 3939 Clothing, family
- 3772 Clothing, men's & boys'
- 3913 Clothing, women's
- 3756 Shoe stores
- 3954 Other apparel & accessory stores

Automotive & Service Stations
- 3558 Gasoline service stations
- 3319 New car dealers (franchised)
- 3533 Tires, accessories, & parts
- 3335 Used car dealers
- 3517 Other automotive dealers (motorcycles, recreational vehicles, etc.)

Building, Hardware, & Garden Supply
- 4416 Building materials dealers
- 4457 Hardware stores
- 4473 Nurseries & garden supply stores
- 4432 Paint, glass, & wallpaper stores

Food & Beverages
- 0612 Bakeries selling at retail
- 3086 Catering services
- 3095 Drinking places (bars, taverns, pubs, saloons, etc.)
- 3079 Eating places, meals & snacks
- 3210 Grocery stores (general line)
- 3251 Liquor stores
- 3236 Specialized food stores (meat, produce, candy, health food, etc.)

Furniture & General Merchandise
- 3988 Computer & software stores
- 3970 Furniture stores
- 4317 Home furnishings stores (china, floor coverings, drapes)
- 4119 Household appliance stores
- 4333 Music & record stores
- 3996 TV, audio & electronic stores
- 3715 Variety stores
- 3761 Other general merchandise stores

Miscellaneous Retail Stores
- 4812 Boat dealers
- 5017 Book stores, excluding newsstands
- 4853 Camera & photo supply stores
- 3277 Drug stores
- 5058 Fabric & needlework stores
- 4655 Florists
- 5090 Fuel dealers (except gasoline)
- 4630 Gift, novelty & souvenir shops
- 4838 Hobby, toy, & game shops
- 4671 Jewelry stores
- 4895 Luggage & leather goods stores
- 5074 Mobile home dealers
- 4879 Optical goods stores
- 4697 Sporting goods & bicycle shops
- 5033 Stationery stores
- 4614 Used merchandise & antique stores (except motor vehicle parts)
- 5884 Other retail stores

Trade, Wholesale—Selling Goods to Other Businesses, etc.
Durable Goods, Including Machinery, Equipment, Wood, Metals, etc.
- 2634 Agent or broker for other firms— more than 50% of gross sales on commission
- 2618 Selling for your own account

Nondurable Goods, Including Food, Fiber, Chemicals, etc.
- 2675 Agent or broker for other firms— more than 50% of gross sales on commission
- 2659 Selling for your own account

Transportation Services
- 6619 Air transportation
- 6312 Bus & limousine transportation
- 6361 Highway passenger transportation (except chartered service)
- 6114 Taxicabs
- 6635 Travel agents & tour operators
- 6338 Trucking (except trash collection)
- 6551 Water transportation
- 6650 Other transportation services

- 8888 Unable to classify

★U.S.GPO:1991-0-285-174

Income Tax Forms: Schedule C **225**

Index

A

accountants, 218
accounting, 205-221
accounts
  banking, 208
advertising, 118-121
  catalogs, brochures, 119
  freebies, 121
  giveaways, 121
  labels, 120-121
  mass media, 118-119
  plan, 121
after the sale, 144
approach to selling, 3-4
artisanship, 4-5
assistance, 12, 26-30
  government resources, 27-29
  independent business associa-
    tions, 29-30
  professional services, 26-27
attitude, 1-2, 17-18
  confidence, 2, 17-18

B

balance entries
  deductions, 44-46
balancing the budget, 43-46
bank accounts, 208
bookkeeping, 205-221
  accountant, 218
  accounting, 205-221
  analysis, 220
  assets, 216-217
  balances, 214-221

bank accounts, 208
employment, 217-218
expenditures register, 209-214
financial records, 207
net worth statement, 218-219
payments, 217
publications, 218
receipts, 214
samples, 207-221
tax year, 215
tips, 215-216
brainstorming, 23-26
budget entries, 44-46
  monthly and yearly balances,
    46
  revenue, 44
budgeting, 40
business and professional cli-
    ents, 175-176
  selling tips, 175-176
business deductions, 71-73
  capital expenses, 72
  cost of goods, 71
  deductible expenses, 72-73
  general requirements, 71
business forms, 15, 38, 39, 41,
    57
  activities schedule, 15
  taxes, 222-225
business image, 52-53
business plan, 20-21, 33-50
business structure, 47-50
  choosing a structure, 47-48
  incorporation, 50
  partnership, 49-50
  proprietorship, 48-49

C

cash, 208-209
  petty, 208-209
catalogs, 119-120
  brochures, 119
closing the sale, 142-143
  inducements, 143
  tips, 142-143
cost factors, 104
cottage industry (see home-
    based business), 3
craft fairs, 115
craft show sales, 183-192
  demonstrations, 192
  display techniques, 188-191
  procedure tips, 187-188
craftsmanship, 4-5
customer satisfaction, 108
customer service, 85-87
  advice, 86-87
  greeting visitors, 85-86
  showroom, 86

D

deductible expenses, 72-73
demand (see price levels), 104
developing a working plan, 33-50
  documentation, 34-36
  outline, 36
  size, 35
direct marketing, 136
distribution decisions, 114-116
  craft fairs, 115-116
  local markets, 115
  other methods, 116
  store displays, 115

dividing expenses (*see* tax breaks), 80
documentation, 34-36
  contents, 34-36

E

effective workplace, 81-85
  efficiency, 81-85
  environment, 82-83
employee management, 65-66
  family employment, 67-68
  federal identification number, 66
  labor legislation, 66-67
  plan of, 65-66
employment practices and laws, 63-64
  independent contractors, 64
enthusiasm, 141
equipment and supplies, 201-202
ethics (*see* price levels), 103
evaluating your selling success, 144-146
exhibit tips, 137
exhibiting, 178
expenditures register, 209-214
expenditures, 42-43

F

fair pricing, 104
family employment, 67-68
  advantage, 68
  laws, 68
federal identification number, 66
fictitious names, 54
finance, 12-13, 37-44, 195-197, 207
  capital borrowing of, 195-197
  sources, 196-197
finance tips, 12-13
financial plan, 37-43
  balancing the budget, 43-44
  budgeting, 40
  business forms, 38-39, 41
  expenditures, 42-42
financial records, 207
functional office, 83-85

G

goals, 37
  action oriented, 37
  budgeting, 40
goals and objectives, 18-20
  terms, 18-19
government resources
  other assistance, 28-29
  Small Business Administration, 28

state and local, 27-28
government resources, 27-29

H

handmade appeal
  construction, 96
  unique features, 95-96
home-based business, 75-89
  advantages, 75-76
  cottage industry, 2-3
  potential problems, 76
  steps before starting, 78
home parties, 152-172
  accessories, 156
  closing remarks, 166
  closing the party, 166
  demonstrations, 165-166
  displaying your crafts, 156
  incentives, 154
  miscellaneous, 157
  motifs, 155-156
  opening your party, 160-166
  order techniques, 167-168
  packing your crafts, 156
  parking, 158
  pricing, 155-156
  questions and answers, 164-165
  refreshments, 155
  responsibilities, 153-154
  reviewing the party, 168-171
  scheduling, 154-155
  selection of crafts, 152-153
  setting up your party, 158-160
  variety, 155-156

I

incorporation, 50
independent contractors, 64
insurance
  government programs, 69
  private coverage, 69-70
  types of, 70-71
insurance, 69-71
Internal Revenue Service requirement, 15-16, 51-73
interviews and surveys, 112
inventory control, 107-109

K

keys to future sales (*see* product tips), 108-109

L

labor legislation, 66-67
legal requirements, 51-73
  business forms, 57
  IRS, 52
  licenses and permits, 54-68

naming your business, 52
  registration, 53-54
  zoning ordinances, 56, 58-60
licenses and permits, 54-68
  sales tax, 54, 56
  tax exemption, 56
local markets, 115

M

marketing your product, 111-128
  interviews and surveys, 112
  observation and analysis, 113
  research, 112
  targeting the consumer, 111-114
  variations and appeal, 114
materials and workmanship, 101
monthly and yearly balances, 46
moonlighting, 11

N

names and slogans, 118
naming your business, 52
net worth statement, 218-219

O

objections, 141-142
  personal factors, 142
  product related, 141-142
observation and analysis, 113
observation and preparation, 13
open house sales, 179-183
  promotions, 180-181
order and organization, 21
  brainstorming, 23-26
  scheduling, 22-23
  workplace, 22
organization for production, 98-100
  batching, 99
  increase productivity, 99
  purchasing, 100
  the work area, 99
other requirements
  federal laws, 61-62
  local and state, 61
  pension plans, 63
  self employment and taxes, 62-63
  social security, 63

P

partnerships, 49-50
personal referrals, 138
practice, 6
price levels, 101-107
  cost factors, 104
  demand, 104
  ethics, 103

fair pricing, 104
market value, 102-103
profit, 103
pricing strategies, 105-107
accessories, 106
discounts, 106
increases, 107
promotions, 107
psychological, 106-107
pricing, 100-107
problem minimization
control, 77
interruptions, 76-77
product tips, 108-109
product variations and appeal, 114
professional services (*see* assistance), 26-27
proprietorship, 48-49
public appearance, 116-118
marketing yourself, 116-117
names and slogans, 118
printed matter, 117-118
public relations, 124-128
alternatives, 124-125
appreciation, 126
clientele, 125-126
public speaking, 124
public speaking, 124
publicity, 121-123
activities plan, 122
displays (*see also* distribution decisions), 123
media coverage, 123
special services, 126-128

Q

quality, 100-101

R

receipts, 214
record keeping, 199-221
equipment and supplies, 201-202
files, 201
material, 204-205
scheduling, 202-204
registration, 53-54
fictitious names, 54
trade names, 54
research, 112
risk minimization, 10-14
assistance, 12

finance tips, 12-13
learning, 11
moonlighting, 11
observation and preparation, 13-14
steps to, 10
timetables, 14-15

S

sales
follow up, 173-174
open house, 179-180
sales presentation, 139-141
enthusiasm, 141
sample, 139-141
tips, 141
sales tax, 54, 56
scheduling, 22-23
self employment and taxes, 62-63
selling events
practical choices, 147-151
selling approach, 3-4, 129-146
confidence and character, 131-132
consumer oriented, 130-131
difficulties, 136
exhibit tips, 137
hard sellers, 130
orders, 130
other sources, 138-139
personal referrals, 138
process of, 133-135
product knowledge, 131-132
rules to observe, 132-133
special events, 137-138
selling events, 147-172
advantages, 148-149
alternatives, 149-151
craft shows, 150
home parties, 151
media sales, 150-151
methods, 149
opportunites, 149
store sales, 150
tips , 148-149
selling success and expansion, 173-197
selling tips
for business and professional clients, 175-176
selling your product, 91-109
benefits, 93
consumer concerns, 93
customer perception, 94

handmade appeal, 95-96
observation, 94-95
what consumers want, 91-93
setting up your business, 9-10
showroom tips, 178-179
Small Business Administration, 28
special deductions (*see* tax breaks), 80-81
starting your business, 8-32
risk minimization, 10-14
setting up, 9-10
stepping out, 87-89
flexibility, 88
security, 87-88
steps before starting, 8-9
home based business, 78
storage, 84-85
store displays, 115
store sales, 193-197
carts and kiosks, 193-194
storefronts, 194-195
strengths and weaknesses, 4-6

T

tax breaks, 79-81
dividing expenses, 80
qualifications, 79
special deductions, 80-81
tax exemption, 56
tax forms, 222-225
tax year, 215
taxes (*see also* IRS requirements), 15-16, 51-73
telemarketing, 136
terms, 18-19
timetables, 14-15
trade names, 54

V

variances and rezoning, 58-59
variety and quality, 96-98
a broad line, 97-98
color and decoration, 98

W

window displays, 177-178

Z

zoning ordinaces, 58-60
home occupations, 59-60

W

workplace, 22